SWEET CHARIOT 2

HEROES AND HEARTBREAK

RUGBY WORLD CUP 2007

With contributions from:
MICK CLEARY
STEPHEN JONES
ALASTAIR HIGNELL
JILL DOUGLAS
JIM NEILLY
JOHN INVERDALE
MATT DAWSON
EDDIE BUTLER
CHRIS JONES
ANDREW COTTER
TERRY COOPER

RUGBY WORLD CUP 2007

SWEET CHARIOT 2

HEROES AND HEARTBREAK

EDITED BY Ian Robertson

This book has been produced for Green Umbrella Publishing
by Lennard Books
a division of Lennard Associates Ltd
Windmill Cottage
Mackerye End
Harpenden
Herts AL5 5DR

This edition first published in the UK in 2007
by Green Umbrella Publishing
The Old Bakehouse, 21 The Street,
Lydiard Millicent, Swindon SN5 3LU

ISBN 978 1 905828 29 6

Production Editor: Chris Marshall
Design Consultant: Paul Cooper

Printed and bound by
Butler & Tanner, Frome

The publishers would like to thank Getty Images for providing
all the illustrations for this book and would also like to acknowledge
the contribution of all their photographers:
Dave Rogers, Shaun Botterill, Alex Livesey, Warren Little
Stu Forster, Laurence Griffiths, Jamie McDonald
Richard Heathcote, Ross Land, Cameron Spencer, Julian Finney
Tertius Pickard/Gallo Images and the Getty Images/AFP team

CONTENTS

Introduction

11 Vive La Difference! – ALASTAIR HIGNELL

The Pools

21 POOL A
No Two-horse Race – MICK CLEARY

35 POOL B
Fiji Steal the Show – STEPHEN JONES

49 POOL C
The Scrap for Second Place – JILL DOUGLAS

63 POOL D
Pumas Top the Pile – JIM NEILLY

Quarter-Finals

77 Australia v England – MICK CLEARY

89 New Zealand v France – JIM NEILLY

101 South Africa v Fiji – STEPHEN JONES

113 Argentina v Scotland – ANDREW COTTER

Semi-Finals

125 England v France – MICK CLEARY

135 South Africa v Argentina – STEPHEN JONES

Third-Place Play-Off

145 France v Argentina – DAVID HANDS

The Final

155 England v South Africa – JOHN INVERDALE

Looking Back

173 Tales of the Unexpected – ALASTAIR HIGNELL

Highlights

177 Player of the Tournament: Victor Matfield – EDDIE BUTLER

179 Rugby World Cup 2007: World XV – MATT DAWSON

183 The Highs and the Lows – CHRIS JONES

187 **Statistics**

foreword

Royal London Group is delighted to once again be the main supporter of this book, which provides a magnificent record of the sixth Rugby World Cup.

From the opening game, this has been a real rollercoaster of an event, with the "underdogs" triumphing on several occasions. One particularly welcome feature was the continuing emergence of the "new" nations who, even when not winning, have often provided a refreshing reminder of many of the traditional values of the sport.

The 2007 Rugby World Cup will be remembered for many and varied reasons – the new levels of fitness and power achieved by many of the teams; the upsets; the passion and the pride; the skills and the flair of individual players. And while South Africa were undoubtedly worthy winners, the defending champions England demonstrated terrific courage and willpower in once again reaching the final.

This book is a wonderful record of all the games, capturing the colour, the disappointments and the triumphs. I am sure rugby fans everywhere will enjoy reading it and keeping it for the lasting memories of a great tournament.

John Deane

Chief Executive
Royal London Intermediary

THE RUGBY WORLD CUP 2007

THE TEAMS

The headquarters building of Capgemini in Paris displays a makeover as France gears up for RWC 2007.

INTRODUCTION

VIVE LA DIFFERENCE!

ALASTAIR HIGNELL

After five increasingly successful tournaments, the International Rugby Board was confident that rugby was ready for a new challenge. Of course, the first priority was for a bigger and better Rugby World Cup, making larger profits and reaching a wider audience than ever before, but by handing the tournament to a francophone country for the first time, the game's rulers affirmed that rugby was also mature enough to speak a new language.

The horse-trading that seems inevitably to accompany such decisions did mean that Wales, Scotland and Ireland – until the redevelopment of Lansdowne Road got in the way – were all promised home fixtures, but right from the outset there was never any doubt that this was to be a World Cup with an overwhelmingly strong French accent. *'Oui, je parle rugby'* was not just the title of a guide targeted at the expected 450,000 visitors to France in September and October, it was adopted, or so it seemed, as the mantra of a whole country.

New president Nicolas Sarkozy – mindful of the the impact of France's 1998 football World Cup final victory on then president Jacques Chirac, who despite not knowing the names of half the team saw his poll ratings leap – restyled himself as a rugby fan and insisted government ministers attend matches in order to reap as much political gain from what most of France assumed would be a clear path to at least the semi-finals.

Big-hitters of the French business world – Peugeot, EDF, SNCF, Société Générale, Orange, Capgemini – piled in as

sponsors. The French Ministry of Foreign Affairs took charge of organising the event in partnership with the Economic Interest Group and made its International Conference Centre on Paris's Avenue Kléber available to host the 4000 journalists expected to cover the tournament. An official from the Protocol Department was seconded to make sure the 250 foreign dignitaries and VIPs arriving for the event received the sort of welcome that France could be proud of.

The French cities staging matches at the tournament – Toulouse, Bordeaux, Lens, Saint-Etienne, Lyons, Nantes, Montpellier, Marseilles and Paris – fell over themselves, and chopped down a few forests, to trumpet their attractions, not just as short-term tourist destinations but as long-term business investment opportunities, too. Six thousand volunteers were recruited by the Organising Committee to take part in what Tournament Director Claude Atcher described as a 'unique and remarkable human adventure', while the sport's values of solidarity, sharing and friendship were stressed in '*Rendez-vous 2007*', a project whereby some 80 teenagers from 32 countries on 5 continents were invited to attend the tournament by the Jeune Planète Rugby association.

Rugby's reputation for compassion was underlined by further commitment to the World Food Programme and its 'Tackle Hunger' campaign, while France's commitment to eco-friendly policies was borne out in a barrage of bulletins detailing, for instance, how the near 800 tonnes of garbage expected to be produced by the event would be recycled, how efficiently the 4.7 million kilowatt-hours of electricity would be generated, where the 2600 metres of solar panels had been installed and how ferrying teams around the country by high-speed TGV trains would reduce the carbon footprint of the whole event.

By midsummer it was clear that the whole nation – and not just the traditional southwest rugby heartland, 'L'Ovalie' – was behind the event. Articles on rugby and rugby players appeared in the unlikeliest of places. The celebrated French intelligentsia embraced the hitherto ignored or disparaged; much was made of the primitive, manly physicality of rugby. Sale forward Sébastien Chabal, with his flowing black hair and full beard, was dubbed '*l'homme des cavernes*' and endowed with all the characteristics that had made cartoon characters Asterix and Obelix such national icons. And, after forking out 80 million euros for this tournament and the next, France's most popular television station, TF1, set out to turn the French team into household names, while coach Bernard Laporte – a charismatic figure with the sharpest of business brains – could be found endorsing 17 different products, including ham and dog food.

LEFT Sébastien Chabal in action for France against Wales in an RWC 2007 warm-up match. The charismatic forward was known as '*l'homme des cavernes*' (the caveman) by French fans. **FACING PAGE** Montpellier, one of nine French cities hosting matches during RWC 2007, gets in the mood.

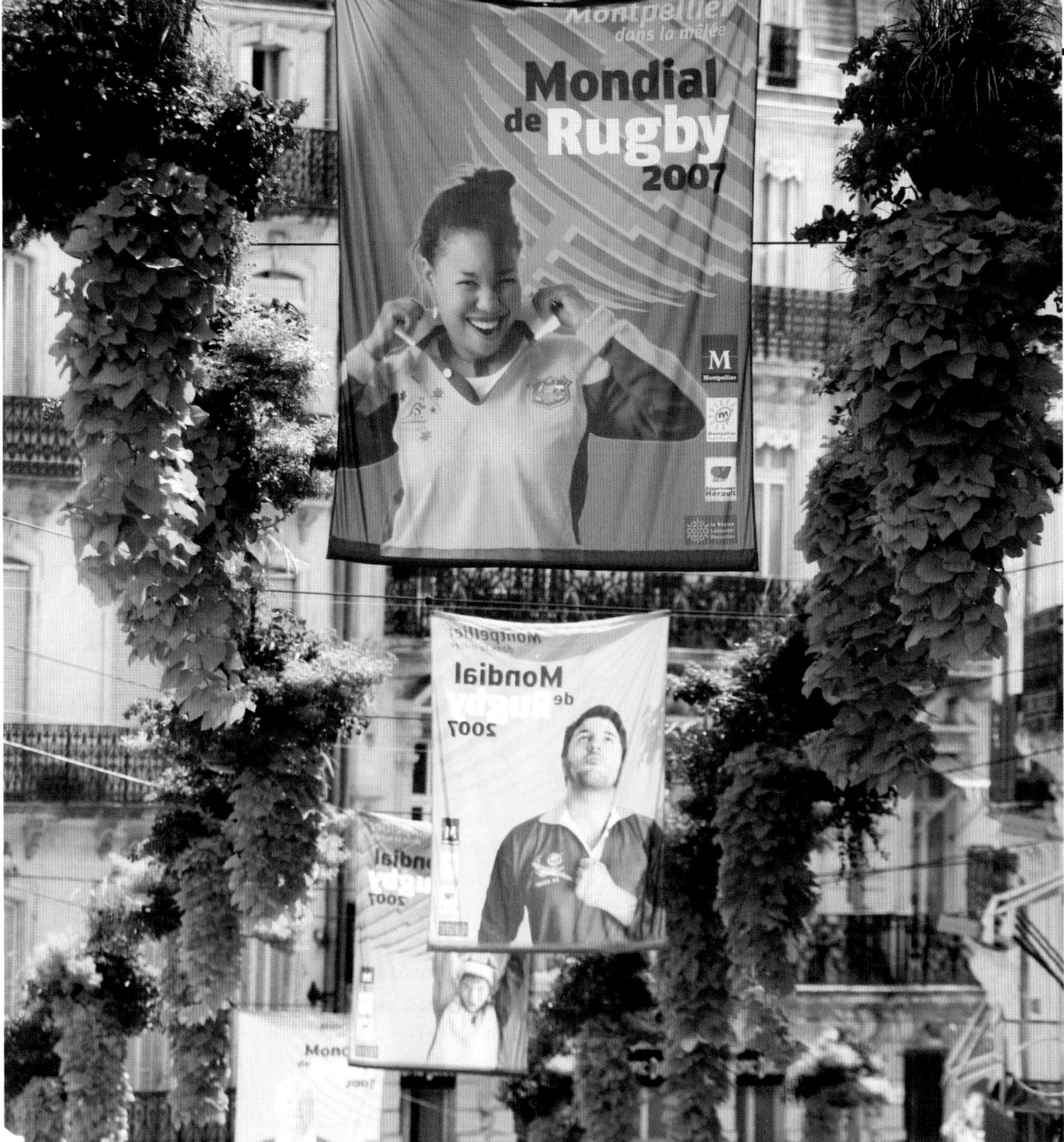

But by the time the tournament started at the beginning of September, France had also embarked on a mission to win over the rest of the world – and in particular the estimated 450,000 visiting fans, who would contribute to combined attendances of over 2.4 million in the coming weeks. With the competition budget growing from 204 million euros to 218 million euros, the Organising Committee threw its full weight behind the Ministry of Foreign Affairs' *'Oui, je parle rugby'* campaign to create a common language between hosts and visitors.

'The World Cup is an opportunity for us to highlight the diversity of French … a dynamic and living language, adapted to today's world and open to outside influences and talents,' declared Bernard Kouchner, Minister of Foreign Affairs. It was also, though he didn't say it, an opportunity to soften the reputation for French surliness towards English-speakers. With 12 of the competing 20 teams hailing from English-speaking countries, the *'Oui, je parle rugby'* scheme was given full prominence. First, it showed a series of films involving 12 Francophile internationals to give an account of their special relationship with France and its inhabitants. Then it produced an interactive CD-ROM entitled *Le français dans la mêlée* which was distributed by a network of 436 French cultural institutions to give foreign supporters a 15-lesson course in French as it applies to rugby. Finally it printed nearly half a million copies of a guidebook called *Kit de survie en français*, for distribution at stadia, tourist offices and at airports and railway stations.

The booklet contained the 250 sentences thought to be indispensable to any self-respecting rugby fan at the tournament – from *je voudrais acheter ce maillot de rugby* (I want to buy this rugby jersey), through a section on technical terms (translations of props, hookers, flankers, gumshields and penalties come with handy illustrations), to the more convivial *la hola* (the Mexican wave), *allons boire un coup* (let's have a drink), *c'est moi qui paie* (it's my round) and the inevitable *j'ai la gueule de bois* (I have a hangover). It also featured all the World Cup dates, information on host towns, useful numbers and humorous illustrations – everything, in fact, to take the fans' minds off the huge price they were being asked to pay to get into the matches.

Ticket prices ranging from 100 euros for some of the smaller games to 2100 euros for certain tickets for the final underlined the business imperatives of the tournament. Each previous World Cup had made a bigger profit than its predecessor, and RWC 2007 had every intention of bettering the $A150 million in revenue posted in Australia four years before. The selection of high-capacity football stadia in France – in addition to the use of Cardiff's 73,000-seater Millennium Stadium and Edinburgh's Murrayfield, which could hold 68,000 – was one strand of the policy. As always, though, the real money was to be made from broadcasters who had been left in no doubt by previous tournaments of the commercial value of the Rugby World Cup.

Four years previously the tournament's worldwide television audience had exceeded 3 billion, confirming the event's status as the world's third most-watched event – well short of the football World Cup (30 billion in 2006) but within shouting distance of the summer Olympics (4 billion in 2004). And the reach of Rugby World Cup was all set to increase. When Setanta secured exclusive live rights to RWC 2007, the tournament became the first RWC to be shown on a dedicated network in the United States and Canada, leaving Setanta's Robert Ryan confident that 'this will definitely be the most-watched Rugby World Cup in the U.S. so far'.

French commercial broadcaster TF1, having taken over rights from France Télévisions, was equally bullish. Network executives expected to average an audience of 5 million viewers for each of the 20 matches that TF1 was to air, which included all of the France games, and predicted that it would turn a profit on the event, in contrast to the hefty loss it took on last year's soccer World Cup. A 30-second spot on TF1 during the opening game of RWC 2007 was selling for 100,000-115,000 euros, rising to a possible 205,000 euros during the final.

In Britain, ITV once again had exclusive rights to the event and planned to air all 48 matches, spread over two channels, with ITV carrying the big games, and ITV4 the others. Everything was also to be available for streaming on the broadcaster's website, and expectations – based on the coverage of the 2003 Rugby World Cup, which despite the huge time difference attracted 15 million viewers to the final and averaged more than 7 million at England's other matches – were high.

Indeed, the expected level of interest in Britain had email and web content security vendor Marshal predicting decreased productivity for UK plc, with 10 per cent of the workforce expected to down tools for at least 30 minutes each day as they kept up to date with developments. Michael Clifford, EMEA vice-president at Marshal, said: 'Rugby is one of the country's most popular sports which will mean many people will be glued to their screens over the next six weeks. We estimate that one in ten workers will spend at least half-an-hour each day catching up on the World Cup which will result in more than 31m hours of lost productivity and will result in losses of around £461m.'

With 48 matches over 44 days involving 20 teams in 5 pools in 3 countries, those errant workers would have plenty of distractions. Every match could be either seen live on television or downloaded via a delayed feed to be watched later. The intensity of the media rivalry meant that with podcasts, vodcasts, dedicated websites, blogs and online diaries as well as all the more established outlets of newspapers, television and radio the consumer would be engulfed by an avalanche of news, analysis, information and gossip at any hour of the day or night.

In Pool A most of the pre-tournament speculation concerned England, whose fall from grace had been spectacular since that dizzy November night in Sydney when they became the first northern hemisphere side to win the World Cup. While key players such as Martin Johnson and Matt Dawson had retired, others had been dogged by injury – Steve Thompson and Trevor Woodman forced to call it a day; dropped-goal hero Jonny Wilkinson only available for eight England matches in four years. Results, too, had taken a tumble – only ten out of twenty Six Nations matches were won – while coaches had come and gone. First, Sir Clive Woodward walked off in a huff, then his successor, Andy Robinson, was sacked ten months before the start of RWC 2007. New man Brian Ashton had inherited a team in disarray and spent the first six months on the horns of a dilemma: whether to stick with the older, more experienced survivors or to trust his instincts and gamble on youth. After watching an understrength squad being thrashed by South Africa in the summer, he opted to put his trust in age and experience for the defence of the world title.

The Springboks, by unlucky coincidence, were England's main rivals in the group. They were out for revenge for defeat at the same stage four years previously, and those 50-point drubbings of England in the summer were indications that South

RIGHT Jonny's back! After four injury-filled years, the hero of Sydney was fit for RWC 2007. Here he slots a penalty in a warm-up game against France in Marseilles. **FACING PAGE** The US team, their campaign assured TV coverage back home, is welcomed at Paris's Charles de Gaulle airport.

ABOVE The All Black high command, Richie McCaw and Graham Henry, chat before the 2007 Tri-Nations decider against Australia, which New Zealand won 26-12. Could anyone stop the All Blacks from coming away from France with their first World Cup since 1987? **FACING PAGE** The waiting is almost over. France and Argentina parade ahead of the opening match of RWC 2007 at the Stade de France.

Africa and England were seemingly headed in opposite directions. Springbok coach Jake White could boast a settled side that had been maturing together for several years and had, in Bryan Habana, probably the fastest wing in world rugby. Such was South Africa's focus on World Cup success that White had chosen, much to the annoyance of Australia and New Zealand, to rest his key players for the second half of the Tri-Nations.

Also in Pool A were the USA, starting to stir under new CEO Nigel Melville with the promise of a professional league and greater television exposure; Samoa, RWC quarter-finalists in 1991 and 1995 and grouped with England and South Africa for the second World Cup in succession; and their Polynesian neighbours Tonga, so strapped for cash earlier in the year that they had seriously considered pulling out of the tournament.

Wales were to fly the Six Nations flag in Pool B, with their key fixture against Australia scheduled for the Millennium Stadium. Wales had also changed coach, Gareth Jenkins having replaced 2005 Grand Slam winner Mike Ruddock. Although their form since that 2005 success had taken a dip, and despite the fact that the Wallabies had beaten them twice in the summer, Wales still fancied their chances on home soil.

Australia's coach John Connolly had survived a loss-laden start to his tenure, but both his half backs had passed 100 caps for their country and in Chris Latham, Matt Giteau and Lote Tuqiri he had plenty of potential match winners. As the only team to have won the World Cup twice, in 1991 and 1999, Australia – who had also, against expectations, reached the final in 2003 – knew all about peaking for the big occasion.

Fiji, beginning to emerge from a fallow period, and Canada, muscular and committed as ever, were regarded as the teams most likely to cause an upset in Pool B, while Japan, as skilful as any side in the tournament, could be relied on to provide both excitement and entertainment.

Pool C was the only group with an out-and-out favourite. Graham Henry's New Zealand were the reigning Tri-Nations champions and for the preceding two years had been playing rugby on a different planet from everyone else. In captain Richie McCaw and outside half Dan Carter, they had two players already touted as all-time greats; the rest of the squad was littered with world-class players. Yet the question could still be asked: were they destined, like their predecessors in the previous four tournaments, to be labelled as 'chokers'? New Zealand had won the first World Cup in 1987 and had entered every tournament since then as favourites. But they had finished on

the wrong end of some of the most extraordinary matches in recent rugby history – and that hurt. Graham Henry and his men knew that the whole of rugby-mad New Zealand expected them to deliver this time and that they dare not let the nation down.

Scotland once again found themselves paired with New Zealand but were entering the group with their sights firmly set on quarter-final qualification as runners-up. To reach the last eight, though, they would have to beat Italy, to whom they had lost at Murrayfield in the recent Six Nations Championship. Both teams expected to beat Romania, still a long way from the force they had been in the 1980s, and new boys Portugal, who had emerged from a qualifying tournament involving a record 86 nations from 5 continents to claim the last place at the finals.

Pool D was dubbed the 'pool of death'. Namibia, in their third World Cup, and Georgia, in their second, were given no hope against three teams ranked in the top ten in the world. Argentina, packed with players who had honed their talents in Europe, had beaten England at Twickenham only recently; Ireland – with Brian O'Driscoll, Paul O'Connell and Ronan O'Gara in their prime – were the reigning Triple Crown champions; and France had finished top of the Six Nations in three of the four years since the last World Cup.

And all the pressure was on France – from broadcasters TF1, who had already released the news that it needed Les Bleus to at least reach the final from the point of view of advertising revenue; from President Sarkozy, looking for a feel-good factor as he launched a painful programme of reforms; from a government hoping that a successful competition would attract an extra 1.6 million tourists per year, generate an extra 8 billion euros over the next four years and boost France's chances of obtaining the Olympic Games after losing out to London for 2012; and finally from the French public, still living off the memories of the outpourings of pride that engulfed the nation the last time France had staged a World Cup. As French Rugby Federation President Bernard Lapasset put it: 'We're all dreaming of 1998 and of a win for Les Bleus.'

A whole nation had got behind its team, and a whole nation had got behind the event. Never before had the words of the Marseillaise been belted out with such pride – and such longing: '… *Le jour de gloire est arrivé*!'

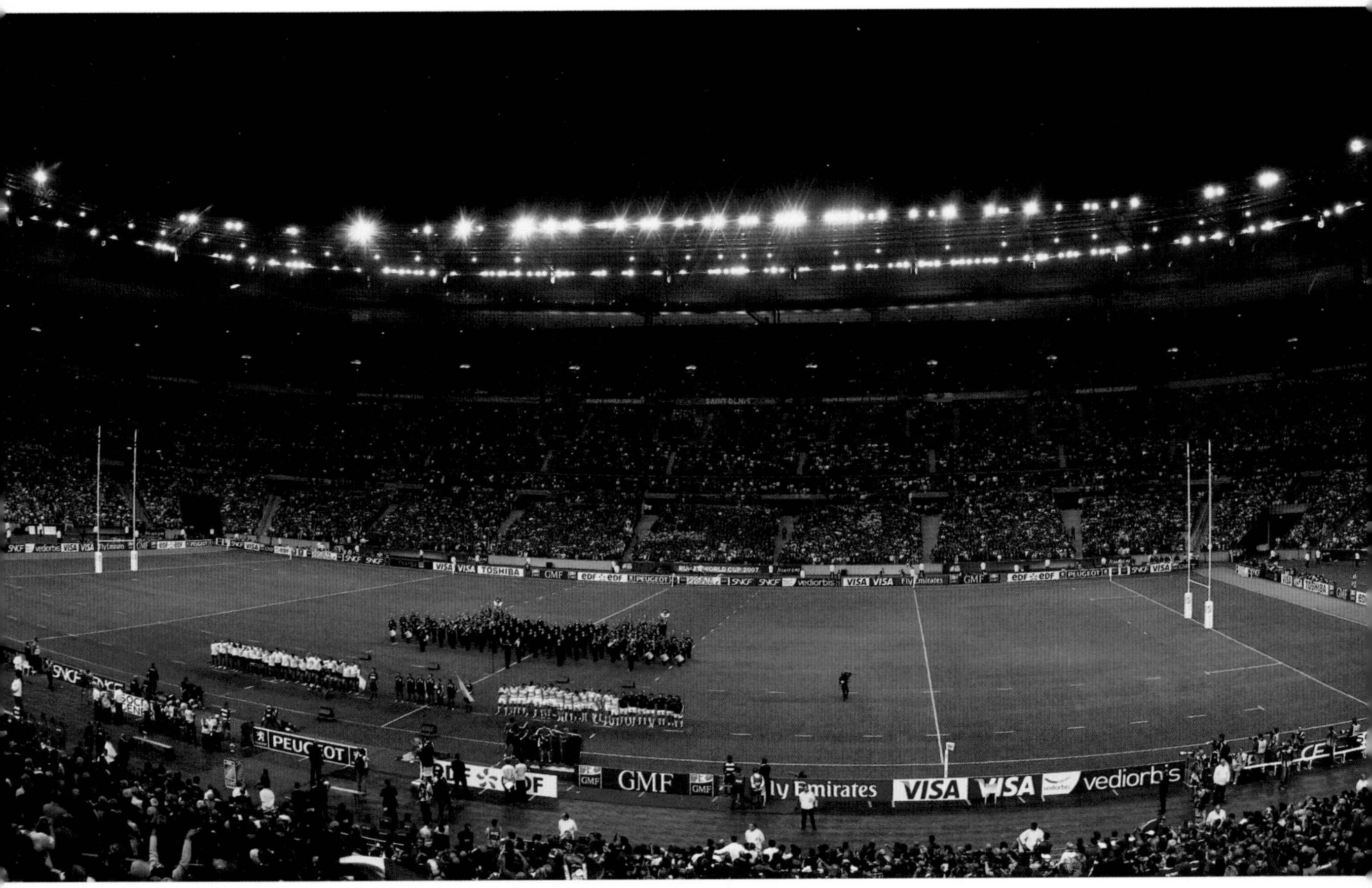

'07

O2

As armas! As armas!

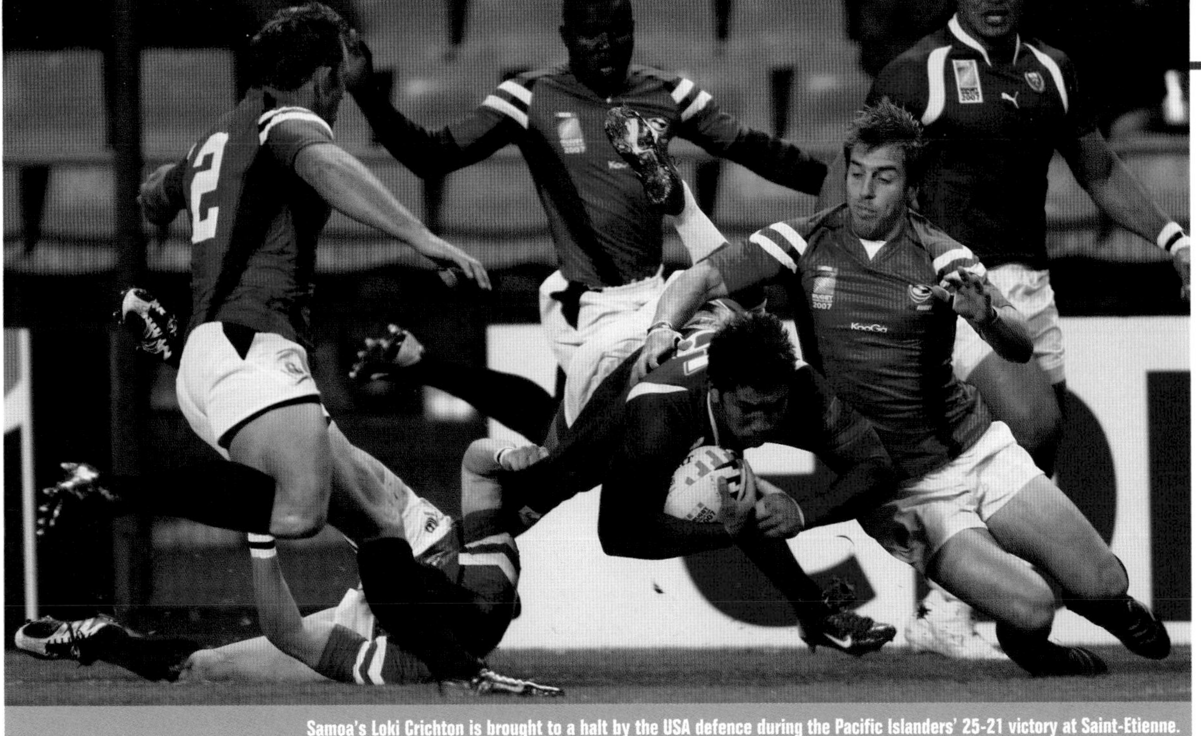

Samoa's Loki Crichton is brought to a halt by the USA defence during the Pacific Islanders' 25-21 victory at Saint-Etienne.

POOL A

NO TWO-HORSE RACE

MICK CLEARY

One game. One shot at glory. One face-off. That's what Pool A was going to be all about. A heavyweight tussle between familiar foes. Another round in what had become a feature of recent World Cups.

England and South Africa knew each other well. They had experienced the elation of victory as well as the slumped shoulders of defeat. Each had nudged the other into the margins of previous World Cups. Each knew the significance of victory. This sporting soap opera was due another episode. Watch that and fast-forward to the real drama of the knockout stages. Yep. That's what Pool A was all about.

Same as in Perth four years earlier. The two countries had tussled and duelled back then, the Boks showing the survival instincts of the desperate and the damned. They had been backed into a corner, fighting for their very credibility. They gave every last bit of their being, but the would-be world champions had that extra bit of class. On went England to glory. On went South Africa to tame defeat by New Zealand and vilification back home.

In 1999 England and South Africa met at the quarter-final stage in Paris. Fly half Jannie de Beer landed dropped goal after dropped goal. Five in all. England sank to their knees as if he had planted his boot in their nether regions. Back then, it was England who trudged home, chided for their tame resistance.

More of the same then for the 2007 Rugby World Cup? Another exclusive showdown between two of the game's superpowers? Well, it was an ingredient, albeit in a staggering guise. But there was far more on offer in Pool A than just a slug-fest between the old rivals. As befitted the tone of RWC 2007, everyone brought something to the table. No one was there merely to make up the numbers. No one was there as cannon fodder. Each and every team came with hope in their heart and abundant skill in their boots. Each and every team was fit and ready and prepared to dare. They were not going to lie back and be trampled on by the big boys. They were no mere punchbags. They were no patsies.

Tonga, Samoa and the USA all left their mark on Pool A. Certain individuals left their mark on the opposition, too, it has to be said, with two notable citings in the first game. USA centre Paul Emerick was banned for five weeks for his tip tackle on Olly Barkley and exited the tournament at the first. England captain Phil Vickery also copped it, cited for his crude, reckless hack on Emerick, for which he was suspended for two matches. It was a bad start for England, who were flat and leaden throughout, getting home 28-10 but without either swagger or conviction. And they'd lost their captain.

Samoa centre Brian Lima was also to leave his own trademark imprint. First 'the Chiropractor', in his record fifth World Cup, took a heavy hit when flying up on Springbok Andre Pretorius, sustaining a concussion which was to rule him out of the game against Tonga. Then Lima, who was to retire after the tournament, had his career brought to a premature end with a three-match ban for a wild tackle on Jonny Wilkinson. Tonga flanker Hale T Pole also joined the bad boys, banned for one week for his piece of mayhem against his Pacific Island cousins.

No, Pool A was not a gentle place to be. But it had heart and soul and empathy. The Islanders brought not only their traditional good cheer and fearsome rugby presence. They also brought no little good practice to bear on the field of play – notably Tonga, who eclipsed their Pacific rivals Samoa.

What was truly heartening was that there was a real sense that the injection of cash from the International Rugby Board was actually paying dividends. For so long, we have all wrung our hands and tut-tutted about the scandalous plight of the Pacific Island countries, upbraiding the IRB for their seeming neglect of these proud rugby tribes. And now, what do we see? A sense of structure. A semblance of planning and cohesion. A hint of what might be.

BELOW Olly Barkley is upended by Paul Emerick in England's opening match. The USA centre received a five-week ban for the tackle, although Barkley later played down the incident. **FACING PAGE** Tonga replacement Viliami Vaki seals the match v USA with a try ten minutes from time.

'The IRB funding means that we can run academies and help nurture talent for the future,' said Samoa coach and former All Black Michael Jones, who was to step down after the tournament. 'That might help give young Samoans a future rather than just relying on getting a scholarship to New Zealand. The next step would be for us to try and develop our own professional competition within the Islands, perhaps contract the top 40 players or so. That's the dream. At least, though, we've got things rolling.'

And so they had. Samoa, in fact, had a disappointing World Cup, falling below their customary high standards. But the scales were balanced, because as they went down, Tonga came up. Tonga beat Samoa for the first time in seven years, winning 19-15 in a fractured, disjointed match in Montpellier. The Tongans were not the slightest bit bothered about the quality of the game. The result was all that mattered for them. They had always been seen as rich in promise but poor in delivery, often running out of steam or lacking in organisation.

Tonga had come into the game on the back of an encouraging 25-15 win over the USA at the same Stade de la Mosson in Montpellier just four days earlier. (Once again, it was disturbing to note how it was always the so-called minnows who had to endure the quick turnarounds between games. They didn't moan. They just got on with it. You can only imagine the hue and cry if it had been a New Zealand or an England that had to suffer such hardship.)

Tonga substitute Viliami Vaki scored the match-clinching try against the Eagles ten minutes from time. No. 8 Finau Maka, a familiar figure on the European circuit for his Afro hair as well as for his barnstorming performances for Stade Toulousain, set his side on their way with a try after two minutes. Tonga showed that they had much to offer up front as well as out wide, with Maka touching down from a rolling maul. Tonga's robust, disciplined forward play was to be a feature of their campaign.

USA prop Mike MacDonald helped his side get back into the game with a try eight minutes into the second half. The scores seesawed thereafter, Tonga captain Nili Latu setting up wing Joseph Vaka for a try before Eagles second-row Louis Stanfill clattered over in the 67th minute. With the score at 18-15, Tonga had good cause to celebrate Vaki's winner.

That Tonga were able to last the distance was due to many factors, one of which was the presence of Australian trainer Brian Hopley in their ranks. Hopley introduced several facets into their training regime, from the use of inspirational motivational quotes from the likes of Winston Churchill to regular pool sessions following a game. 'It was a challenge at first because some of the players were non-swimmers, so they didn't like the

RIGHT Tonga flanker Hale T Pole lets referee Jonathan Kaplan know in no uncertain terms that Epeli Taione has scored against Samoa. The Tongans later hung on with 13 men to beat their Pacific Island rivals 19-15.

water and didn't understand why they had to jog round a pool,' said Hopley, who had been part of the Wallabies' World Cup-winning camp in 1991.

Tonga's gutsy performance against Samoa showed that their opening win was no fluke. They had to really draw on each other to come through, finishing the match with 13 men after Hale T Pole was sent off and then yet another yellow card was handed out. Michael Jones paid due compliment to Samoa's opponents, saying that it was the best Tonga performance he had ever seen. Centre Epeli Taione scored the only try of the

ABOVE Springbok back-rower Schalk Burger takes out Junior Polu. Penalised at the time, Burger was eventually banned for two games for a dangerous tackle on the Samoa scrum half. **FACING PAGE** Sukanaivalu Hufanga crosses for a try as the Tongans rattle the Springboks in Lens.

match on the hour, making amends for his own yellow card in the 28th minute. Toma Toke was the other Tongan to be sin-binned. Tonga competed ferociously in every phase of play.

'The Tongans, when they're in that mood, it doesn't matter which game plan you throw at them, they're going to knock you over, smash you over,' said Jones. 'They were awesome. We have to eat humble pie.'

Tonga had announced themselves. They were going to be a handful for any side that took them lightly. There was a distinct impression that Samoan minds were on the game against England a week later in Nantes. 'We wanted this one more than Samoa,' said Tonga captain Latu. 'I said to the boys before the game, "Today you either die or come back to the changing room with nothing."'

Tonga's win was no fluke, no mere blip upwards. As Samoa were gathering themselves to give England a lively challenge in Nantes, so Tonga were on the brink of causing one of the greatest upsets Rugby World Cup had ever known. Their game against South Africa in Lens had appeared as if it would follow a predictable pattern, similar in tone and outcome to Samoa's opening pool game against the Boks.

Samoa had been hearty and competitive throughout the opening phases of that match at the Parc de Princes, pushing South Africa hard in every phase. They might have sustained their challenge still further if it hadn't been for some harsh judgments from referee Paul Honiss.

A litany of marginal calls went the way of the big boys. There was a key about-turn in scoring just after half-time. Samoa thought they had scored when Joe Tekori picked up and plunged over. Honiss took advice from touch judge Lyndon Bray and ruled offside. Within minutes, South Africa had scored down the other end, entirely legitimately, when centre Jaque Fourie sliced through to kill the game at 28-7.

Small wonder that Samoa feel that the dice are loaded. 'That was a critical turning point,' said Samoa coach Jones. 'It seemed pretty straightforward. A try then would have seen a totally different outcome. We might not have won but it would have lifted our boys. As it was, the wind went out of our sails. I'd like to think that refs don't go into games with the perception that lesser teams infringe.'

Thereafter South Africa galloped away to victory, 59-7, with wing Bryan Habana scoring four tries and veteran full back Percy Montgomery, two. However, the Boks didn't escape unscathed. Flanker Schalk Burger was cited for a wild, high challenge on Samoa scrum half Junior Polu. Burger had been penalised at the time but was to be banned for four matches, reduced to two games on appeal. Like Vickery, he too was to be left kicking his heels for the supposed showdown at the Stade de France.

As for Tonga, they were to show that they had far more in the locker than Samoa when it came to seriously troubling South Africa. The Boks played into their hands by taking them lightly. Jake White left out a number of his big-hitters, expecting the understudies to account for Tonga. Wrong call. Big wrong call.

The game will go down as one of the best of the tournament. It had everything: twists and turns, a potential major upset, vivid, dramatic rugby, a packed stadium and uncertainty right to the last.

South Africa came through 30-25, but they had been given one hell of a fright. How the Stade Félix-Bollaert rose to acclaim

Tonga at the end. Only the decisive intervention of a raft of high-powered substitutes from the Springbok bench saved South Africa. They trailed 10-7 early in the second-half before the cavalry – featuring, among others, Percy Montgomery, who became the most capped Springbok, eclipsing Joost van der Westhuizen – arrived on the scene to calm nerves.

The revamped Boks scored 20 unanswered points during a purple patch to seemingly rescue the game. Wrong again. Back came Tonga, who scored tries through Sukanaivalu Hufanga and Viliami Vaki to set up a nail-biting finish. Pierre Hola kicked a penalty to close the scores still further. Montgomery pushed South Africa out to five points, but the heartbeat of an entire nation stilled as a last-second kick-through bounced the wrong way for Tonga. 'I'm obviously relieved,' said White afterwards. 'I thought Tonga were outstanding.'

Tonga's next game was against England. No danger of any complacency there. No danger of England taking Tonga lightly. The world champions weren't good enough to even consider that. They might have done eight years ago. No wonder. Tonga were thumped 101-10 by England in the 1999 World Cup.

Tonga had improved since then. And England, in this tournament at any rate, had gone backwards. Their opening game against the USA ought to have been a loosener: tough in parts, but none too taxing in the grand scheme of things. How could it be otherwise? The USA were a motley crew of enthusiastic part-timers. Only a handful of them had anything like a full-time contract. The rest did what they could when they could. Former England scrum half Nigel Melville was now the chief executive of American rugby, charged with planning for the future. He knew what his team would be up against.

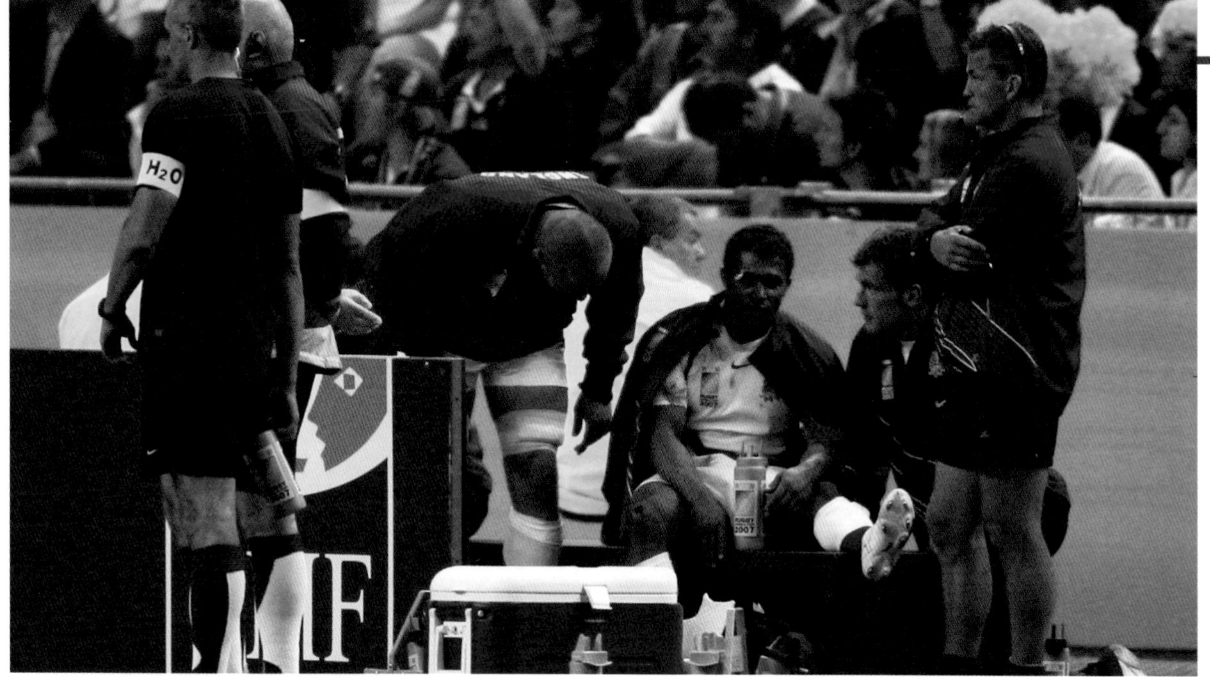

ABOVE Jason Robinson, his injured leg elevated, sits out the last quarter v South Africa. Fears that his World Cup, and career, were over proved unfounded. **FACING PAGE** Juan Smith heads for the line for the first try as the Boks rack up 36 unanswered points against England.

'Most of them have made huge sacrifices just to be here,' said Melville, who took up his post in January 2007 after ten years coaching at Wasps and then Gloucester. 'They'll just do bar work or labouring so that they can have time to train and play rugby. It will be amateurs against professionals, a throwback in some ways. Our boys feel immensely privileged to be here, to have the chance to play against the best. They won't have seen much top-level professional rugby. They'll have read about these people so, although they won't be overawed, there will be a lot of excitement about getting out there. They hope to gain the respect they deserve.'

There were only a few names in the squad familiar to a UK audience: fly half Mike Hercus, once of Sale, and injured lock Luke Gross, who had plied his trade in the Premiership and is now at first division Doncaster. Centre Paul Emerick has a contract with Newport Gwent Dragons while prop Mike MacDonald is with Leeds. Nevertheless England barely got out of first gear, tries from Jason Robinson, Olly Barkley and Tom Rees helping them to an unconvincing 28-10 win. Prop Matekitonga Moeakiola scored for the Eagles, and, indeed, the USA were to register at least one try in each of their games. One of their two scores in the 64-15 defeat against South Africa would be a candidate for try of the tournament, high-speed wing Takudzwa Ngwenya blazing past Bryan Habana, no less, from halfway to cap a move that began deep in the USA half.

That there was trouble in the England camp, though, was evident. Their woes deepened as they looked to build towards the key game against South Africa. Jonny Wilkinson was already sidelined after turning an ankle in training prior to the USA game. There had been no one near him at the time. Fast-forward seven days, Ashton names his side, gives the number 10 shirt to Barkley, who'd been Man of the Match against the USA, then watches in disbelief as another fly half limps off before the end of the training session with a hip injury. The gods didn't think much of England.

Step forward Mike Catt, who was charged with directing the game for England from fly half. He hadn't played there at Test level for eight years. Andy Farrell was named at inside centre, although there was no end of mischief-making by England as they tried to conceal just who would be wearing the number 10 shirt come kick-off. Initially they made the pretence that Farrell would be thrust into the role. As things turned out, it wouldn't have mattered a damn who played there. Farrell was also to be the principal goal-kicker, a wretched state of affairs given that he'd barely ever taken a pot at goal in union.

Three seasoned internationals had paid heavily for the lame-duck showing against the USA, Wasps back-rowers Lawrence Dallaglio and Joe Worsley as well as Sale's Mark Cueto all getting the axe. England were on their uppers. 'It will be backs-to-the-wall stuff,' said the RFU's Elite Rugby Director, Rob Andrew.

England put on a show of defiance in the build-up to the game. 'We want to draw strength from adversity,' said stand-in skipper Martin Corry. 'And we've had our fair share. But that's great. It's pulled us together. We know we've let ourselves down, our supporters down, our country down. In situations like this, the ideal game for us is a game against South Africa, in terms of the challenge they're laying down, in terms of the

physicality they offer. Nine o'clock on Friday night can't come soon enough for us.'

South Africa were in much better health, the suspension of Burger notwithstanding. Centre Jean de Villiers was, though, also missing through injury. His place was taken by the gifted Francois Steyn. Wickus van Heerden stepped in for Burger.

The Stade de France was a wonderful place to be prior to kick-off. The stands were packed. There were some 40,000 white-shirted England fans determined to make the most of the experience. Then the game kicked off and it all fell horribly flat.

England were dreadful. Simply dreadful. Long before the final whistle those self-same devotees to the English cause were to be seen streaming out of the stadium in disgust. Jason Robinson was a lone point of resistance. He alone managed to inject some urgency and devil into proceedings. But once again England were to be cursed on the injury front. Robinson pulled up suddenly around the hour mark, clutching his hamstring. By then the game was long up. England had been outfought and out-thought on a colossal scale.

If one man could be said to sum up the difference between the teams it was Springbok scrum half Fourie de Preez. He was bright, smart, alert and blindingly fast. England were none of these things. Du Preez had a direct hand in all three of his side's tries. He had the presence of mind after supporting an initial

LEFT Samoa No. 8 Henry Tuilagi runs into a welcoming committee of Joe Worsley, Nick Easter and Andy Gomarsall as England defeat Samoa 44-22. **BELOW** Wing Paul Sackey brings the crowd to its feet as he beats his opposite number, Alesana Tuilagi, to top off England's win over Samoa.

break in the fifth minute to keep his balance on one knee and find Juan Smith inside for the try-scoring run. A minute before half-time he spun away from Farrell and made huge yardage before finding wing JP Pietersen in support. Montgomery was doing damage with the boot as well, and South Africa were finding clear water. They were 20-0 ahead at the break. England were forlorn and clueless. It was only a matter of time before Pietersen added another, with du Preez again the prompt. England were shell-shocked, going down 36-0. 36-0!

There was further bad news on the injury front with centre Jamie Noon ruled out of the tournament with knee damage. England's wounds, though, were more psychological than anything. Defence coach Mike Ford was blunt in his assessment 36 hours later; honest, too, about the emotional impact.

'There was a lot of anger, a lot of embarrassment too,' said Ford. 'My stomach is still in turmoil. But we've all got to go through the mix on this one. What we can't do is sit around and feel sorry for ourselves. If we do that, we'll soon be going home. We're so disappointed for all the fans. Confidence is a fine-line thing and at the moment we haven't got it. In 2003 we had six or seven players that would make a World XV. I'm not sure how many would get in now. I'm not saying that we haven't got great players but that other teams have overtaken us. South Africa scrum half Fourie du Preez made a massive difference. We haven't got that sort of world-class player. We are where we are with some of the players we've got. Selection is a problem. We're finding out about players as the game unfolds, about how they cope with pressure and that tells us things we'd maybe not known before.'

England did manage to regroup, the return to action of Jonny Wilkinson helping them to an encouraging 44-22 win over Samoa in Nantes in which he scored 24 points. Even then, England allowed Samoa to sneak up after building an early lead. Samoa closed to within four points at 26-22. England, with a brace of tries each in the game for Martin Corry and Paul Sackey, managed to pull clear only in the closing stages. Samoa full back Loki Crichton scored 17 points, Junior Polu getting a generous verdict from the Television Match Official for Samoa's only try.

England were going through the wringer. They did at least do enough to qualify, finally subduing a spirited challenge from Tonga, winning 36-20 at the Parc des Princes, wing Paul Sackey again bagging a brace of tries. It was far from convincing. South Africa finished top, with England runners-up. The final placings may have been predicted before the start. The tale within the tale was anything but predictable.

BELOW Team-mates Dallaglio, Moody, Gomarsall and Chuter rush to congratulate Andy Farrell, who has just scored England's fourth try – the centre's first in an England union jersey – against Tonga in Paris.

Brian Lima, retiring after a record five World Cups.

What they said...

South Africa: Bryan Habana (wing)

"The first three weeks of the tournament have been great for us."

South Africa: Jake White (coach)

"Our performances send us into the knockouts with genuine confidence that's based on our heavy win over England and a substantial victory over USA when we had already qualified."

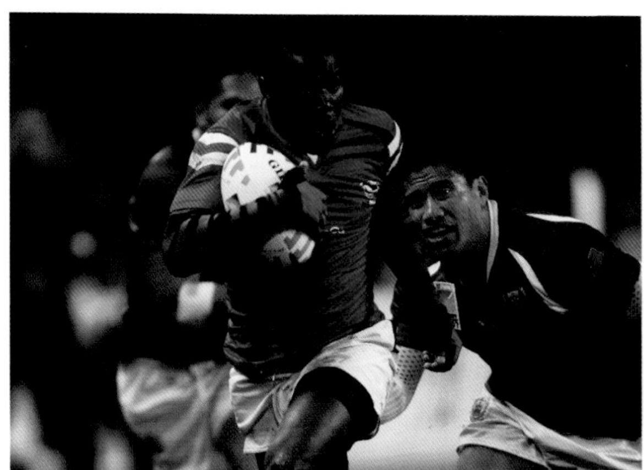

ABOVE USA flying machine Takudzwa Ngwenya – outstanding tries against Samoa and South Africa. **RIGHT** Jason Robinson and Josh Lewsey of England challenge South Africa's Bryan Habana at the Stade de France.

England: Brian Ashton (coach)

"It won't have done us any harm to fight our way out of the position we were in after losing badly to South Africa and needing to win both games against the Islanders. Still, we know we have to improve hugely against Australia."

England: Ben Kay (lock)

"After the loss to South Africa the squad was very down. Many were close to tears. We glimpsed the possibility of elimination. That would have been the lowest point of all our careers. We had to find the right answer to a couple of million-dollar questions."

Samoa: Michael Jones (coach)

"It's just wonderful finally to get a win. We were hanging in for that, because we have never gone through a World Cup without winning."

Tonga: Quddus Fielea (coach)

"We have made big strides and achieved milestones, but our rugby is desperately short of funding and needs help from other Unions."

USA: Peter Thorburn (coach)

"The little teams don't seem to get any close referee decisions. I'm very proud of the performances. We've got only four professionals and we played against two major nations and two who make top teams work hard."

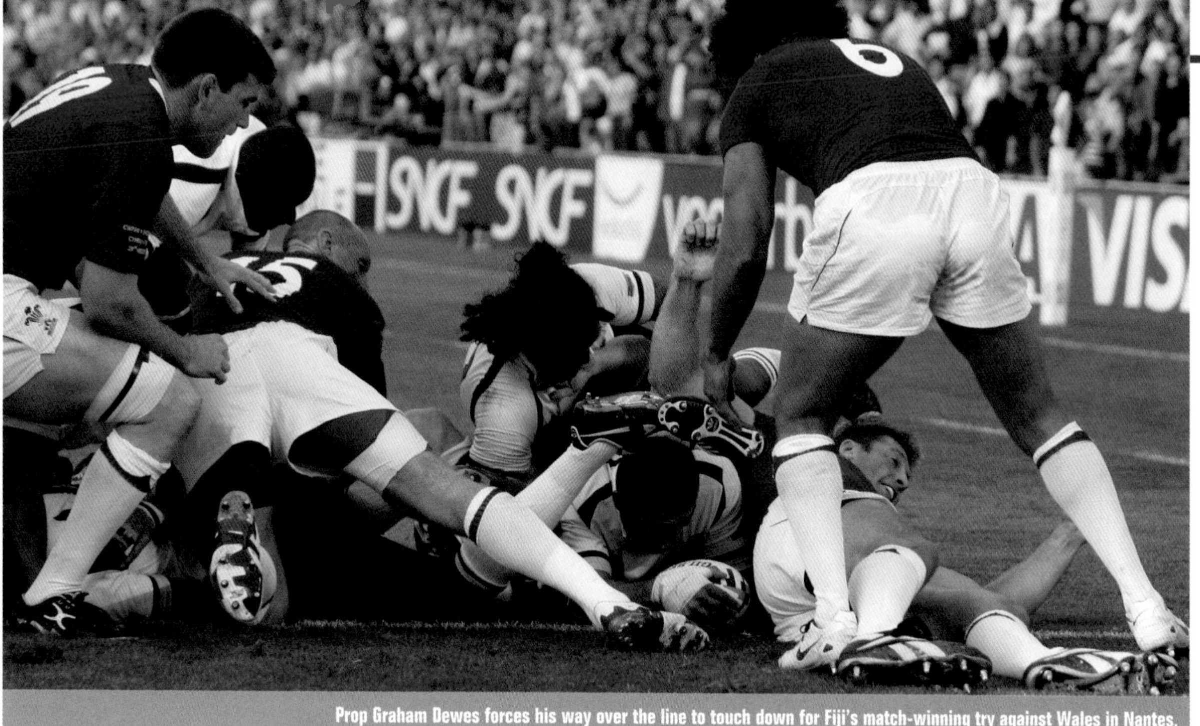

Prop Graham Dewes forces his way over the line to touch down for Fiji's match-winning try against Wales in Nantes.

POOL B

FIJI STEAL THE SHOW

STEPHEN JONES

This was the pool that had everything. It had seismic shocks, huge attendances and rugby of high calibre played by every team in the pool bar none.

In its way, the pool typified the whole tournament, because whatever the predictions were before it began, things never really turned out quite as you expected. All of the five teams – Australia, Fiji, Wales, Canada and Japan – contributed something of palpable worth, and although the pool featured the Australia against Wales game as its centrepiece, in the end the focus was elsewhere.

Indeed, the focus was on the Wales v Fiji game, which completed the pool action for both teams on a staggering afternoon in Nantes, towards the west coast of France. This was a game which almost burnt the stadium down, such was the soaring magnificence of both teams. Of its type, Fiji's epic 38-34 victory over Wales was the greatest World Cup match ever played. And yet it was no carefree romp. There was forward play and back play of high class, and even though Wales were ejected sensationally from the tournament by this defeat, they played a full part.

There was a price to pay, because within 24 hours of the end of the game, Gareth Jenkins, the Wales head coach, had stepped down amidst a searching inquest. It was little consolation to the Welsh squad and the Welsh nation that they had taken part in a match which raised attacking rugby to new levels.

Staggeringly, Fiji pulled away to a 25-3 lead with rugby from the gods during a period of only around 12 minutes in the first half. Even though Stephen Jones opened the scoring for Wales with a penalty, Fiji began to strike without mercy and with brilliant precision, with Seru Rabeni and Seremaia Bai conjuring in midfield. An attack heavily involving these two led to a try by flanker Akapusi Qera. Soon after that, Vilimoni Delasau added to Fiji's lead with a spectacular try, chipping ahead and dragging the ball down to score inches inside the dead-ball line. Nicky Little, the anchorman at fly half, added two penalties, and it was suddenly 18-3.

There was more to come. Another spectacular attack and clever handling sent Kele Leawere over, and it was 25-3. That was still the score near to half-time, but then Wales pulled a masterstroke of their own, with Alix Popham scoring after a period of Welsh scrummage dominance. Qera was sent to the sin-bin soon afterwards, and so although Fiji had taken the breath away with the brilliance of their three tries, there was still a chance for Wales if they could come out strongly in the second half. And did they ever! In fact, Wales now scored three tries which matched, in terms of sweeping attack, anything that Fiji had produced. Shane Williams scored his sixth try of the tournament after he unleashed an amazing series of sidesteps on the end of a lightning Welsh counterattack. Gareth Thomas and Mark Jones then both scored after movements involving handling and precision and sheer pace. It was Wales at their best, and the kicks took them into a 29-25 lead.

Yet not the least of Fiji's qualities on this blessed day was their resilience. Their forwards picked up the pace and Little kicked a penalty to bring Fiji to within a point, and then another to see them edge in front by 31-29.

We did not know, though, at that stage, as Fiji dominated territory and reeled off a series of attacks, that the real drama was yet to come. Little had a pass intercepted in Welsh territory and Martyn Williams raced half the length of the field to score, and although James Hook missed the conversion, Wales now led 34-31 with just six minutes remaining.

Afterwards, Little confessed that the coolness of the Fijian squad behind their posts amazed him. Apparently, even the

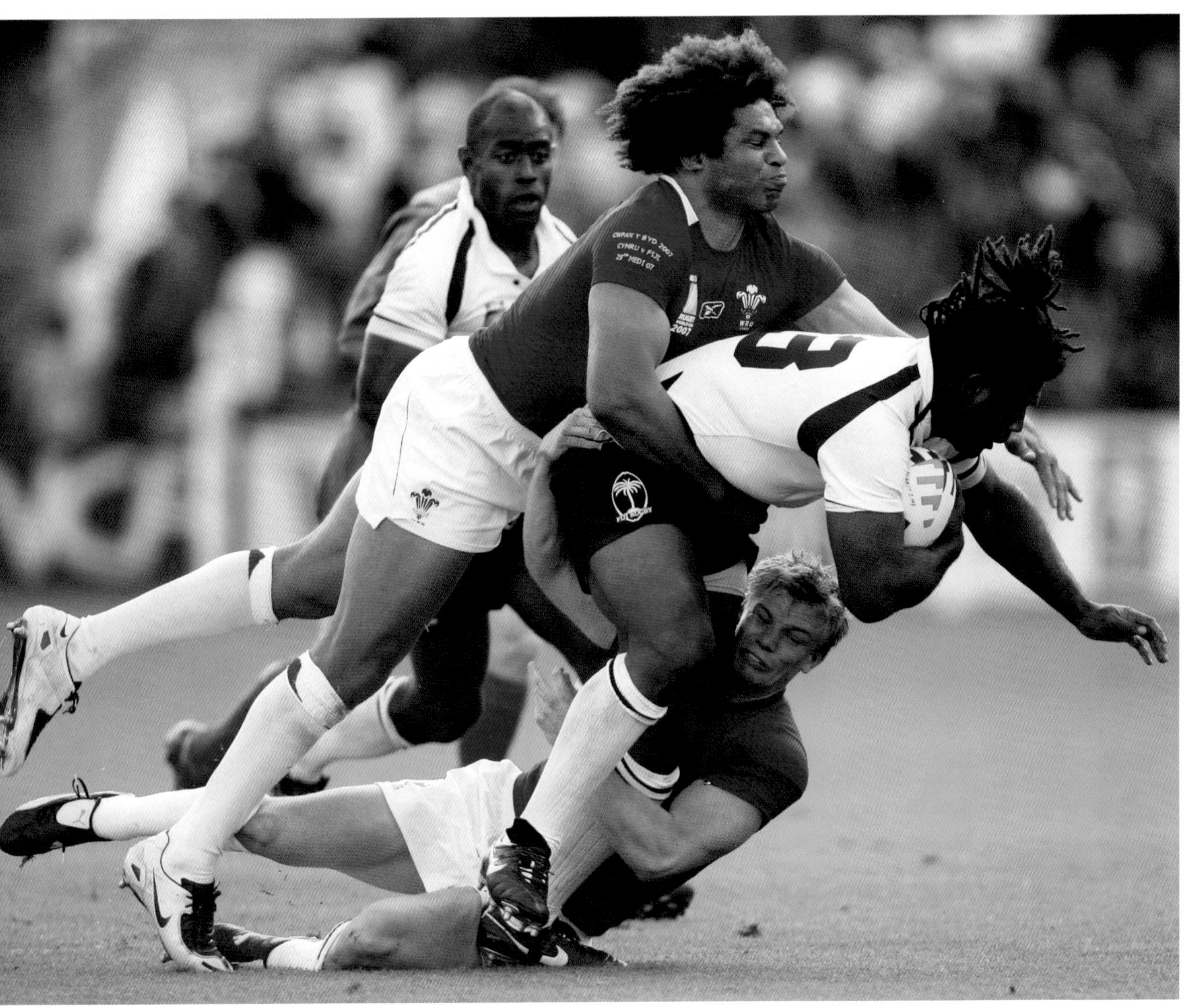

younger players were convinced that Fiji could still do it. Delasau made some brilliant runs in the closing stages, and after he was held just inches short of the Wales line, prop forward Graham Dewes came up and forced his way over. The try was given, after a suitably dramatic pause, by the video referee, and Little's conversion put Fiji four points ahead.

Was there to be another twist? It was always on the cards, but Fiji's defence held firm in the face of desperate Welsh attacks, and the epic of the tournament was over, apart from the warmest of receptions from the Nantes crowd.

It was the Wales v Australia game at the Millennium Stadium that was meant to decide the pool. It was a disappointing occasion in the sense that it was a one-off in Cardiff, far removed from the real World Cup in France and a victim of political manoeuvring. For all that, there was a large crowd who were in optimistic mood. Yet frankly, even though Wales came back strongly in the second half to lose by only 32-20, they were well out of the game from the early stages and their comeback was always going to fall short.

The young Australian fly half Berrick Barnes gave a superb performance as he came in to take the place of the injured Steve Larkham. Wales targeted Barnes for special attention, but he

BELOW Flanker Martyn Williams sets off for the Fijian line to score Wales's fifth try after latching on to an interception less than ten minutes from time. **FACING PAGE** Colin Charvis and Dwayne Peel bring down the hard-running Seru Rabeni, one of Fiji's danger men.

kept his cool and controlled the match with confidence. Indeed, it was a splendid break by Barnes which set up an early try for Matt Giteau, and this was instrumental in taking the Welsh team and the Welsh crowd out of the game.

Stirling Mortlock had to leave the field at half-time after sustaining a shoulder injury, ironically when he was in the process of scoring his team's third try. But in a tempestuous match, two tries by Chris Latham from full back, one after he gathered his own kick, frankly left Wales with very little hope of a victory. They did come back from being 25-3 down at the interval, inspired by Jonathan Thomas forcing his way over, but this was the day when the world realised that Wales had not made the necessary improvements in the months before the tournament and also that Australia were by now potential semi-finalists, at least.

The Wales forwards had been strongly fancied before the tournament, but in the continued absence of lock Ian Evans, who only reappeared in time for the last pool match against Fiji, Wales could not summon the firepower. They had a decent pack but not a dominating pack, and, frankly, the link at half back between Dwayne Peel and either Hook or Jones never appeared to spell much in the way of danger to the opposition. Indeed, Wales often attacked with real bite only when Mike Phillips, the reserve scrum half, arrived in matches as a replacement.

Nor were Wales much cop tactically. They did play some wonderful rugby against Fiji in the second half, but the idea that they allowed themselves to be sucked into what can only be described as a Fijian-type game grew and grew.

BELOW Chris Latham hurls himself over the Wales line to score in Australia's 32-20 win in Cardiff. The full back finished the pool stages ninth in the all-time list of international try scorers. **FACING PAGE** Wallaby lock Daniel Vickerman accepts line-out ball in Cardiff. **FOLLOWING PAGES** Drew Mitchell of Australia, top try scorer in the pool stage with seven, leaves Japan's Tomoki Kitagawa behind in Lyons.

It was unclear as the pool stage ended how many other Welsh notables would follow Gareth Jenkins in leaving the international scene, but apart from Gareth Thomas, the veteran captain, the Welsh squad is youthful and may well be able to regroup under the next coach.

Australia, for their part, seemed to be erasing some of the question marks which had appeared over their team ever since the 2003 World Cup final, when they were hammered up front by the English pack. Against the Welsh and in Australia's other pool games, it seemed that players such as Guy Shepherdson and Matt Dunning had improved somewhat. Certainly, even though the Wallaby scrum was never dominant, at least it appeared to be mounting a holding operation. Australia's backs were shown in a splendid light against Wales. Mortlock and Giteau appeared to be a superb centre combination and Latham was in the form of his life. It was probably here that all their likely opposition in the knockout stages realised that Australia had to be fingered up front to take their backs out of the game.

'07

The pool had opened in rather disappointing fashion, especially for those who hoped that the number of gigantic thrashings in this tournament would be well down. In fact, the number of thrashings was well down by the end, but Australia did begin with a remorseless 91-3 victory over Japan in Lyons.

The smaller teams in the tournament were always given far less time to recover than the bigger sides, and after this savaging at the hands of the Wallabies, fears grew that Japan could be wiped clean out of the event. So it was massively to their credit that they reappeared four days later and took part in an absolutely wonderful match against Fiji. It ended in a 35-31 victory for the Islanders, who scored four tries to three by Japan. But it was here that Japan showed some of their attacking potential. The final five minutes provided one of the highlights of the World Cup because Japan retained the ball through a multitude of phases in a desperate attempt to score the winning try. The move rolled on and on and on and space often seemed to be appearing in the Fijian defence. But Fiji managed one final turnover and held out.

By this time, Wales had beaten Canada 42-17, although not before Canada had pulled well clear in the first half. Canada's fate of finishing bottom of the pool with only one draw – against Japan – suggests that they were weak. In fact, they were anything but. In terms of fitness, sophistication and quality, this was the best Canadian team to appear in a World Cup since the 1991 heroes reached the quarter-finals and took New Zealand all the way in a memorable match in Lille.

This time, coached by a clever and wise owl in Ric Suggitt and led by the experienced Morgan Williams at scrum half, they were distinctly lively. They had a decent mixture of youth and experience, the latter provided by two wonderful old warriors in Rod Snow and Jon Thiel, the props, who were 69 years old between them. Thiel provided one of the stories of the World Cup by playing well even though it was not much more than a year since he had undergone heart surgery.

For many people, Canada were the most unlucky team in the whole tournament. Even though they lost 29-16 to Fiji in Cardiff, the scoreline made a mockery of the run of play. Canada were trailing by less than a converted try and were hammering away boldly in the closing stages, often within inches of the Fijian line and also near the posts should a conversion have been required. In the end, though, Kameli Ratuvou ran the length of the field on an overlap turnover to score his second try. Canada were also desperately unfortunate to have a try ruled out by the Television Match Official (TMO). Mike Pyke, their full back, appeared to ground the ball properly when his momentum took him over. But the try was disallowed.

ABOVE Canada seem unable to believe that referee Tony Spreadbury is referring Mike Pyke's (with ball) scoring attempt against Fiji upstairs. In the end the try was disallowed. **FACING PAGE** Shane Williams slides in in Wales's 72-18 win v Japan. He scored a pair in this match and another brace against Canada and ended his World Cup with six tries in all.

This was by no means the only time that Canada fell foul of the officials. They were leading Japan by seven points towards the end of another enjoyable group match in Bordeaux. Frankly, Canada could easily have been further in front, because Morgan Williams appeared to have been denied a valid try earlier in the match. With the clock showing that time had run out, Canada kicked the ball safely out of play and were about to begin the celebrations. Yet amazingly, we discovered that the prominent stadium clock was not necessarily the sole arbiter of time.

Apparently, because of some lack of communication between the stadium clock operator and the referee, there was still time remaining. This was quite appalling, and Canada did well to take their ill fortune with relative grace afterwards.

Japan used the time well. They launched a desperate series of attacks, and the TMO was called in again in controversial circumstances, ruling that Williams had batted the ball illegally out of play. He may well have done, although no camera angle existed which proved conclusively that the ball was not already out of play when he made contact. Japan duly attacked again, scored a converted try for a 12-12 draw, and Canada's hopes of a rare World Cup victory were dashed. Afterwards, the impressive Suggitt urged his men to hold up their heads. 'The process of putting Canada back towards the top of the rugby tree is in progress, it may take ten years but we will get there.'

Canada played bravely only four days later, going down 37-6 to Australia in Bordeaux. Later that same day, Wales completed the pool with their extraordinary defeat at the hands

of Fiji. A satisfying number of the ten pool games had ended closely, and indeed, it was probably this pool more than any other which showed in a ridiculous light the notion peddled by the International Rugby Board that the tournament should be reduced to only 16 teams.

The shaking ground on which this plan first rose was that the tournament was a little too long, and also that there were too many big scores. Granted, Japan did concede a total of 163 points in their games against Australia and Wales alone, even though they were fiercely competitive in their other matches. But the progress of Fiji demolished any sporting or moral argument to reduce the number of teams in the finals from 20

FACING PAGE DTH van der Merwe crosses for Canada's second try against Japan. **LEFT** The Japan team show solidarity as Shotaro Onishi lines up the conversion that would give them a draw against Canada. **ABOVE** The conversion is on its way, snatching victory from Canada at the very last.

to 16. They were curiously ill at ease in a 55-12 defeat at the hands of Australia in Montpellier, but in beating Canada, Japan and Wales, they stuck up for the rights of all the smaller nations to be present. Indeed, the IRB should surely be investigating as a matter of urgency the idea of producing 24 teams to contest the 2015 World Cup, which seems likely to be held in England.

It is ironic that the IRB's own successful funding programme has helped Fiji enormously, giving them proper back-up and, in the shape of the new Pacific Nations Cup, an event in which to hone their skills and teamwork. The other great factor in their improvement has been the fact that so many Fijians now play tough professional rugby in France and England.

There was nothing flashy or fluky about Fiji's play in this tournament. It was based on sound principles, and all those who claimed that they were merely playing glorified Sevens rugby missed the point. The likes of Rabeni and Bai were good enough to unlock the best of defences, often with first-phase ball.

So it was Australia and Fiji who were to progress from this colourful pool. As for Wales, there had seemed an outside chance that, given the enormous benefit of home advantage for two of their games, they could take the pool title. But they never really gelled; they never appeared to have a real structure and purpose. It was supremely ironic that Wales only clicked into gear when way behind against Fiji; and even more ironic that the day of their deepest gloom was the day when the sport itself shone brightest.

BELOW Fiji players celebrate their remarkable victory over Wales in one of the great matches in World Cup history.

Gareth Thomas – 100 caps, a try and heartbreak v Fiji.

What they said...

Australia: John Connolly (coach)

"There are question marks about whether we have had enough hard games and there is a plus and minus to that. Sometimes the hard games can drain you and other times you can build from them."

Fiji: Ilie Tabua (coach)

"Our goal was to get to the quarter-finals and to achieve it is an amazing feeling. It shows that the tier-two nations can compete, and that there is more competition for the level-one teams."

ABOVE Canada's Mike James wins line-out ball v Australia in his last match before his retirement from international rugby. **RIGHT** Wales coach Gareth Jenkins after Wales bowed out of RWC 2007. Though after the defeat to Fiji he expressed a wish to continue in his job, within 24 hours he had gone.

Wales: Gareth Jenkins (coach)

"We're bitterly disappointed. People outside international sport cannot comprehend our bitterness. There's not one of us here who's not bleeding emotionally, but it was probably the game of the tournament so far."

"Personally, my ambition is to continue coaching Wales, simple as that. We've had the result we didn't want, and I did say I would be judged on the World Cup."

Wales: Gareth Thomas (captain)

"I think the emotion as a rugby player is difficult because when you've played rugby forever you don't feel like you've let yourself down. But you do feel like you've let your nation down. We really believe that we've let down a nation of passionate rugby people."

Canada: Mike James (lock)

"We are very disappointed not to have won one game and I am tired of Canada coming to the World Cup as a tourist. We need to make changes in the way Rugby Canada deals with the sport."

Japan: John Kirwan (coach)

"Japan played their four games in the short burst of 18 days and I can't fault our courage in any way. We walk away with a lot of respect."

Strong, masculine, totally unnecessary metal clasp.
Spurious ceramic stopper to flick while drinking.
Bulging neck to grasp decisively at the bar.
Glass nobbly bits. Why not?
Deeply authentic Teutonic heritage featuring some bloke from SomeWaria in Bavaria.
To be pronounced viss a Mittel European furrin' accent.
Deep brown 0.756 litre bottle. Because you're a man.
Brewed only with female hops found in the Upper Volta.

17 99
GREENE KING
IPA
Ale.
The pint with nothing to prove

GREENE KING
IPA

BRITAIN'S FAVOURITE CASK ALE

Replacement hooker Ross Ford goes over for the last of Scotland's eight tries against World Cup new boys Portugal in Saint-Etienne.

POOL C

THE SCRAP FOR SECOND PLACE

JILL DOUGLAS

A bracing dip in the North Sea and a jog along the beautiful West Sands beach in St Andrews gave the rugby world a glimpse of what the Scotland squad would bring to the World Cup.

The muscular, toned torsos were the product of a heavy summer workload, overseen by fitness coach Mark Bitcon, and their appearance on the beach in early August caused quite a stir. The team management had realised they needed to be bigger, stronger and more powerful if they were to compete on the world stage.

But Scotland's careful World Cup preparations could have come unstuck with unrest and speculation concerning the future of the Edinburgh pro team and the exodus of top players at the end of the domestic season. Scott Murray, Marcus Di Rollo and Simon Taylor were just three of the Scotland stars in the squad who would not be requiring a return flight from France at the end of the tournament after signing contracts with French clubs. But when would they be free and available to join their new clubmates?

When the make-up of the RWC 2007 pools was announced, it was clear that Scotland's success in France would depend on their performance on the last weekend of round-robin matches, against Italy in Saint-Etienne. With the group also containing nailed-on favourites New Zealand, no one was in any doubt that the second team to progress to the quarter-finals from Pool C would be the winner of this crunch match on 29 September.

And Scotland had good reason to fear the Italians. The Scots finished the 2007 Six Nations with only a Wooden Spoon to show for their efforts and were stunned by Italy at Murrayfield when the Azzurri scored three tries in the first six minutes. Pierre Berbizier's men went on to win, recording their first away victory since joining the championship. Ahead of the World Cup, many believed the Italians could seriously challenge for a place in the last eight for the very first time.

Chris Paterson put it plainly, 'Italy are a top team. They're above us in the world rankings, and

that's all you need to know to appreciate how difficult the game will be for us. But we know we can beat them and if we get our game right then we will beat them.'

Scotland had summered well and received an enormous boost when it was confirmed that their barnstorming, tough-tackling captain Jason White had recovered from major knee surgery and would be available for the forthcoming campaign. Scrum half Mike Blair was also back in action, so Frank Hadden had a full squad to take to France.

Before heading south, Scotland played two warm-up matches at Murrayfield and enjoyed a gutsy win against a disappointing Ireland and a spirited display against a classy Springbok side. Four days later they were on their way.

The Tartan Army was all too familiar with the Scotland base for the World Cup. Saint-Etienne is in the Massif Central, about 60 kilometres south of Lyons en route to Toulouse. It is a beautiful city, renowned for its art and design, but will always be best remembered by Scottish football fans as the scene of their exit from France 98, when they lost to Morocco in the city's football stadium. Rugby fans hoped to enjoy better fortunes in

BELOW New Zealand stand-off Dan Carter chips past his Italian opposite number, Roland de Marigny, as the All Blacks win 76-14 in Marseilles. **FACING PAGE** All Black Mils Muliaina, at centre for New Zealand's opening game, and Italy wing Marko Stanojevic challenge for a high ball.

the Stade Geoffroy-Guichard, known locally as *le Chaudron* (the Cauldron) or *l'enfer vert* (the green hell), an allusion to the colours worn by the local football team, AS Saint-Etienne. The Cauldron would play host to Scotland's opening match against Portugal, the day after the first game in Pool C between tournament favourites New Zealand and Italy in Marseilles.

The Mediterranean port is famed for the Mistral wind that sweeps through the city, but it was the All Blacks who blew Italy away in the Stade Vélodrome and gave an early indication of what the Scots and the rest of the world could expect in the weeks ahead. New Zealand made their intentions very clear, demolishing the Italian defence in the opening quarter and

RUGBY
WORLD CUP
2007
SCOTLAND

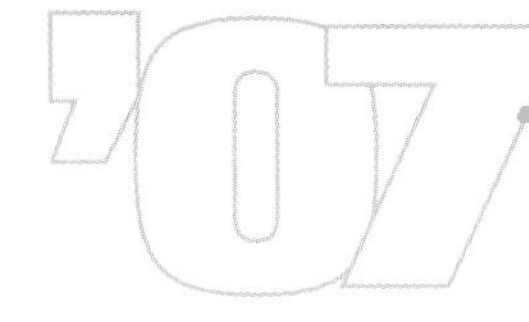

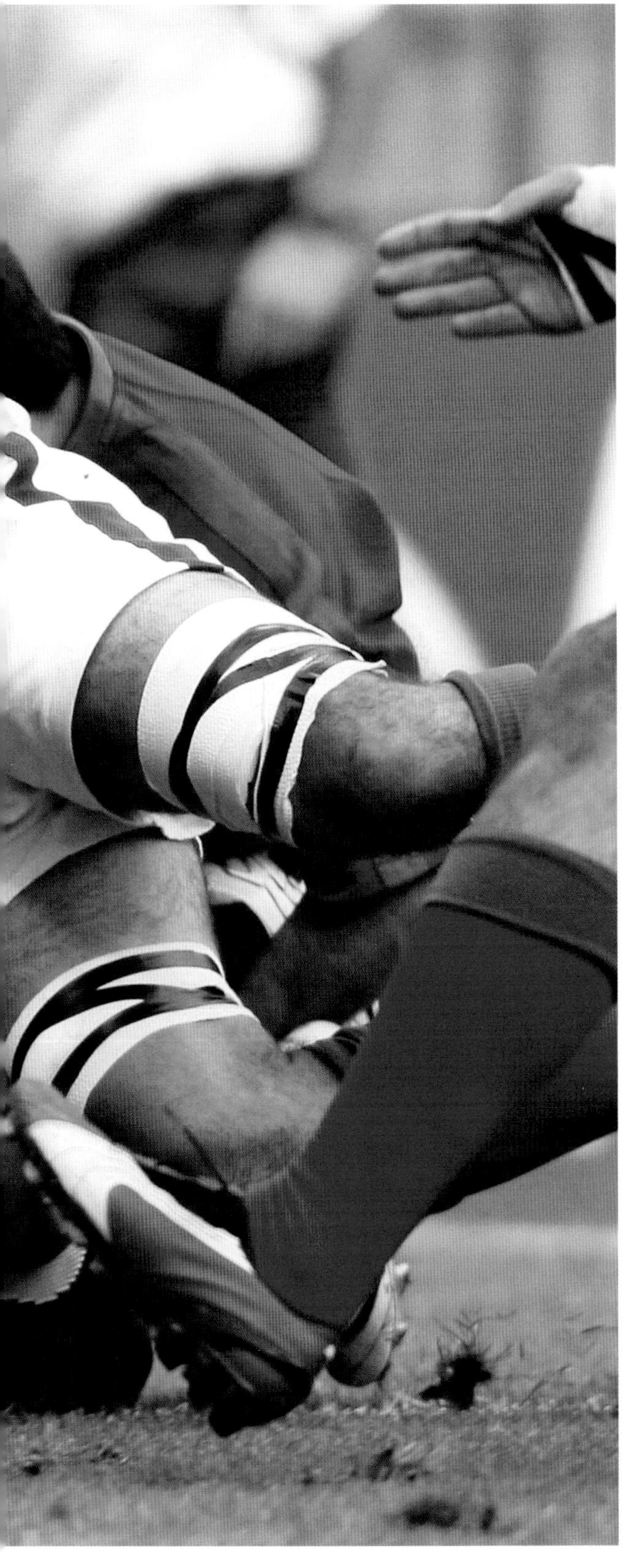

punishing their opponents for not giving the pre-match haka the proper respect. Captain Richie McCaw spearheaded the 11-try romp. He was first to cross the Italian line and was followed by Doug Howlett, Mils Muliaina and Sitiveni Sivivatu in the first half-hour to put the result beyond doubt long before the half-time whistle blew. Dan Carter contributed 17 points to give the New Zealanders a comfortable 76-14 victory, with Italy scoring tries through Marko Stanojevic and Mirco Bergamasco.

If it was All Black in Marseilles, Scotland hoped it would be all blue in *l'enfer vert* 24 hours later. A cranky start to their 2003 World Cup campaign against Japan meant the Scots would take nothing for granted against Portugal, a side of part-timers. Hadden opted to play Dan Parks at stand-off, re-igniting the debate on where Chris Paterson should play in the back line. The competition appeared to stimulate Parks, who played one of his best games in the number 10 jersey, orchestrating a Scottish victory that was convincing, if not polished. He contributed 15 points, and his final act was to convert his own try before being replaced by Paterson in the second half.

Rory Lamont made the most valuable contribution, crossing the Portuguese line twice in Scotland's eight-try haul. Hooker Scott Lawson, making his first start in over a year, gathered a Parks cross-field kick to add his name to the scoresheet before the break. A Portuguese try through left wing Pedro Carvalho gave the neutrals in the 34,500 crowd something to cheer about, but the result was never in doubt. Hugo Southwell, Rob Dewey and Allister Hogg all opened their World Cup accounts, with late tries from Kelly Brown and Ross Ford rounding off a comfortable 56-10 Scotland win.

The organisers' persistence in asking for Man of the Match contributions when only 60 minutes of the game had been played resulted in Portugal's captain, Vasco Uva, receiving the plaudits, and that was all the Portuguese had to celebrate as twilight descended in *le Chaudron*. Parks's post-match comments summed up the mood in the Scottish camp: 'They were very good on the breakdowns; we were less so. We'll work on our defence, we're happy enough but there's still plenty of work to be done.'

A break of nine days allowed the Scots to regroup and recruit prop Alasdair Dickinson, who celebrated his twenty-fourth birthday with the Scotland squad after being called up as a replacement for the injured Allan Jacobsen. Dickinson arrived

LEFT **Scotland's Rory Lamont, younger brother of Sean, scores against Portugal. The full back touched down twice in this game, following up with another brace against Romania in Scotland's next match.**

in time to prepare for their next match against Romania, and to see how Italy would respond to the battering they received at the hands of New Zealand on the opening weekend.

Italy coach Pierre Berbizier made six changes to the team that lost to the All Blacks and his side made a solid start against the Romanians in Marseilles. They scored an early try thanks to some innovation from recalled fly half Ramiro Pez but looked less than impressive in defence and found themselves trailing after leaking two tries in the first ten minutes of the second half. Some solid pressure on the Romanian line eventually led to Italy being awarded a penalty try by referee Tony Spreadbury. This, and a series of penalties from the boot of Pez, spared Berbizier's blushes, and Italy were able to hang on for a 24-18 win.

A few days later the New Zealand juggernaut rolled on, crushing Portugal 108-13 in Lyons. The All Blacks became the sixth team in World Cup history to break the 100-point barrier, with the fourth highest score by a team in the competition. In response to concerns over the mismatch, New Zealand coach Graham Henry said ahead of the game that his side would be 'sensitive'. That sensitivity saw the All Blacks run in 16 tries and afterwards he said: 'I'm delighted the way the guys handled this particular game. They didn't get over-physical, they showed their skills and treated the opposition with a lot of dignity.'

Scotland had home advantage for their second match of the tournament, though had to settle for the visitors' dressing room at Murrayfield for their game against Romania. The 31,000-strong crowd witnessed another steady performance from the Scots, as they registered a 42-0 victory.

Right from the start Dan Parks was again the playmaker. He hoisted a huge garryowen into the Romanian 22 within the first minute, the ball came back to Paterson, who chipped over the Romanian defence, collected and scored to open the Scots' account. The Television Match Official was called into action, but Paterson, and the Murrayfield faithful, had already celebrated the score, and the wing, now recognised as one of the best goal-kickers in world rugby, added the conversion. This was the first of six Scottish tries, Allister Hogg grabbing a hat-trick and the Man of the Match award. 'Obviously Ally got the

Man of the Match for loitering on the wing and I'm sure the other back-row players will be congratulating him when they get back to the dressing room,' was Frank Hadden's wry response in the tunnel immediately after the final whistle.

Hadden was more impressed by the Scots' defence: they did not yield to the bruising Romanians despite the statistics showing the Scottish scrum lost four against the head, a staggering match fact in World Cup rugby. Rory Lamont added two more tries to his tournament tally and the Scots celebrated a sound victory, with their captain Jason White delivering the following verdict: 'I am disappointed in some aspects but delighted to win. We knew Romania was going to be hard. We will learn and improve for the next game against the All Blacks on Sunday. That wasn't good enough to beat the All Blacks.'

Frank Hadden's selection policy for the New Zealand game six days later split the nation. With only a further six days between the New Zealand match and the all-important date with destiny and Italy in Saint-Etienne, Hadden had a decision to make. Should he select his best side against the world's top-ranked team and build momentum going into the Italy match, giving his star players the chance to take on the favourites for the Webb Ellis Cup? Or should he sideline his key players and give the remainder of the squad an opportunity to feature in an epic encounter with New Zealand's all-star cast? The rugby public felt they might be cheated by Frank fielding a 'second-string' XV, though many had sympathy with the coach's dilemma.

ABOVE Three-try Ally Hogg breaches the Romanian defence at Murrayfield on his way to the Man of the Match award in Scotland's 42-0 victory. **FACING PAGE** Alexandru Manta attempts to charge down Paul Griffen's kick as the Azzurri struggle to overcome Romania 24-18 in Marseilles.

Frank played safe and made 13 changes to his starting line-up from the Romania match, with only Chris Paterson and

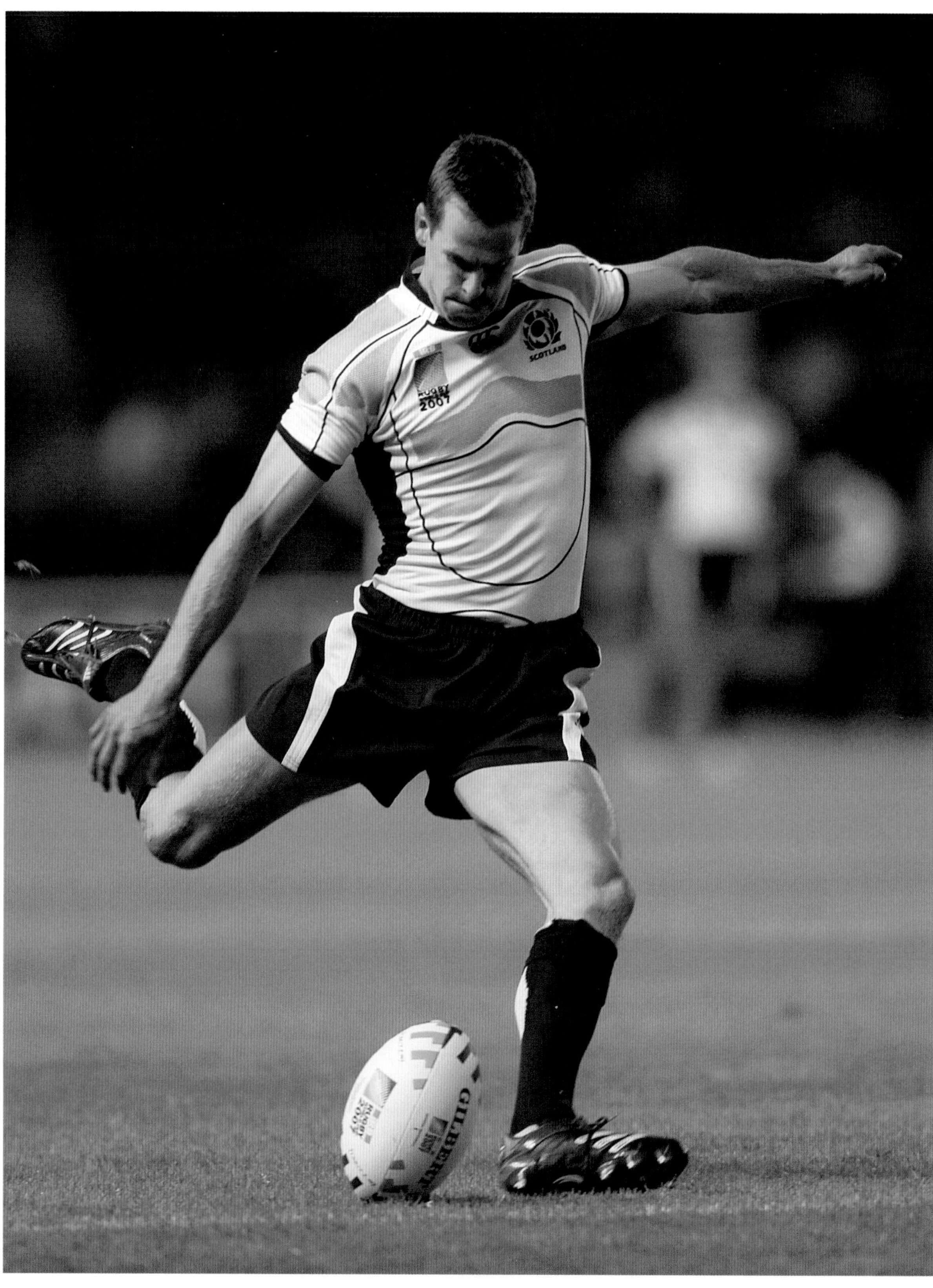
SCOTLAND
RUGBY
2007
GILBERT

speedster Simon Webster retaining their places in the XV to start against the All Blacks at Murrayfield. The debate continued in the press, on radio and television and in bars across the country. Was it a tactical master plan on the part of Hadden or abject defeatism? In all honesty, would it have mattered either way?

As it was, despite a 40-0 defeat at the hands of the All Blacks, Scotland probably emerged the happier of the two camps. There is no embarrassment in conceding 40 points against the world's best when you field your understrength side, and the New Zealanders' error-strewn performance could only be attributed partly to the fact that the two sides' jerseys were virtually indistinguishable. The clash of shirts made it sometimes impossible to tell the two sides apart. Scotland wore their new jerseys that sport lots of white alongside the traditional blue. The All Blacks were in their 'silver fern' second strip with a liberal amount of black thrown in.

But the jersey clash could not take the full blame for a below-par performance from Dan Carter and the slapdash handling of his fellow backs. Richie McCaw was first to breach Scotland's defences five minutes into the match, and there was an audible groan around Murrayfield as the Scottish fans feared the worst. But the New Zealanders squandered their early chances and made hard work of their opportunities to lead 20-0 at half-time.

The errors did not end with the break, and a series of forward passes, knock-ons and missed kicks thwarted the New Zealanders' desire for points. Indeed, it says much for Henry's side that they can accumulate 40 points while playing this badly.

Doug Howlett scored twice to set a new all-time New Zealand try-scoring record, with Byron Kelleher, Ali Williams and Dan Carter accounting for the remaining touchdowns. It was a

BELOW Doug Howlett dives in for a try against Scotland at Murrayfield. The wing registered two tries in New Zealand's 40-0 victory, his first making him the All Blacks' top try scorer of all time, passing Christian Cullen's total of 46. **FACING PAGE** Mr 100 per cent. Chris Paterson slots a conversion against Romania. By the end of the pool stage, Paterson had yet to miss a kick at goal in RWC 2007, succeeding in all 15 attempts.

ABOVE Portugal hooker Joaquim Ferreira crashes over for the opening try of the match against Romania. Although they went down 14-10, the Portuguese put up a heroic performance in close-fought match, turning over ball after ball. **FACING PAGE** Alessandro Troncon, in his 101st international, scores the only try of the decider against Scotland, but it was not enough to see Italy into the quarter-finals.

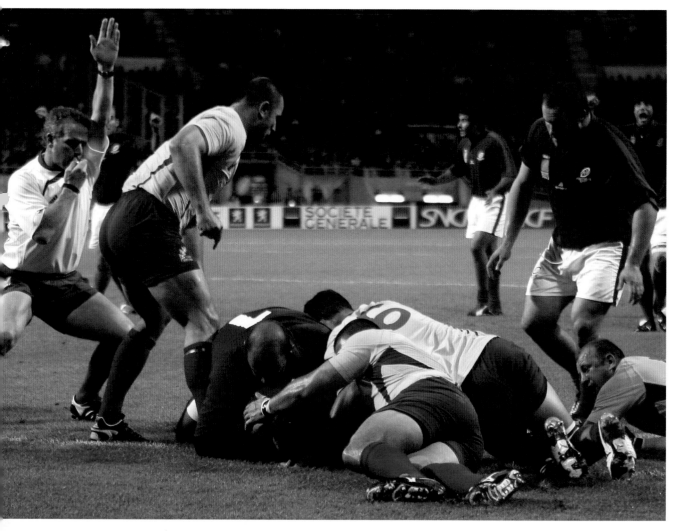

comprehensive win but by no means a walkover, and Henry himself conceded afterwards, 'we could have done better'. New Zealand completed their trouble-free passage to the quarter-finals with an 85-8 win over Romania in Toulouse.

As far as Frank Hadden was concerned, he was perfectly justified in his controversial selection and said: 'At least I have a team to train tomorrow. When I saw the tournament schedule, I could not believe it, but I had to work with it and this way I got to put out two fresh teams, one in this game and another next week against Italy.'

If Frank felt pressurised by the pool's schedule, imagine how Portugal reacted when they realised they would have to face Italy just four days after their New Zealand encounter. Italy secured the win 31-5 and so, as we had all predicted, it came down to a winner-takes-all head-to-head in Saint-Etienne.

The build-up to the match was intense. Rumours abounded of Italian players being promised a huge cash bonus for making the quarter-finals, and expectations in the country were high after their Six Nations success. But they were denied the services of their inspirational captain, Marco Bortolami, who was ruled out after suffering a spinal injury in their win over Portugal.

Taking over the armband in his swansong for Italy was Alessandro Troncon, an equally passionate servant of the Azzurri, and for many the natural leader of the side. Ramiro Pez was preferred at fly half. Frank Hadden's selection was reasonably predictable, though Scott Murray, Scotland's most capped player, was a surprise omission from the 22. Ahead of the match, Hadden was asked to comment on Bortolami's injury and whether it showed he was right to 'rest' his top players against New Zealand. 'We knew it was a brave decision because we knew we'd get pelters for it, but that didn't stop us making the decision because we are extremely ambitious and have a lot of faith in this squad to go a long way in this competition.'

Just how far Scotland could progress would depend solely on the outcome in the rain-drenched *le Chaudron*. Careful to avoid a repeat of the previous meeting in February, Scotland made a solid, if conservative, start, with Chris Paterson knocking over two early penalties to give the Scots a six-point lead. And when the Azzurri were reduced to 14 men as a result of the sin-binning of Mauro Bergamasco, it looked as though the Scots would have the composure to capitalise. But it was Italy who seized the initiative, scoring the match's only try through Troncon, with David Bortolussi adding the conversion. A hefty penalty kick followed to put the Italians 10-6 up. Game on.

Chris Paterson is deceptively powerful, a clever runner and a talented ball player, but it is his ability to slot goals which sets him apart, and he kept his side in the hunt, punishing Italy's indiscretions and kicking two further penalties to relieve the pressure and give Scotland a narrow lead at the break.

Into the second period, the newly signed Gloucester player continued in his flawless style, two further penalties giving the Scots an eight-point advantage. But Italy would not lie down and Bortolussi narrowed the gap by three points after Nathan Hines was sin-binned for a high tackle. The Italy full back then guaranteed a nerve-jangling finale to the game by slotting another kick, and with the scoreline poised at 18-16 in Scotland's favour, he was given the opportunity to win the match with a penalty kick just five minutes from time.

Ironically it was Chris Paterson who saved Scotland's World Cup four years ago in Australia, when he kicked a last-minute

conversion to seal them a place in the last eight. Bortolussi was given the same opportunity but pushed it wide and Scotland hung on for a memorable victory, exorcising the memories of Murrayfield in February.

For Italy coach Pierre Berbizier, it marked the end of his time with the Azzurri as he was to return to France post-World Cup. He had been key to the Italians' progress and promotion up the world rankings. After conceding that Scotland had perhaps handled the conditions better than Italy, he reflected on his time with the side, saying: 'I have had two wonderful years. I would like to thank Italian rugby for having allowed me to work with the national team. Now I wish them very well. It's been an amazing experience for me.'

Frank Hadden, meanwhile, was relieved to see his side progress to the quarter-finals and paid tribute to Chris Paterson, who earned his eightieth cap in the match, and Dan Parks, who enjoyed one of his best days in a Scotland jersey. 'Chris Paterson and his goal kicking was sensational, as was Dan Parks. We knew when the rain came down it was going to be a match with limited opportunities.

'It's not so much a sense of relief, it's more having an opportunity to continue to show the progress we have made in the past two years.'

Captain Jason White acknowledged the match had been tough and looked forward to the next stage, saying: 'The main thing is worrying about ourselves. We'll be taking a bit of pride from today, but stay reasonably grounded and look to improve.'

BELOW Moment of madness. Italy's Mirco Bergamasco trips Man of the Match Dan Parks at Saint-Etienne. Though the offence went unpunished at the time, the centre was later cited and received a two-week ban.

Alessandro Troncon of Italy won his 100th cap v Portugal.

What they said...

New Zealand: Richie McCaw (captain)

“All the games have been physical encounters and to get the results, the All Blacks had to do things right. They managed that, but none of the wins has been easily achieved and the gap was not as big as some expected.”

New Zealand: Graham Henry (coach)

“We want perfection. We want to win 250-nil.” (after New Zealand's 85-8 victory over Romania)

Scotland: Frank Hadden (coach)

“After the hours and hours of practice Paterson does, he thoroughly deserves the accolades.”

ABOVE New Zealand's Joe Rokocoko, who scored three tries in the match, attempts to evade Romania's Csaba Gal in Toulouse. **LEFT** Marcus Di Rollo is tackled by Diogo Mateus and Federico Sousa as Portugal, in their debut match in an RWC finals tournament, take on Scotland in Saint-Etienne.

Italy: Alessandro Troncon (scrum half)

“Elimination is a bitter pill to swallow with many players in tears. This is the biggest disappointment I have had as a player and will be very difficult to erase.”

Portugal: Tomaz Morais (coach)

“It couldn't be better. The players dignified our country with their attitude to playing rugby with heart.”

Romania: Daniel Santamans (coach)

“It's difficult to score points because we were always defending against Italy, Scotland and New Zealand.”

Argentina rejoice after beating Ireland at the Parc des Princes to top Pool D and avoid a quarter-final against tournament favourites New Zealand.

POOL D

PUMAS TOP THE PILE

JIM NEILLY

Containing three of the top six teams in the IRB rankings, Pool D was, not surprisingly, dubbed the 'pool of death' long before RWC 2007 got under way.

While it was always going to be a case of France, Ireland and Argentina competing for two quarter-final places, few would have predicted that Ireland would bow out so ignominiously and France would find themselves playing in Cardiff for a semi-final spot. France, having looked so impressive in their wins against England and Wales, seemed to be in top form, and while Ireland lost to Scotland, albeit with a second-string side, and just squeezed past Italy in Belfast, all the pre-tournament indications were that the teams that had finished in first and second places in the 2007 Six Nations would go through, most likely in that order. It was a plot that hadn't been presented to Marcelo Loffreda and his vastly experienced Pumas squad, 18 of whom had been involved in RWC 2003; and if that script had been perused, Agustín Pichot tore it up with disdain.

As the other 18 teams relaxed in their respective hotels around France and, ludicrously, in Wales and Scotland, the hosts and Argentina contested the opening game of the competition at a packed Stade de France. The scene was set for France to pick up where they had left off in the Six Nations and to take a positive step towards a home quarter-final, thus avoiding a clash with New Zealand in Cardiff. Alas for Bernard Laporte, nobody had told the Pumas.

For the third successive World Cup, Argentina had not only been drawn in the same pool as the host country, but were required to play in the opening game, presumably on the basis that, while they would not only be competitive and provide a meaningful challenge, they would lose, as they had done against Wales in 1999 and Australia in 2003.

No fewer than ten of the Pumas were playing in their third successive tournament, and with skipper

Pichot starting his fourth, and with the bulk of the side plying their professional trade in Europe, they had few weaknesses, as France were to discover.

Marcelo Loffreda, poised to take over the reins at Leicester, opted for Juan Martín Hernández to start at fly half in preference to Felipe Contepomi and Federico Todeschini. Not only did Hernández justify his selection, but he produced a variation that left the French bewildered, and his towering positional kicks caused mayhem in a nervy French defence.

A predominantly French crowd couldn't believe what was going on, and the Pumas swept into a 17-9 half-time lead against an experienced French side led by Raphaël Ibanez and containing former skipper Fabien Pelous plus another ten World Cup veterans. The Pumas started by far the better, with Contepomi, recently qualified as a doctor from Dublin's College of Surgeons, kicking an early penalty, but within two minutes David Skrela replied in kind for France, who were starting to look less than comfortable, their forwards under constant pressure from a grizzled Pumas pack, and seemingly at a loss at how to cope with Hernández' relentless bombardment. Contepomi restored the Pumas' lead with a second penalty, and came close with an attempted dropped goal after centre Damien Traille left the field with a nasty head wound and was replaced, to rapturous acclaim, by Freddie Michalak. The pace had quickened, with France raising home hopes following a huge tackle by Serge Betsen on Contepomi, which resulted in a surge for the Argentine line and required some desperate defence.

The Pumas regained their composure, nailing the French deep in their own territory, and had the Argentinians' finishing been as proficient as their approach work it would have been all over as a contest by the interval. As it was, Felipe Contepomi kicked his third penalty for a deserved 9-3 Puma advantage.

ABOVE France wing Cédric Heymans has his kick charged down by Argentine No. 12 Felipe Contepomi as the Pumas shock the host nation on opening night. **FACING PAGE** Argentine full back Ignacio Corleto leaves the French defence behind as he sprints away to score the game's only try.

It was about to get worse for the French. Centre Traille – now back on the field, with Skrela reverting to fly half – burst through the Argentine defence and linked with flanker Rémy Martin, but his speculative pass was intercepted by Horacio Agulla and he sent full back Ignacio Corleto in for the tournament's first try, stunning the home support. Contepomi's conversion hit the post, but the Leinster player, in his third World Cup, went on to land a fourth penalty to a couple from Skrela to give the Pumas a 17-9 half-time lead.

France brought on Sébastien Chabal and Dimitri Szarzewski for tiring veterans Ibanez and Pelous, and Skrela, who had kicked a fourth penalty, gave way to Michalak as France strove to break down the most parsimonious defence in the tournament. Yet it was Argentina who looked the more likely to score, with Corleto scorching away, only to deliver a poor pass to Contepomi.

Michalak, France's star of the 2003 World Cup, missed with a straightforward penalty, and the crowd knew that it would all end in tears, with Argentina holding on 17-12 for the greatest victory in their rugby history. France were left contemplating, at best, an unenviable trip to Cardiff to face the All Blacks.

Back in Bordeaux, Ireland's coach Eddie O'Sullivan, having watched his reserve side lose both Tests in Argentina three months earlier, pronounced himself 'very impressed' with the Pumas, reaffirming his belief that the final Pool D game, between his side and Argentina, would be the crucial one in the group. With 17 survivors from the 2003 campaign, and with Brian O'Driscoll, Malcolm O'Kelly and Alan Quinlan in a third tournament, Ireland had a vastly experienced squad, with most positions occupied by leading cap winners.

O'Sullivan, who had agreed a four-year contract extension, and all of Ireland had been expecting comfortable bonus-point wins against first Namibia and then Georgia, thus leaving nothing to chance in terms of the mathematics. When O'Driscoll collected his own clever kick ahead to twist over the Namibian line for a try after just four minutes, Ireland's World Cup seemed to have got off to the perfect start.

O'Driscoll's try was his thirtieth for Ireland, breaking the record he held jointly with Denis Hickie, who had announced that he was to retire from rugby at all levels after the World Cup. Ronan O'Gara, soon to be the subject of intense speculation about his personal life, added the conversion and then a penalty just after Hickie put down a perfectly decent pass which would have allowed him to get back on level try-scoring terms with O'Driscoll. While Ireland didn't seem unduly troubled by Namibia, there was the impression that here was a team struggling to find its form.

O'Gara took a quick tapped penalty and launched a perfect cross-kick which was gathered by Andrew Trimble, who was on the right wing for the recovering Shane Horgan, for Ireland's second try. O'Gara failed with the conversion and was similarly off-target after a forward surge brought a third Irish try courtesy of flanker Simon Easterby, before Namibia's fly half Emile Wessels, who had played for Esher for a couple of seasons, slotted a penalty for a 20-3 Irish lead at the interval.

Job done? Not quite, as it turned out, though a penalty try eight minutes after the restart, converted by O'Gara, gave

BELOW Ireland did not have things all their own way against Namibia. Here Gordon D'Arcy is wrapped up by Bradley Langenhoven and Jacques Nieuwenhuis. **FACING PAGE** Grigol Labadze gets the better of Juan Martín Fernandez Lobbe during the clash between Georgia and Argentina.

Ireland the bonus point they needed and they seemed capable of repeating the 64-7 trouncing of the Namibians of four years earlier. With their captain Kees Lensing, one of the few players with Super 14 experience, limping off, Namibia looked to be well out of it.

To everyone's surprise, Namibia stormed back against an out-of-sorts Ireland, scoring two excellent tries in the space of five minutes, the first from back-rower Jacques Nieuwenhuis following a splendid run by wing Ryan Witbooi, and the second from centre Piet van Zyl, in just his second Test. Wessels kicked both conversions to close the gap from 24 to 10 points. A late Jerry Flannery try, unconverted, saw Ireland home 32-17, but Namibia had come from a 57-point deficit in 2003 to just 15 in 2007, so which side had made the greater progress?

Argentina, given an impossibly tight schedule in 2003, this time found themselves back in action just four days after they upset the French in Paris. Marcelo Loffreda made only six changes in his starting line-up for the game against Georgia in

Lyons, and the Pumas struggled for most of the first half. They went behind to a penalty from Georgia fly half Merab Kvirikashvili and, despite a clear advantage in terms of territory, turned around just 6-3 ahead, with Felipe Contepomi kicking a couple of penalties.

As the Georgians wilted in the second half, Argentina started scoring tries, with Lucas Borges getting two, Patricio Albacete a third, and, right on the final whistle, a dreadful defensive howler let Federico Martin Aramburu in for what was to prove to be a vital 33-3 bonus-point win, given Ireland's failure to achieve that target against Georgia four days later.

A fit-again Shane Horgan for Andrew Trimble at right wing was Ireland's only change as Eddie O'Sullivan offered a vote of confidence in the players who had underperformed against Namibia. There had been ever-increasing stories of unrest in the Irish camp, and a French journalist enraged both O'Sullivan and Brian O'Driscoll at a press conference by asking them to comment on reports of Ronan O'Gara's alleged gambling activities. A French plot to unsettle the Irish? Surely not.

Once again in Bordeaux, Ireland were, if possible, even worse than in their opener against Namibia, failing to match the sheer muscularity of a Georgian pack who had been playing second or third division rugby in France. Any notions of Ireland repeating their two previous wins against Georgia of over 60 points were quickly dispelled, and O'Sullivan's men went into half-time just 7-3 up, Ronan O'Gara having converted Rory Best's try, and Kvirikashvili having kicked a penalty for the buoyant Georgians.

The old order was stood on its head four minutes after the restart as Peter Stringer's pass to O'Driscoll was intercepted by Giorgi Shkinin, who legged it for the Irish posts; Kvirikashvili's conversion gave Georgia the lead, sending their supporters and the French neutrals into paroxysms of glee. Ten minutes later, a nervy and totally unsettled Ireland responded with Girvan Dempsey finishing off a decent move, O'Gara converting to put his side just four points ahead.

The final quarter saw Georgia, who had tired in the same period against the Pumas, batter the Irish line. Kvirikashvili missed with a couple of dropped-goal attempts, and in the final minute only a desperate tackle by Denis Leamy stopped Georgia from snatching a winning try, Ireland ending up 14-10 victors. Amazingly, Eddie O'Sullivan felt that his side had performed better than in the first game.

Lambasted by the French press, Bernard Laporte, who had nine days to reflect upon the loss to Argentina, made 12 changes to his side to play Namibia in Toulouse, and, cleverly, included seven Toulouse players in his starting XV. With the African qualifiers down to 14 men following the sending-off of No. 8 Nieuwenhuis, Laporte got the win and the confidence boost he needed as France overran Namibia 87-10, scoring 13 tries, including a hat trick by Vincent Clerc and a couple from

LEFT Namibia can't hold Sébastien Chabal as he drives to the line to score during France's 13-try victory in Toulouse. Chabal, playing at lock, started this match, having appeared as a replacement against Argentina.

Sébastien Chabal, the second of them a typical crowd-pleasing effort from halfway.

Having left Yannick Jauzion out of the starting XV for the Namibia game, Laporte retained the entire back division for 'Le Crunch' against Ireland at the Stade de France, sticking with a half-back combination of Jean-Baptiste Elissalde, who had led the side against Namibia, and Freddie Michalak. Olivier Milloud and Raphaël Ibanez returned to the front row, Jérôme Thion came in to partner Chabal in the second and Serge Betsen displaced Yannick Nyanga in the back row.

Whether or not Peter Stringer's wayward pass against Georgia was a significant factor, Ireland's most capped scrum half, who had started 79 of Ireland's previous 85 Tests, was axed by Eddie O'Sullivan as he was poised to start with Ronan O'Gara for the fifty-third time, which would have set a new northern hemisphere record for a half-back pairing. Isaac Boss, Stringer's Six Nations understudy, was leapfrogged by Eoin Reddan for his first international start, having made his Test debut as a last-minute replacement at Stade de France in the 2006 Six Nations.

O'Gara was lucky to survive, but it seemed that O'Sullivan either was still harbouring notions that his tried-and-trusted men would deliver or had little faith in their understudies, a situation which – though the truth of it remained unclear – was reported to have been a contributory factor to unease in the camp. Denis Hickie was also dropped, with Andrew Trimble starting on the left wing and Jerry Flannery coming into the middle of the front row for Rory Best, who had dislocated a thumb against Namibia. Having failed to get a bonus point against Georgia, and with tries and match points in short supply, O'Sullivan wasn't inclined to experiment, with the prospect of a winner-takes-all game against Argentina now looking more and more likely.

Having won only once in Paris in 35 years, Ireland were rank outsiders at the Stade de France, and, after a lively start, all the ongoing frailties re-emerged, with a disturbing inability to create in midfield all too evident. While Brian O'Driscoll was firefighting all over the park, Ronan O'Gara and Gordon D'Arcy were having yet another forgettable evening, and a forward pack that had impressed in the Six Nations Championship looked distinctly overcooked and underpowered.

Try-scoring opportunities were a rarity in the first half, and Irish mistakes, which were all too frequent, were punished by Jean-Baptiste Elissalde, who kicked four penalties to one dropped goal by O'Gara for a 12-3 half-time lead to France. When Elissalde kicked his fifth goal at the end of a dull third quarter, France were all but home and dry.

Both hookers were replaced, with Frankie Sheahan, who hadn't made a match-day squad in Australia, coming on for a first World Cup appearance. Dimitri Szarzewski and Lionel Nallet

ABOVE Vincent Clerc scores his second try of the match against Ireland. **RIGHT** Clément Poitrenaud, Cédric Heymans and Clerc look happier after victory over the Irish puts France's campaign back on track. **FACING PAGE** Brian O'Driscoll arrives in the nick of time to help deny Poitrenaud.

replaced Ibanez and Chabal, with Elissalde assuming the captaincy. Four minutes after the bustling scrum half had opened up that 12-point gap, Ireland conceded a crucial try which was to see them off.

Andrew Trimble came in off the left wing, assuming, it appears, that Vincent Clerc was going to attack from a five-metre scrum. But Clerc stood his ground, and Michalak, who had been kicking like a drain all night, dropped a neat punt into his wing's hands and he went in for his fourth tournament try. Paul O'Connell's sin-binning didn't help the Irish cause, and Clerc got in again to seal an emphatic, if paradoxically unimpressive, 25-3 win for the hosts. As France celebrated, Eddie O'Sullivan, showing extraordinary levels of stoicism, maintained that his side, while short of match time, was getting better, and that a win against Argentina was still a reality, even after the Pumas put Namibia to the sword the following evening.

The Pumas were ruthless, showing Ireland what could and should have been achieved, rattling up nine tries in an emphatic

63-3 win, the bonus-point victory in the bag by half-time. Namibia's World Cup was to end in a fourth straight defeat as they went down 30-0 in Lens to Georgia, who recorded a first World Cup win.

Ireland returned to Parc de Princes for the first time in almost a dozen years, never having managed a win in 14 visits, their preparation overshadowed by the sudden illness of prop forward Simon Best, who had captained the side against the Pumas in both Tests the previous June. The genial Ulsterman had been relaxing in Bordeaux with his team-mate Paddy Wallace, when he complained of a headache, loss of feeling in one arm and difficulty with his speech. Wallace immediately contacted the Irish management, and Best was rushed to hospital where tests revealed that there was no neurological problem, and that, as was confirmed at a second hospital, and upon his return home, he had a hitherto unrevealed heart irregularity.

Best's brother Rory, due to take over the Ulster captaincy on his return to Belfast, was magnificently positive about the situation, and within hours, Simon's wife, Katie, and his father, John, had flown to Bordeaux, where the Irish team doctor, Gary O'Driscoll, had been ever present at Best's bedside. That the prop had not suffered a stroke and would make a full recovery – though his rugby future was far from certain – gave the Irish camp a major boost.

The situation at the top of Pool D produced mathematical permutations of mind-blowing complexity, with Argentina weighing up the likelihood of winning the pool or finishing third and out of the quarter-finals. France's straightforward win over Georgia, who went down 64-7 in Marseilles, copper-fastened a place in the last eight, though the Georgian forwards again did themselves proud. Nine tries, including two from veteran wing Christophe Dominici, indicated the French superiority in the threequarters, and then it was a case of the French getting behind Ireland, who if they could secure a four-try bonus-point win and deny the Pumas a loser's bonus point would ensure that France stayed in Paris for a home quarter-final.

Eddie O'Sullivan was forced to call upon Geordan Murphy, a player with whom he had, it appeared, an indifferent relationship, to replace the injured Girvan Dempsey, in the wake of tales that Murphy had to be recalled to the Irish camp from the airport at Bordeaux, having decided to quit the World Cup. Denis Hickie, in his eleventh season of international rugby, replaced Andrew Trimble, who was then forced to withdraw from the replacements' panel with an infected finger. In all, the Ireland coach started just 19 players throughout the campaign, two fewer than in the four pool games in Australia in 2003.

Again, O'Sullivan was convinced that his side was on an upward curve, and, with three games under their belts, he believed that his players would perform against a side that hadn't conceded a try throughout. Even so, Ireland were relieved that France had gained a bonus point against Georgia, since, if they hadn't, O'Sullivan's men would have been out of the tournament well before kick-off at Parc des Princes.

There was an eerie feeling of déjà vu at the old concrete edifice, so many times the scene of gallant Irish defeats, as well as a few utter tankings, and the gusto with which the Pumas sang their anthem was indicative of their resolve as they prepared for another memorable night in their rugby history. No. 8 Gonzalo Longo was the only change from the side that had ambushed the French in the tournament's opening match.

Ireland began at a frantic pace, but the loss of their opening line out and some impoverished kicking by Ronan O'Gara didn't bode well, despite a territorial advantage. Again, Gordon D'Arcy was a shadow of the player who had excelled in several Six

BELOW Felipe Contepomi and Shane Horgan chase a loose ball towards the Irish line. In the end Denis Hickie, following on, showed a great turn of speed to touch down ahead of the Pumas' centre. **FACING PAGE** Georgia celebrate the opening try of their maiden RWC win, against Namibia.

Nations campaigns, and while the Irish pack were far from overwhelmed, they lacked the abrasive thrust of the Pumas' eight, six of whom were more than 30 years of age.

A rare penalty miss by Felipe Contepomi, who was playing against four of his Leinster colleagues in the Irish threequarter line, gave Ireland some brief respite as Argentina survived early but misdirected Irish pressure. Then the Pumas exploded with some slick support and wonderful probing from the ebullient Pichot, who sent Lucas Borges past and through Hickie and David Wallace for the game's first try.

Four minutes later, O'Gara reduced the gap to two points with a penalty, but from the restart Argentina regained possession, and fly half Hernández, revelling in his new international role, dropped a goal. Ireland scrambled possession from another messy line out, and D'Arcy drifted wide to allow O'Driscoll to take O'Gara's flat pass. Ireland's captain hit the line like a rocket and touched down for his thirty-first Test try, which O'Gara goaled to put the Irish ahead for the first and only time.

Hernández dropped a second goal with five minutes of the half remaining to take his side back into the lead before Argentina conjured up a second try, Horacio Agulla squeezing in at the corner. Contepomi converted and the Pumas bounded off at half-time 18-10 up, confident that they could deny Ireland the hatful of scores they would need in the second period.

Contepomi popped over a penalty just two minutes after the restart before Ireland shone again, with O'Driscoll slipping his marker to offload to Wallace. The flanker, who had spurned a first-half overlap, found Murphy, who ran a lovely angle for the best score of Ireland's campaign. O'Gara failed with the conversion, and the Irish challenge simply faded away. Contepomi kicked successive penalties and Hernández completed a hat-trick of dropped goals for a 30-15 win, and a thoroughly deserved one, for the Pumas.

Argentina remained in Paris to prepare for their quarter-final against Scotland, France came to terms with the enormity of their game in Cardiff against New Zealand, and Ireland, of whom so much had been expected, left for Dublin the next morning. Despite a hammering from the Irish press corps and from the vast majority of Irish supporters, Eddie O'Sullivan was adamant that he had no intention of walking away from his post, a situation confirmed in Dublin by Philip Browne, the IRFU's chief executive.

Whether or not the ultra-conservative O'Sullivan, assuming he will make minimal changes to his squad, can recapture the spirit and enthusiasm that had prompted such optimism remains to be seen. For most Irish supporters, the performances were far more disappointing than the results, and if O'Sullivan does stay in harness will he start building for the 2011 World Cup with immediate effect?

BELOW Argentine left wing Horacio Agulla beats No. 8 Denis Leamy's last-ditch dive to score the Pumas' second try as Ireland go down 25-3 and out of the World Cup at the Parc des Princes.

Denis Hickie retired from Test rugby after RWC 2007.

What they said...

Argentina: Agustín Pichot (captain)

"It's a relief after what happened in the last World Cup when we lost badly to top nations. We came to win the four pool matches in a strong group and we have done it."

Argentina: Marcelo Loffreda (coach)

"We haven't exceeded the level of the Six Nations, but we are level with Europe and have a place in the world. This team can play against any team at any level."

ABOVE Georgia fly half Merab Kvirikashvili kicked 15 points as his side recorded their maiden RWC win against Namibia in Lens. **RIGHT** Yannick Jauzion of France tries to find a way through the Namibia defence in Toulouse.

France: Raphaël Ibanez (captain)

"We've qualified for the quarter-finals, and that was our first objective before we started our 'pool of death'. We live on."

France: Bernard Laporte (coach)

"We are happy to have qualified, but unhappy that one loss to Argentina on the opening day means that we have to play in Cardiff."

Ireland: Brian O'Driscoll (captain)

"We had three options open and we're taking the worst. A lot of the onus has to go on the players. There's only so much coaching that can be done. Maybe we played some half-decent rugby at the end, but it was too little, too late."

Ireland: Eddie O'Sullivan (coach)

"It does not matter what ideas we had about ourselves. The fact is that we were not good enough and are going home. I'm totally committed to this job. It's been a tough World Cup and things haven't gone to plan. But I've never walked away from a challenge and I don't intend to start now."

Namibia: Wacca Kazombiaze (lock)

"We have come a long way, but still the feeling is not good. We set goals and objectives, but they were out of reach, though we made some high scores."

Georgia: Malkhaz Cheishvili (coach)

"We had three games which have been very satisfying. There is a future for our rugby, but we need to create infrastructure."

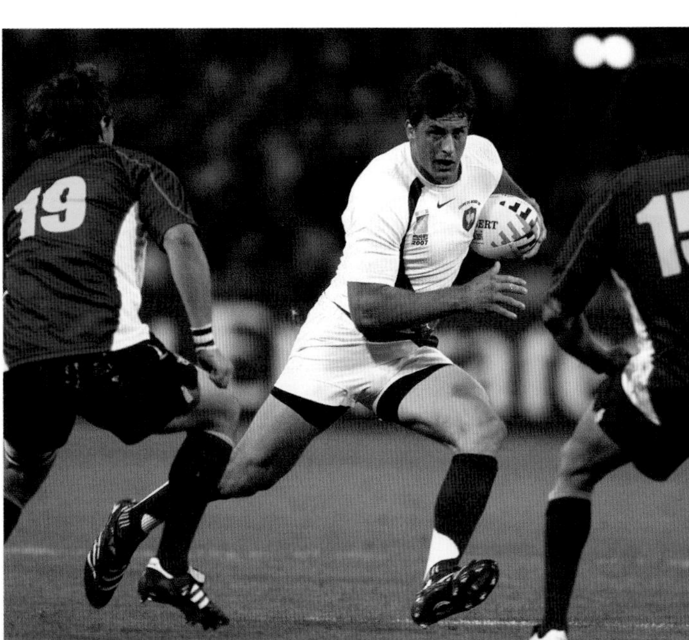

The rampaging Andrew Sheridan, Man of the Match in Marseilles, is brought to a halt on this occasion by Australia's Daniel Vickerman.

QUARTER-FINAL

AUSTRALIA v ENGLAND

MICK CLEARY

Chris Latham wiped a tear away from his eye. Stephen Larkham limped round the field staring vacantly ahead. Several other players slumped to the turf.

Meanwhile, all round, many demented blokes in white shirts jumped and hugged and whooped. Up in the stands of the Stade Vélodrome, those wearing England colours were copying their heroes down below. They too were in an advanced state of delirium. The collective levels of euphoria did not diminish for several hours. If at all.

Only sporting upsets can do this to rational folk. Only the sense of the unexpected that is central to sport's appeal can make people hope and pray and, occasionally, get a return. It was a day for sporting connoisseurs in Marseilles.

From the depths of their being, England managed to pick themselves off the canvas and deliver a knockout blow to Australia. It was unheralded, unforeseen and utterly splendid. Only those within the camp truly believed that it could happen. You wonder how many of them truly believed that it *would* happen.

Fair play to the England squad. They had been criticised, derided and taken to task for the lack of wit and unity in their game. And that was only within the camp. Outside, the level of rebuke was even harsher, for it was tinged with an air of hopelessness.

England may well have been giving their all, but it had proved not enough. They had stuttered and stumbled their way through the group. They had chopped and changed selection. Even for this game there was another raft of changes, and yet another injury problem.

No sooner had Brian Ashton decided to thrust Andy Farrell back into the critical limelight than the former Great Britain rugby league captain strained a calf muscle and was forced to withdraw, a devastating blow for the man himself, who had already seen his union career knocked to bits by constant mishaps.

It was another dig in the ribs, too, for Ashton, who had had to cope with so many enforced alterations to his best-laid plans. The head coach had been under the cosh throughout the tournament. He had not managed to get his ideal XV out on to the field that often, and when he did, players simply failed to live up to expectations. He was also obliged to trim his aspirations to suit the pragmatic moment, always a difficult balancing act.

England's coaches and players were under intense pressure. They had been in knockout mode for a fortnight already, knowing that if they lost they were out of the World Cup and bound for worldwide ridicule. Australia, meanwhile, had had a comparatively easy ride. They had been based in the south of France, embraced warmly by the generous folk of Montpellier and not been unduly troubled by the opposition.

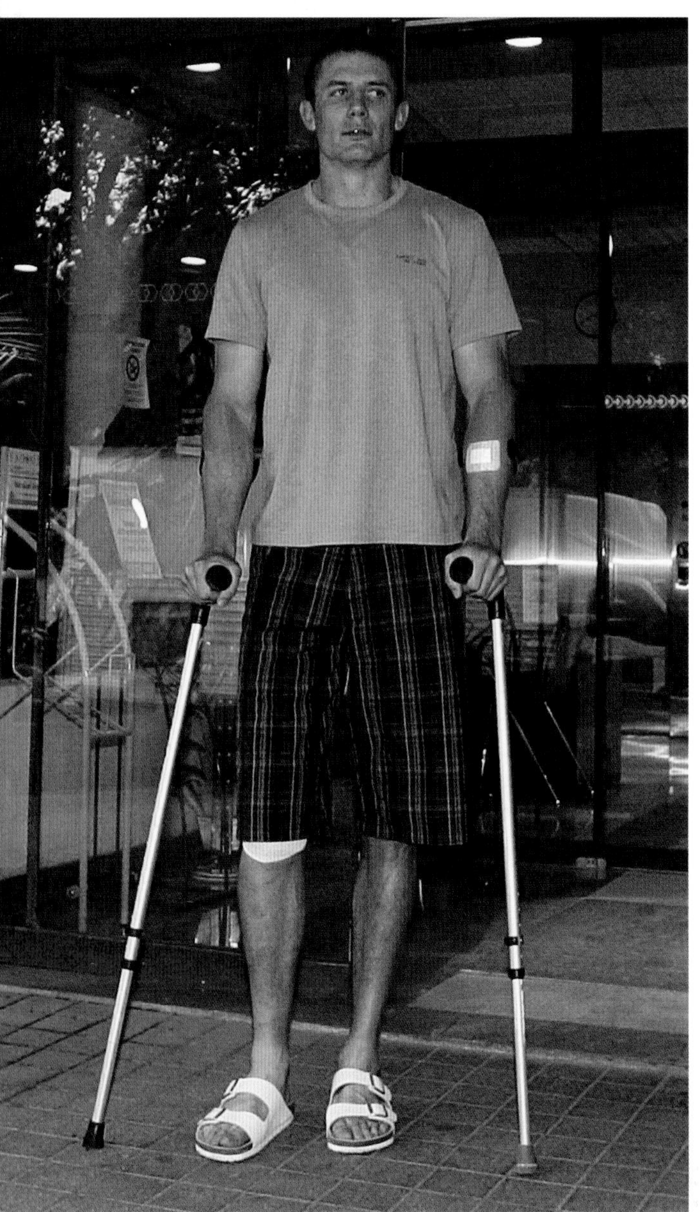

Sure, the flit over to Cardiff had been something to endure. But even that had passed without major mishap. Yes, there had been an unfortunate injury to Larkham to cope with. But how they coped. In came 21-year-old debutant Berrick Barnes. And a new star was born.

Barnes had proved to be a sensation. He ticked all the boxes. In the build-up to this game, he proved easy-going, approachable, the archetypal Aussie. He charmed the European media. When he explained that the wallaby mascot he was carrying under his arm was an age-old Australian custom demanded of the youngest player in the squad, one wag wondered if it might interfere with his ball-handling on Saturday against England. 'Mate, it'll be all right,' said the young Queenslander. 'I'll have it in a baby-carrier.'

On top table, the Wallaby coaches were explaining how it was that they had come to improve their set-piece play. They had England's Andrew Sheridan to thank for that. The Sale prop had done such a number on the Wallaby scrum in November 2005 that the Australian union had no option but to order a complete clear-out of coaching staff.

In came John Connolly and Michael Foley, both once of Bath and men in tune with the hard-nosed school of thought that exists in northern hemisphere coaching circles. The set piece would no longer be seen as a mere means of restarting the game. The Wallaby pack did improve and they were happy to big themselves up. 'Our aim is to be the best in the world,' said flanker Phil Waugh.

Prop Guy Shepherdson echoed those sentiments. 'That's not to say we are the best but that we want to get there,' said Shepherdson by way of clarification. 'It is certainly our aim. Since Michael Foley came in there has been much more attention on the technical aspects of the scrummage.'

So much for all that. Australia appeared to be a in a good place while England had just managed to poke their head out from the dark recesses. But they were coming after Australia. They had no intention of lying down meekly and allowing the Wallabies to avenge the World Cup final defeat of 2003. No, England were not going to go gently into that night. They had the faith, even if no one else did. And they had Sheridan.

'Andrew has the key to this game,' said Sale director of rugby Philippe Saint-André. 'If England can smash the Australian scrum, they can win. They will be on the front foot and this will make it easier for Jonny Wilkinson to manage the game. He will have options to play with and can dictate the tempo and the territory. Australia will have a bit of fear about him.'

RIGHT Mike Catt, last seen at fly half against South Africa, was recalled to face Australia at inside centre after a calf injury to Andy Farrell. **BELOW** Andy Farrell watches a training session in Marseilles after being ruled out of the quarter-final. **FACING PAGE** Wallaby fly half Stephen Larkham leaves hospital in Montpellier after knee surgery. Having featured against Japan at the start, he would take no further part in this World Cup, which was scheduled to be his international swansong.

As things turned out, they were right to.

England picked a side to munch Australia up front. And that is exactly what they did. There were five changes to the side. The men charged with bringing on back the good times to English rugby were a wizened crew, notably prop Phil Vickery, hooker Mark Regan and lock Simon Shaw. Farrell was also initially in the mix, while there was great pleasure in the camp that Jason Robinson had recovered from his hamstring injury.

'The changes we've made signify that we've put a strong emphasis on scrummaging,' said head coach Brian Ashton, who had passed over the claims of Vickery the previous week on his return from suspension in favour of Matt Stevens. 'We felt it was really important to get our most experienced players in the front five on to the field. It's going to be a massive battle area.'

Shaw's return was expected, given that he was rested against Tonga, while Regan's elevation was due to his relish for this type of encounter. 'I'm hoping that there will be a lot of scrums,' said Regan with a glint in his eye. There were. Or at least enough significant ones.

Australia were on the back foot for long stretches of the game. And the reason was simple. The English pack beasted them and bested them at every turn. Australia were hammered at the scrum. The mood was set from the very first engagement. Down it went, a sure sign of pressure. And again. Another reset. At the fourth scrum, England's impatience got the better of them and they charged into the engagement. Penalty to Australia. It was a classic Wallaby sucker punch. They managed to do it again at the next sequence of scrums. Technically, referee Alain Rolland was correct. Morally, he was wrong.

Rolland improved. The Wallabies did not.

England stunned Australia not just by the ferocity of their forward play but also by their brazenness and cleverness all over the field. They went at Australia. And Australia didn't know what was going on.

The presence of Mike Catt in England's midfield was a galvanising influence. Catt was there by default, drafted following Farrell's injury. He had come to the tournament seemingly as the first-choice inside centre. Then he was forced to play fly half against South Africa because of the injury crisis. He hadn't been seen since. 'I suppose he had to pick me,' said Catt ruefully about his selection with Ashton sitting alongside.

The opening 20-minute period set Australia back on their heels. Sheridan and his pals did the damage up front, Catt and Wilkinson mixed and matched their options behind. There was a vibrancy to England's play that had been missing.

BELOW Stirling Mortlock is held by Lewis Moody and Jonny Wilkinson. Like Wilkinson, the Wallaby skipper had a relatively hit-and-miss time with the boot on a day when every point proved crucial. **FACING PAGE** Andy Sheridan and Matt Dunning see eye to eye. **FOLLOWING PAGES** Simon Shaw charges upfield with his England colleagues in pursuit.

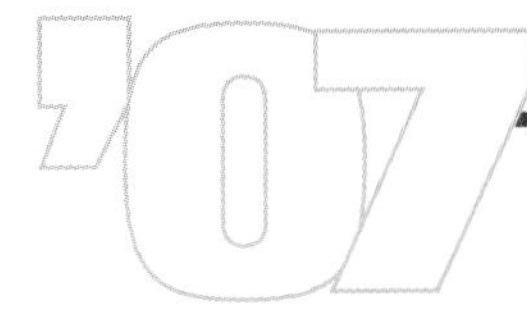

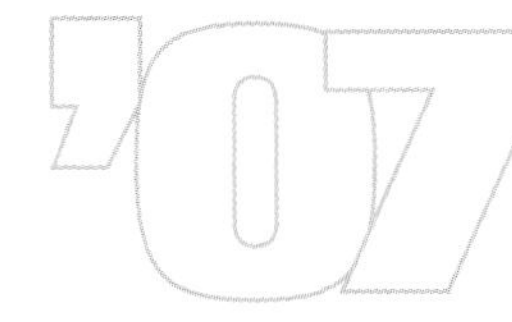

There were mishaps and errors, but England were testing Australia. The only area of fallibility was in their finishing. The Wilko-Catt double act bombed one chance, while a bobbing kick through just evaded the grasp of Paul Sackey.

However, England were in the hunt. They needed points, though, to settle nerves. Wilkinson finally got them there with a penalty goal in the 22nd minute, drawing England level after Stirling Mortlock had opened Australia's account with a penalty in the seventh minute.

Wilkinson had not had the most accomplished World Cup with his kicking. He was struggling to hit his normal levels of consistency. Good but not excellent. He knocked over another in the 26th minute but was to miss two before the half-time whistle. England had need of those points, for Australia struck, and struck hard.

The try came from one of Australia's first periods of sustained attack. They went through the phases, stretching and pulling England. Finally the ball reached wing Lote Tuqiri. He made no mistake. It was his first try of the tournament. As things turned out, it was to be his last.

Thereafter, Australia rarely threatened England's try line. There were glimmers but no more than that. The pulverising that they were taking up front had drained them. England had all the momentum at the breakdown. Wilkinson had two more penalties on the board by the hour mark to leave England 12-10 ahead. That's the way it was to stay. Just.

FACING PAGE Josh Lewsey tries in vain to halt Lote Tuqiri, who is in for the only try of the match. **ABOVE** Wallaby fly half Berrick Barnes launches a long-range dropped-goal attempt deep in the second half. **RIGHT** England scrum half Andy Gomarsall takes off as the final whistle goes to put England in the semi-finals. **FOLLOWING PAGE** England forward heroes George Chuter and Ben Kay congratulate one another on a job well done.

Mortlock had one more shot at goal. There were two minutes fifteen seconds left on the clock when the penalty was awarded against Joe Worsley. The Wallaby captain took his time.

The clock kept ticking. If he got it, then Australia were as good as home on the scoreboard. If he missed, they were as good as home on the airplane.

It was a difficult kick, 50 metres at least with the angle. It set off all right. But then it drifted. And with it went Australia's hopes. It was the end for the Wallabies' 2007 World Cup challenge. It was the end, too, for coach John Connolly and players George Gregan and Stephen Larkham.

For England, though, it was a whole new beginning.

RUGBY WORLD CUP
2007
2003
18

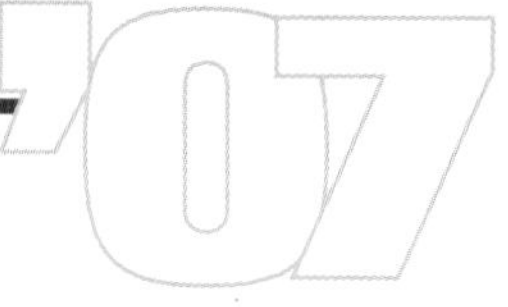

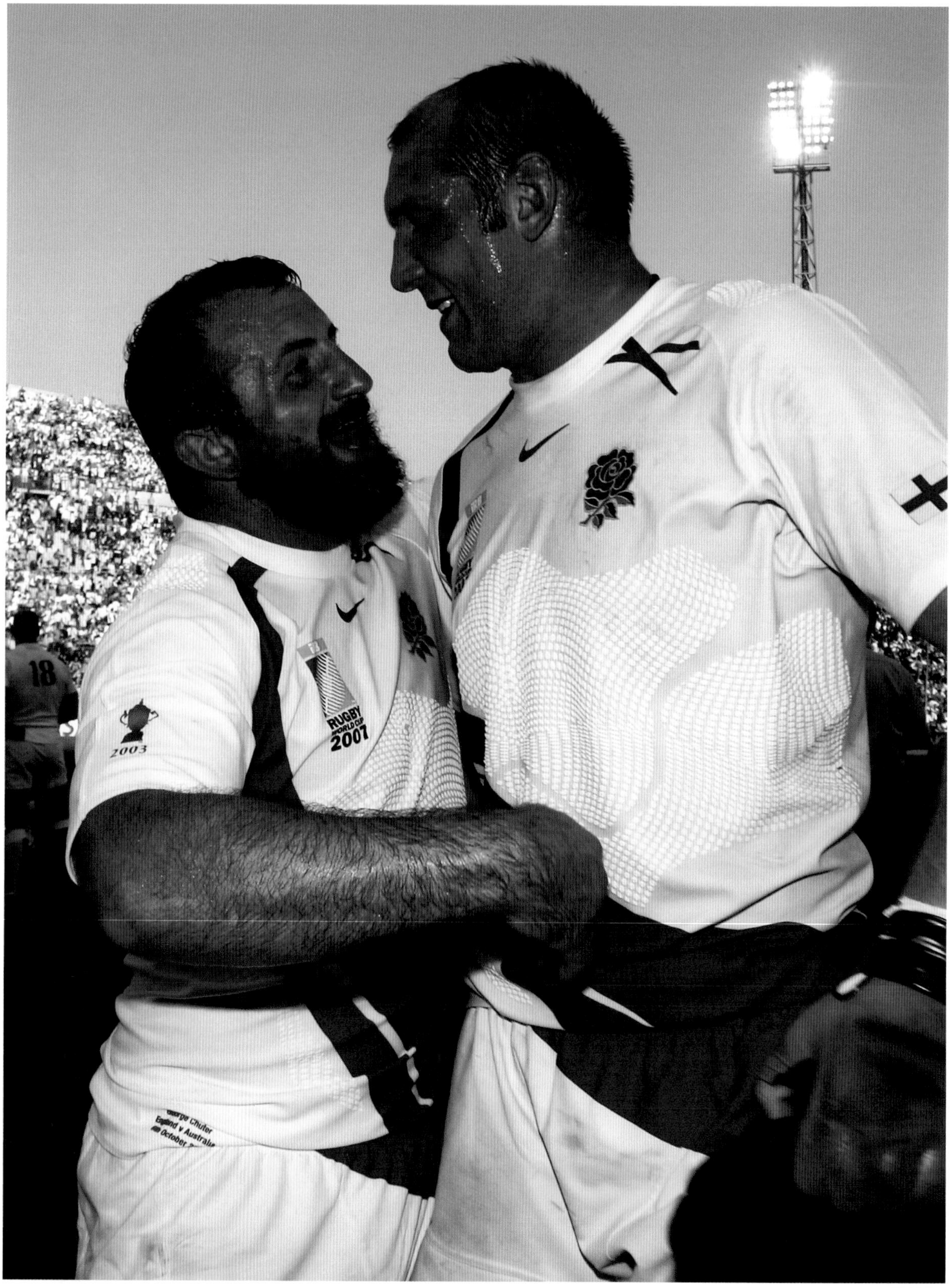

It all sinks in for Daniel Vickerman and Matt Giteau.

What they said...

England: Brian Ashton (coach)

“This victory represents a mountain of effort. The contest was a rollercoaster of emotions – a bit of a nail-biter, especially in the last ten minutes. We took Australia on in a way that people would have expected Australia to take us on, by moving the ball around the field. Today was a more balanced and complete performance than anything we've given in this World Cup.”

“To say the pack was magnificent would probably be an understatement.”

ABOVE Mike Catt and Brian Ashton savour victory. **RIGHT** George Gregan bowed out of international rugby in Marseilles with a world record 139 caps.

England: Phil Vickery (captain)

“Ultimately it was belief and some old-fashioned guts. We're all very proud Englishmen who want to go out and represent our country to the best of our ability.”

England: Mark Regan (hooker)

“I love that pre-match Australian knocking. If they worry about me then it stops them from focusing on rugby.”

England: Lawrence Dallaglio (repl)

“We were battle-hardened after Samoa and Tonga. Australia probably weren't and our belligerence unsettled them.”

Australia: John Connolly (coach)

“It was our worst performance of the tournament. England's scrum got its hits and they controlled the breakdown strongly. I said in advance that their scrum, line out, Wilkinson, the pace they've got outside, would be a massive threat.”

Australia: Stirling Mortlock (captain)

“Personally my goal-kicking was a disappointment. I should have kicked more points. It's an extremely quiet, dull change-room. I think that Stephen Larkham and George Gregan have given so much, not just to Australian rugby, but to the world game. For them to bow out in the quarter-final is extremely sad.”

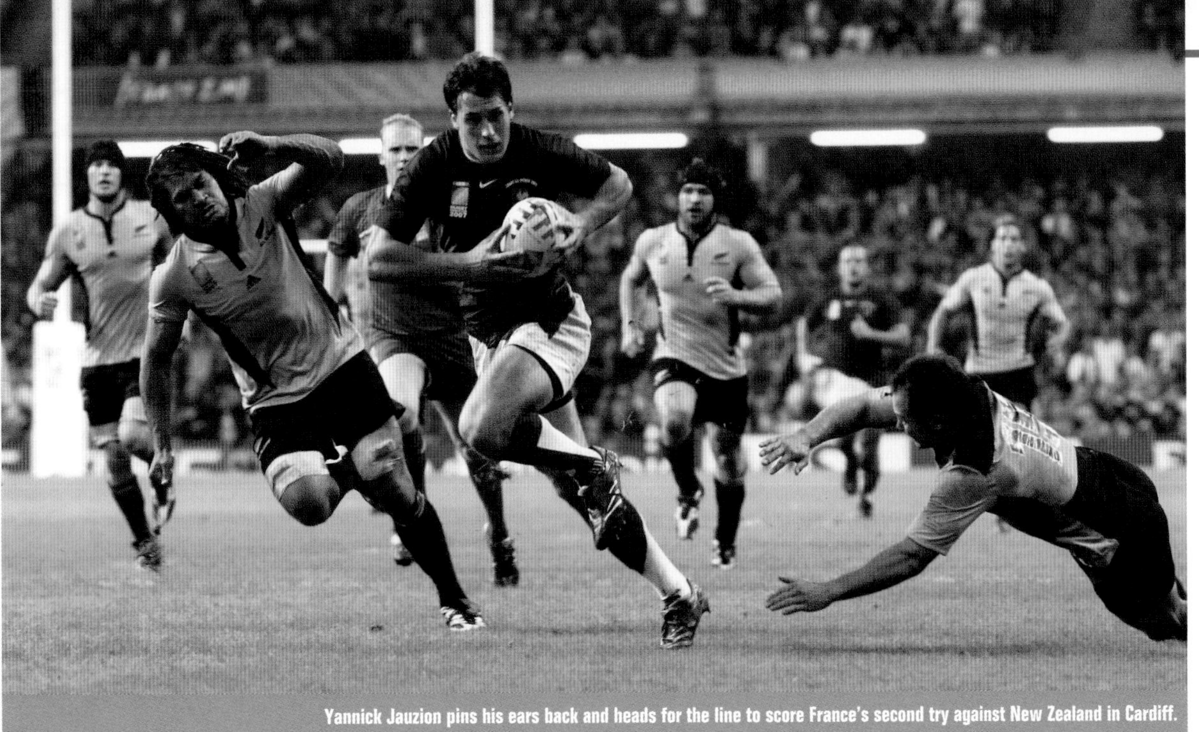

Yannick Jauzion pins his ears back and heads for the line to score France's second try against New Zealand in Cardiff.

QUARTER-FINAL

NEW ZEALAND v FRANCE

JIM NEILLY

Mon Dieu! Incroyable! Quelle surprise! **The sheer unbridled joy on the faces of Bernard Laporte and Jo Maso, and of French President Nicolas Sarkozy and FFR President Bernard Lapasset, was in stark contrast to the death masks of Graham Henry and his assistants, Steve Hansen and Wayne Smith.**

Following a shock loss in their opening game to Argentina, which forced them into an unenviable quarter-final shoot-out in Cardiff, the French had all but revised their World Cup aspirations to a place in the last eight, yet managed to produce a second-half display full of grit, gristle and glorious enterprise to send the All Blacks, the short-priced tournament favourites, crashing out at the Millennium Stadium.

Laporte, scheduled to take up an appointment with the French Ministry of Sport, and Maso, his manager and formerly a precocious centre for Les Bleus, resembled Nosferatu and Harpo Marx on speed as referee Wayne Barnes sounded the end of a game that encapsulated just about all that a World Cup quarter-final could summon up.

Having failed to win the trophy since the inaugural tournament in 1987, New Zealand flopped yet again, prompting Henry to tender his immediate resignation, leaving an entire nation in shreds of bewilderment as, for a fifth competition in a row, the All Blacks were unable to deliver when it mattered most.

Whether it was the dreadful grey outfit or the fact that they hadn't been properly tested in their pool games, making heavy weather of Scotland's second-string outfit, is a matter of conjecture. The fact remained: New Zealand were not going to win Rugby World Cup 2007. *Quelle horreur!*

There has been much debate in recent seasons regarding the validity of the New Zealand haka and its place in the modern, professional game, but as the All Blacks rendered their most traditional version of their time-honoured challenge, the French, an arm's length away, met it with beautifully

underplayed Gallic indifference, responding with casual winks from David Marty and Cédric Heymans and a baleful, malevolent stare from Sébastien Chabal, which, when displayed on the giant screens inside the stadium, put the fear of God into every single spectator and, one suspects, an All Black or two.

Having plumped for 21-year-old Lionel Beauxis of Stade Français, who had started the World Cup as third-choice fly half, and Damien Traille, whose Test rugby at full back had been limited to less than half an hour as a replacement, Bernard Laporte had set out his stall; and with Jean-Baptiste Elissalde following the script to the letter, it was kick, kick and encore le kick from the French from the outset.

The French cause wasn't helped in the early stages by a dreadful line out, with Ali Williams pinching at least four of the early French throws, a situation not helped by appalling throwing from the French captain, Raphaël Ibanez. The early loss of veteran flanker Serge Betsen, who was struck, accidentally, by

BELOW Bernard Laporte opted for Damien Traille (below with ball v Namibia) at full back, giving France extra kicking power. The same plan also saw Freddie Michalak (also pictured) placed on the bench, with Lionel Beauxis starting at fly half. **FACING PAGE** France line up in shirt colours representing the national flag to confront the New Zealand haka.

RUGBY
2007
France 2007
RUGBY
2007

the knee of Fabien Pelous, didn't do anything for French morale, and after Traille was off-target with an attempted dropped goal, it came as no surprise when the All Blacks took the lead.

It was Pelous who incurred the displeasure of English referee Wayne Barnes, the youngest on the referees' panel and with just half a dozen major internationals under his belt. The giant French lock tackled Joe Rokocoko and decided to stay put, allowing Daniel Carter to kick the penalty with 13 minutes gone. Williams proceeded to steal a French line-out ball, pipping Imanol Harinordoquy, and Luke McAlister skinned Beauxis and made decent inroads into French territory before Williams almost made it in at the corner, Vincent Clerc's brave tackle denying New Zealand the game's opening try.

It was a pretty clear sign of things to come. Five minutes later, New Zealand took a quick line-out throw and McAlister made an even more powerful and telling surge from deep, ripping open the French defence and handing on to Jerry Collins who was, in a fine example of classic back-row play, right on his shoulder. Collins took the tackle of Traille and, one-handed, offloaded to McAlister, who steamed over, leaving Carter the formality of the conversion for a 10-0 lead.

It was looking even better for the favourites when flanker Thierry Dusautoir strayed offside at a ruck and Carter popped over the resultant penalty to make it 13-0 with half an hour gone. It seemed as if New Zealand were cruising into a Stade de France semi-final at the expense of the tournament hosts. Amazingly – or perhaps not, if memories of a similar situation in 1999 were to be recalled – the All Blacks didn't score again for another half an hour.

Having realised that their kicking game was getting them nowhere, the French decided that it was time to turn to Plan B, and they started doing what they have done best for a century of Test rugby: run. The All Blacks found themselves in unknown territory coming up to the interval and looked decidedly uncomfortable on the back foot. Williams conceded a penalty at a maul, and Beauxis who had – as had scrum half Elissalde – missed an earlier penalty, nailed a useful kick to close the gap to ten points at half-time.

New Zealand made the better start to the second half, with No. 9 Byron Kelleher making a telling break, but it was France, with Jean-Baptiste Poux on in the front row for Olivier Milloud

LEFT Ali Williams comes mighty close to scoring the first try of the game in the 16th minute. France wing Vincent Clerc (hidden behind Williams and Lionel Beauxis) came in with a last-gasp tackle that nudged the All Black lock just out of play as he touched down in the corner.

just after the break, who came closer to scoring, after Heymans booted downfield. New Zealand managed to slow down the momentum at the ruck, but the French still won the ball, and it looked more than promising as they moved it right, only for Traille to throw an awful pass with the New Zealand line there for the crossing.

Confidence oozing, the French were patient as the crowd sensed that it might not be quite as done and dusted as the half-time scoreline suggested. A rumbling French maul was collapsed near the All Blacks' line. France took the quick tap penalty and Beauxis chipped for the line, only for McAlister to step in front of the galloping Yannick Jauzion. McAlister was shown the yellow card, and Beauxis kicked the penalty, which was the least France deserved, having looked capable of scoring twice in a sustained period of pressure.

A typically All Black pick-and-drive spell followed, with Rodney So'oialo failing to hold a poorish pass. France not only survived but counterattacked almost immediately, Harinordoquy being halted five metres short at the other end as the intensity and tension grew with every passing second.

Displaying a superb level of continuity, France moved the ball left, recycled effortlessly and came right, creating acres of space, and Dusautoir brushed aside Leon MacDonald's tackle to score. Beauxis, with a little help from the post, converted, and it was 13 apiece and very definitely advantage to France.

McAlister returned and New Zealand coach Graham Henry brought on, within a five-minute period, Nick Evans for the struggling Carter, Brendon Leonard for Kelleher, Andrew Hore at hooker for Anton Oliver, Chris Jack for Keith Robinson in the second row and Chris Masoe for Collins at flanker; and the All Blacks reverted to the traditional forward drive. They came close to scoring but were thwarted by a muscular bit of grappling by the crowd-pleasing Chabal, on for Pelous, but New Zealand weren't to be denied and further pressure saw So'oialo barge over. McAlister, crucially, failed with the conversion, but the All Blacks were back in the lead.

Evans, whose quarter-final was to last just 15 minutes, made a telling break, but Beauxis put in a vital tackle before Bernard Laporte replaced his fly half with Frédéric Michalak with just 12 minutes remaining; he also brought on veteran wing Christophe Dominici for Heymans in a bold, attack-orientated selection. Would it be flaky Freddie or fantastic Freddie? The answer came soon enough, and with telling effect.

Traille's initial surge took him past McAlister, who had to move to fly half following Evans's departure, and the full back's pass, perilously close to being adjudged forward, found Michalak, who took it on at pace. Half-checked, Michalak nevertheless retained his composure as he spun out of the tackle to feed the onrushing Jauzion. Having been benched by Laporte for some of the tournament's earlier games, Jauzion, roared on by hysterical French fans, galloped home to reaffirm his world-class status. Elissalde goaled with ease to restore the French lead with 11 minutes remaining.

What followed was a triumph of French determination as New Zealand came at their opponents with mind-blowing ferocity. Given that there was any amount of time remaining for the All Blacks to win the game, the French were magnificent in

FACING PAGE Luke McAlister piles over to score New Zealand's first try as Fabien Pelous (far left) and Vincent Clerc (No. 14) look on in horror. **RIGHT** Damien Traille congratulates Thierry Dusautoir on his 53rd-minute score, converted to bring the sides level. **BELOW** Rodney So'oialo has just driven over to put the All Blacks ahead again after 62 minutes.

LEFT A limping Dan Carter leaves the field just before the hour mark to be replaced by Nick Evans, who himself lasted only 15 minutes. **BELOW** Just moments after coming on for Lionel Beauxis, Freddie Michalak makes the break that sets up Yannick Jauzion's try. **FOLLOWING PAGE** For France – euphoria; for New Zealand – disbelief, yet again.

their ability to soak up all that Richie McCaw's side could muster, though a wayward kick from Michalak after a hard-won turnover must have given Messrs Laporte, Maso and Co. heart failure.

It began to get desperate for New Zealand, who seemed to run out of ideas, and in the final seconds McAlister attempted a long-range dropped goal which finished short and wide of the mark, summing up the All Blacks' World Cup. France survived the drop-out, and Elissalde scampered towards the crowd with the ball like a demented pixie as all of France went into ecstacy.

Bernard Laporte's tactics and his selection had been more than vindicated, and Graham Henry acknowledged that his eccentric opposite number had got it absolutely right, switching from a kicking to a running game, allied to a superb defence.

This was the bitterest of pills for New Zealand to swallow, even more so than the one imposed upon them in 1999, when the French found that little bit extra. The pain of defeat was made even worse by the fact that this loss dashed New Zealand's hopes of hosting RWC 2011 as defending champions.

The French hadn't counted on being in Cardiff, and while the fact that no team had ever won the tournament following a loss in the pool stages hadn't escaped them, their glorious victory ensured a return to Paris and boosted the prospect of their winning a first ever Rugby World Cup.

adidas

Lionel Beauxis – two penalties and a conversion in Cardiff.

What they said...

France: Bernard Laporte (coach)

"They had more possession, but our performance was excellent, disciplined, and we scored two tries from limited ball. We may have beaten the best team in the world. We want to be champions so we had to beat New Zealand."

France: Raphaël Ibanez (captain)

"It is a great victory for all the players, who gave everything. In the World Cup, courage and spirit make the difference and that's what happened. Bernard told us at 13-3 we had to play the last 40 minutes as if they were the most important in our lives."

ABOVE Tension shows among French fans watching in Toulouse. **RIGHT** Graham Henry speaks to the press the day after the match. The NZRU stated that Henry would be replaced as All Blacks coach before the end of 2007.

New Zealand: Graham Henry (coach)

"The players gave their all, but it just didn't happen. The French defence was perfect. The better side won. People will make judgments, but I feel comfortable. I have done everything I can to ensure that we did the best we could. I feel for the families and supporters. It's not a time to think about my future."

New Zealand: Richie McCaw (captain)

"Some guys have played their last Test and that makes the hurt worse. They are pretty shattered. I'm at a loss as to why we didn't play the game together as well as we would have liked. In the second half we lost our composure."

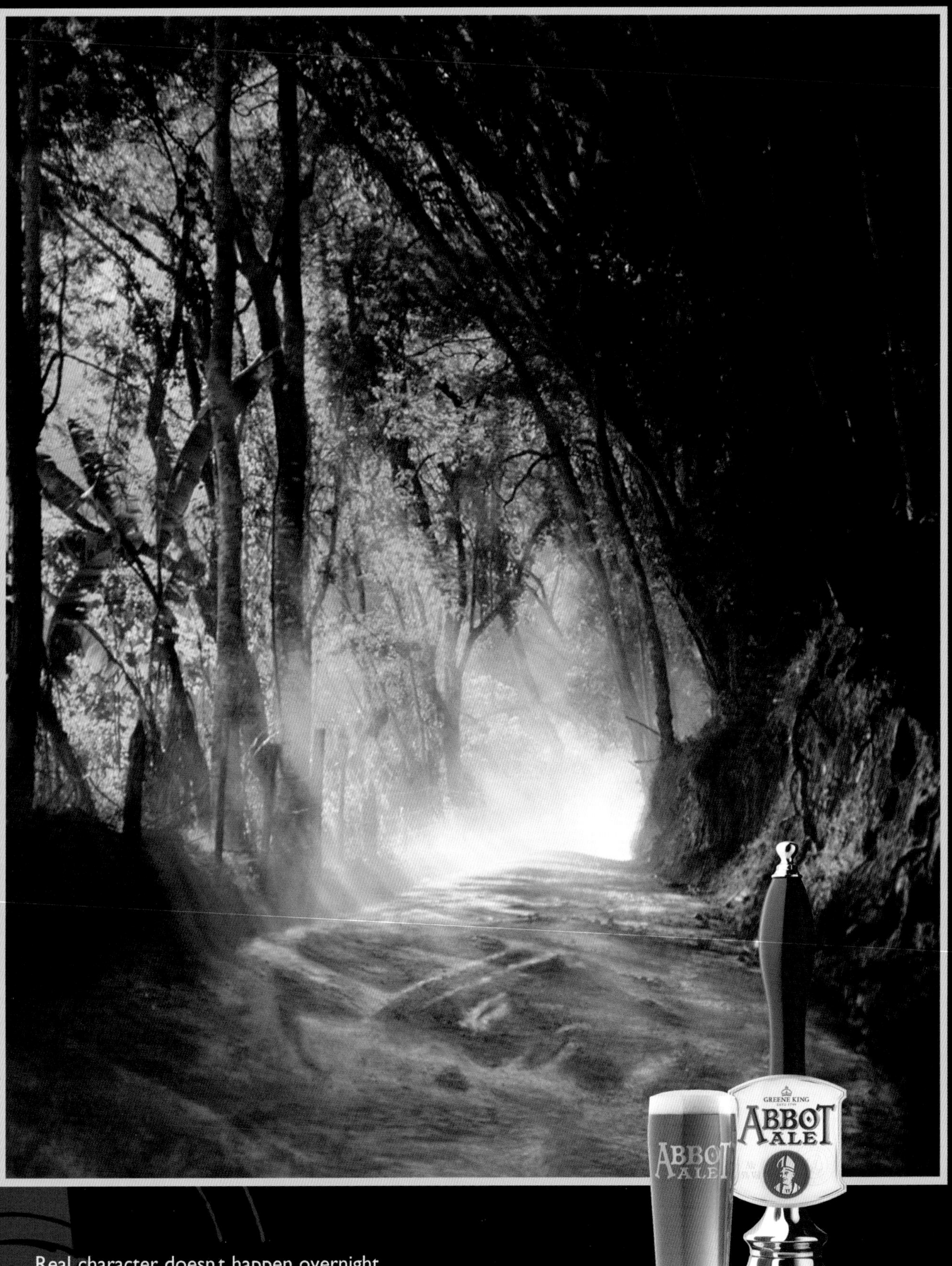
Brewed longer for a distinctive, full flavour
GREENE KING
ABBOT ALE
ABBOT ALE
Real character doesn t happen overnight.
Nor are hidden depths immediately obvious.
But given time, they emerge.
WHEN YOU RE READY, YOU LL FIND IT.

The whistle goes at the end of another extraordinary quarter-final and South Africa are through, having beaten a defiant Fiji 37-20 in Marseilles.

QUARTER-FINAL

SOUTH AFRICA v FIJI

STEPHEN JONES

This was the weekend of shocks. We had already seen England hammer the strongly fancied Australia in the earlier of the two Saturday quarter-finals, then that evening we had seen New Zealand, the tournament favourites, go out to France in Cardiff.

There would be no reverberating shock in this meeting between the powerful South Africans and the talented Fijians. Would there? Surely not. Well, in the end South Africa came through, and the final score hints that it was reasonably comfortable, though not one of the thrashings that the giants habitually hand out to the minnows.

In fact it was anything but comfortable. We knew before the match that this was probably the best team in Fiji's history – well prepared, confident, potentially brilliant behind the scrum and with a new sophistication in their forward game and all-round play. Not to mention a well of courage.

And in a supercharged second half, with the crowd at Stade Vélodrome in Marseilles roaring out their support and near-disbelief, Fiji unleashed a stream of brilliant attacks. They pulled level with the mighty Boks at 20-20, and the white-faced expressions on the faces of the match favourites betrayed a shock and a nervousness.

Even after this, Fiji came within inches of scoring from a series of drives from their valiant forwards. Then, after another Fijian attack of remarkable brilliance, they launched Ifereimi Rawaqa, the big lock, towards the South African line. The only remaining defender was JP Pietersen, the wing.

Yet somehow as Rawaqa dived and clearly crossed the line, the much smaller Pietersen managed to get underneath his man and obtain enough leverage to drag Rawaqa into touch-in-goal with the ball almost trapped off the ground between them. The Television Match Official correctly ruled that it was not a try and South Africa could breathe again.

The Springboks closed out the game with a flurry of late points, showing their professionalism

GMF edf
SOCIETE GENERALE
SNCF SNCF
Orange
VISA VISA TOSHIBA
GMF GMF
edf ENERGY

SNCF
SNCF
vediorbis
VISA
VISA
Fly Emirates
GMF
GMF
edf ENERGY
PEUGEOT
SNCF
VISA

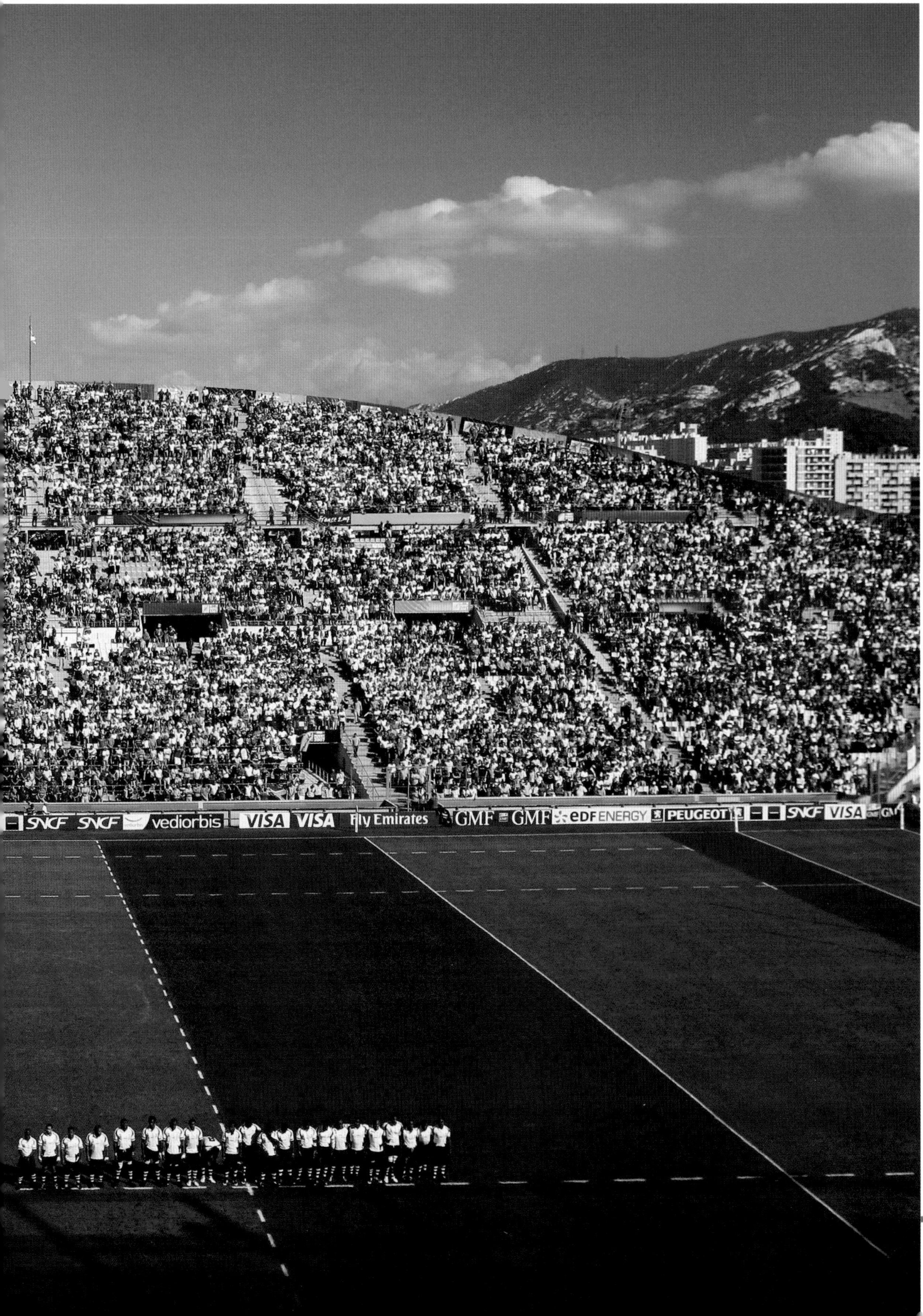

by hemming Fiji into their own territory for most of the last ten minutes. The scenes at the end were typical of the whole World Cup. It had been the most fierce battle; now and again it had been fractious – but the sportsmanship was exemplary.

This was shown when Fiji did their lap of honour. It was a leisurely affair, the Fijians receiving an unforgettable reception from every part of the stadium and at four points they paused as the applause built. It must have taken them a good 30 minutes or more to get round, but when they completed their lap they

ABOVE Centre Jaque Fourie runs in South Africa's first try after 13 minutes. **RIGHT** Referee Alan Lewis blows for the Springboks' second try, registered by hooker and captain John Smit just after the half-hour mark. **PRECEDING PAGES** The teams line up for the anthems on a glorious afternoon for rugby at the Stade Vélodrome in Marseilles.

found the South Africans waiting to clap them off down the tunnel. It was a classy gesture from the winners. It was also another magnificent occasion in the life of this most captivating of World Cups.

The Springboks' powerful driving maul had been their chief weapon. The likes of Bakkies Botha, John Smit and Schalk Burger were outstanding at close quarters and Juan Smith was a belligerent open-side. However, by no means all was well with the South African team, especially behind the scrum. They were taken apart in defence in the second half in remarkable fashion, and on this occasion the link in the midfield between fly half Butch James and Francois Steyn at inside centre did not work. As an attacking unit, South Africa misfired, and the dangerous Bryan Habana was shut out for long periods of the proceedings. This was all food for thought for the team as they headed into their semi-final match with Argentina one week later.

Fiji held on for dear life in the scrums and they were always under pressure whenever South Africa managed to establish

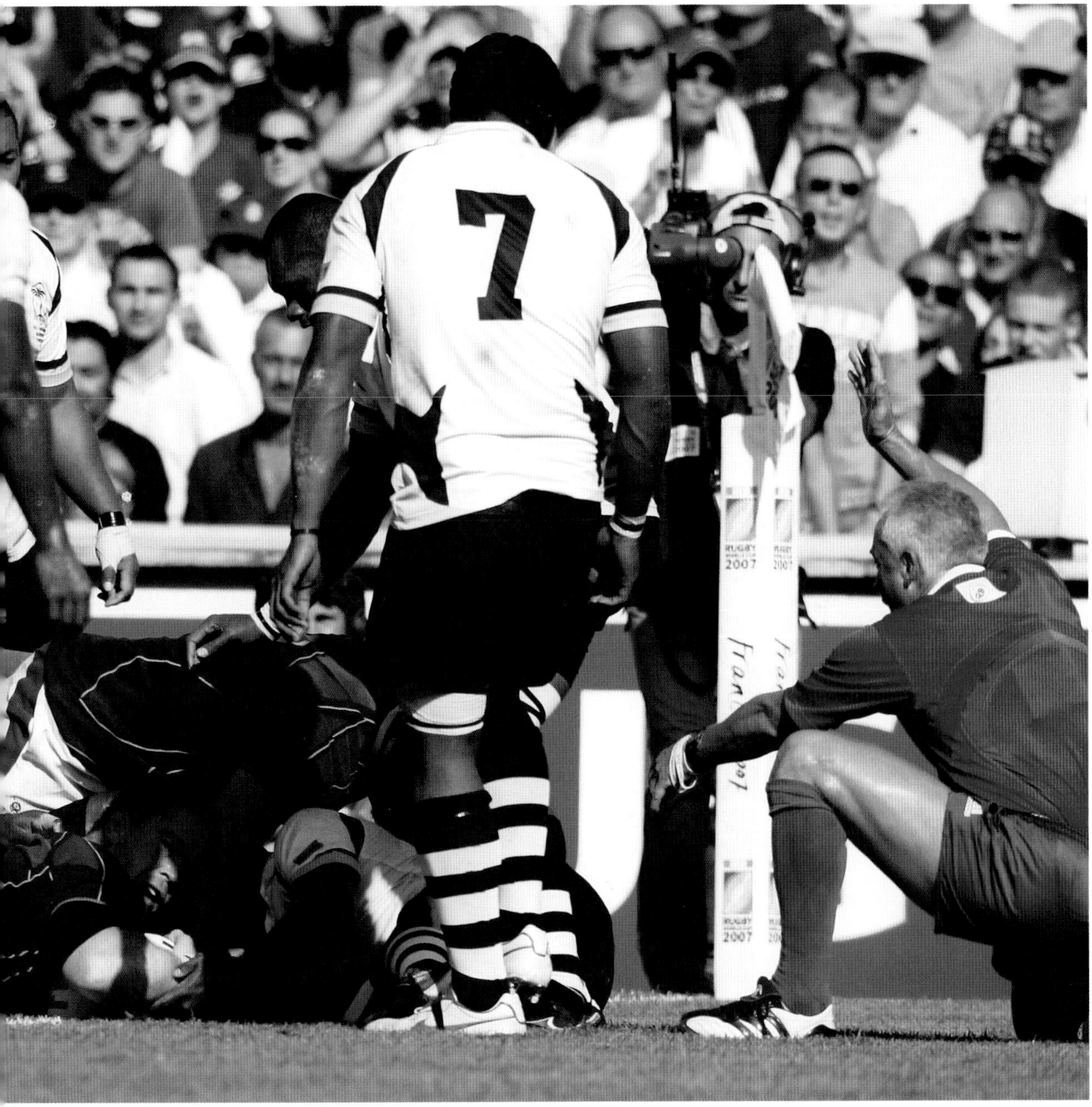

ABOVE South African flanker Schalk Burger and lock Bakkies Botha pursue Fijian captain Mosese Rauluni. **FACING PAGE** Victor Matfield has his work cut out against the Fijian pack on this occasion. In general, though, the South Africans outpowered the Islanders in the forward department.

their driving game. But apart from that the Islanders were the equals of their illustrious opposition. They had, in Sisa Koyamaibole, the forward of the match. The Fijian No. 8 was heroic, not only with his powerful running but also in taking responsibility for clearing up the mess behind the retreating Fijian scrum.

Fiji had lost Nicky Little, their influential fly half, to an injury towards the end of the dramatic win over Wales in Nantes the previous weekend, so Seremaia Bai, normally a centre, stepped across. Bai did a marvellous job, was superb with his stepping and running, and inside him Mosese Rauluni, the captain, was quite wonderful. He sometimes seemed to be bouncing off giant

Bok defenders like a rubber ball. He made breaks, he kicked well, he was inspirational. It was a shame that Seru Rabeni, at centre, had such a poor day with his handling because at his best he would have been a handful for the defence.

Fiji bade farewell to the tournament after this match and returned to a heroes' welcome back in the Islands. The fact that so many of their squad played top professional rugby in France, England and Japan was a double-edged sword for them. On the one hand, their squad had improved no end – hard edges had been added and the pool of players had never been stronger. Little had spoken just before this quarter-final of attending Fiji trials, usually a formality for him, and being genuinely unsure as to whether he would make the squad or not.

Yet the fact that so many players were involved in professional rugby away from Fiji also meant that the full team would be together only infrequently over the next four years. Fiji

still need some means of retaining continuity to maintain their progress. They added a massive vividness to France 2007.

That afternoon in Marseilles there was probably no real hint of what was to come in the early stages, when Fiji appeared to be safely under lock and key. Steyn put South Africa ahead with a fine long penalty and then Jaque Fourie, the centre, scored the first of five South African tries after excellent combination work. Bai did kick a penalty to put Fiji on the board, but Smit scored after definitive close-range work by the forwards and then Pietersen went over after outflanking a defence sucked in by repeated Springbok driving. Bai had kicked his second penalty, but it was 20-6 to South Africa with half an hour remaining.

BELOW Fijian wing Vilimoni Delasau catches up with his own kick ahead to touch down for a magical try to give Fiji hope. **FACING PAGE** The Fijian comeback continues as Sireli Bobo crosses for the Islanders' second five-pointer just two minutes after the first.

Yet Fiji had hardly begun. Vilimoni Delasau started to find space, Rauluni began to cut South Africa up around the fringes and, in particular, Bai commenced shredding the Boks in the midfield. Fiji launched a breathtaking series of attacks from deep, sometimes from stray South African kicks but also from the first phase behind their own struggling set pieces.

Suddenly everything was possible. Delasau scored after a sweeping, devastating Fiji attack that combined continuity with brilliant handling; Bai converted. The Fijians were suddenly back to within a converted try.

Then, incredibly, they scored that converted try. It was another sweeping combination move, more brilliant handling and Sireli Bobo, the wing who had joined the tour party late on, scored a try confirmed by the video official. The conversion from Bai brought it all square.

Fiji continued to come on. Montgomery did put South Africa back in front by 23-20 with a penalty, but it was a highly precarious lead. Rabeni knocked on right at the South African

12
3

line as an attack was building promisingly, and then came the superb defending by Pietersen to stop Rawaqa. It is easy to say that South Africa went on to dominate the last ten minutes, but who can say for sure that Fiji's spirit and skills would not have been able to defend a lead in the closing stages had Rawaqa just been able to ground the ball?

Even so, South Africa asserted themselves splendidly. Juan Smith and Butch James scored late on as the Boks, driven on by John Smit, banished the spectre of defeat and the all-time World Cup shock. Montgomery kicked both conversions, bringing the final score to 37-20, and all that was left was the ritual scenes of sportsmanship after a harsh and yet thrilling battle.

There ended the third of four quarter-finals in what was easily the finest quarter-final round in World Cup history. This was a match that summed up the whole event – great crowds and great and vivid rugby; nothing guaranteed and nothing easy to predict. Marseilles was arguably the finest venue of the tournament, and as Fiji departed and the South Africans strode on, the city and the tournament would miss each other.

BELOW The Fijians are given a rousing ovation by a crowd that recognised their contribution to the match and to the tournament. Meanwhile, the Springboks waited patiently to applaud their opponents from the field.

JP Pietersen scores South Africa's third try v Fiji.

What they said...

South Africa: Jake White (coach)

"We scored five tries to two in a quarter-final, but didn't play as well as we could. We go through with no injuries, what more do you want two weeks out from a World Cup final?"

"John's captaincy was outstanding. The last 20 minutes was the best Test rugby we've played this year."

South Africa: John Smit (captain)

"As much as everyone thought our quarter-final would be easy, it certainly wasn't. At 20-20 the momentum had changed dramatically. We had to start again and hope the boys had enough left to win, but it took us 60 minutes to wake up."

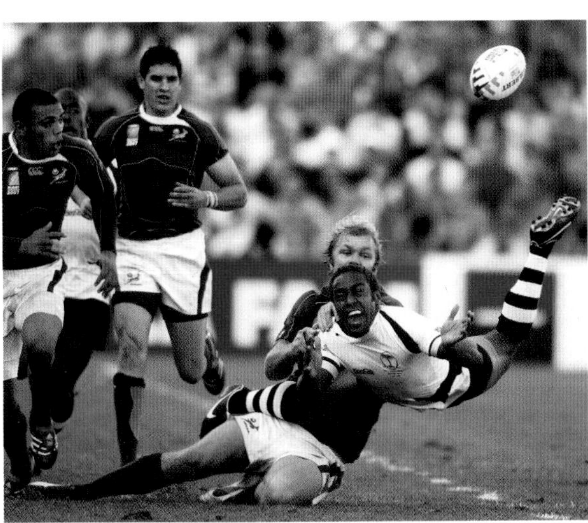

ABOVE Gabiriele Lovobalavu offloads as he is brought down by Schalk Burger. **RIGHT** South African players Os du Randt and Jannie du Plessis share a moment with Mosese Rauluni, the Fijian captain, after the epic encounter in Marseilles.

Fiji: Mosese Rauluni (captain)

"It shows that tier-two nations can take it to tier-one nations. We came in with nothing to lose and South Africa had all the pressure. We found a lot of holes, but were unable to score enough tries."

Fiji: Ilie Tabua (coach)

"In the second half we came back and we would have been back in the game with those couple of missed tries but the bounce of the ball didn't go our way."

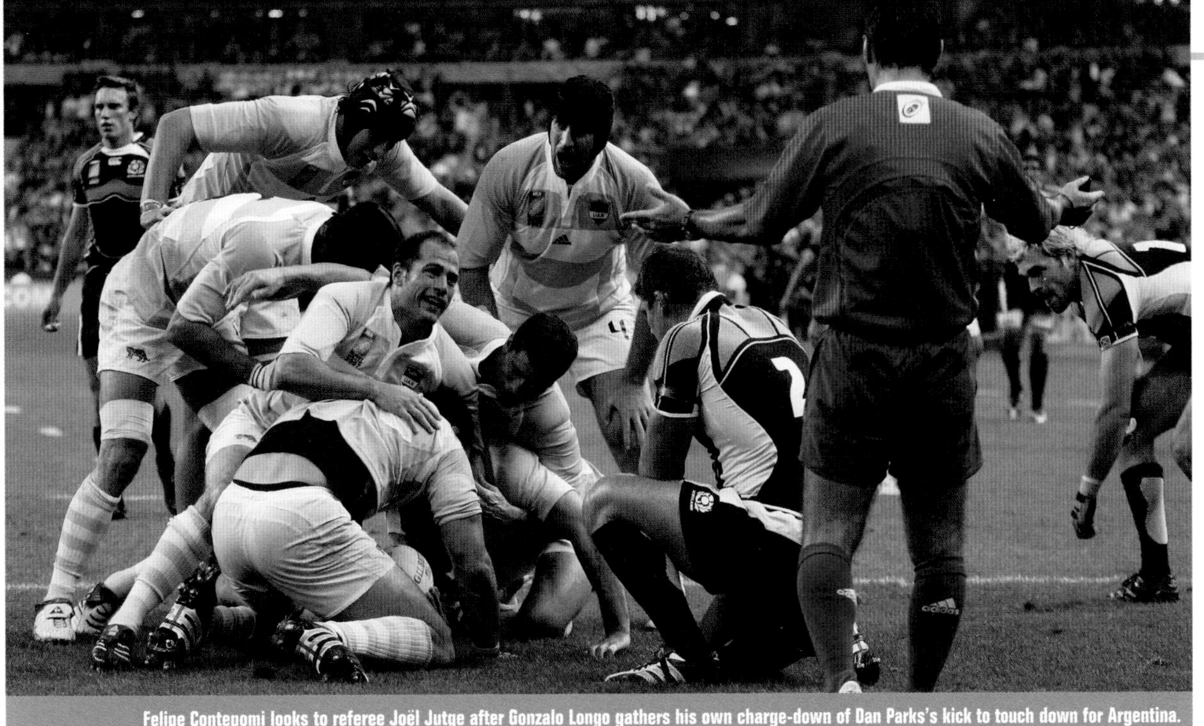

Felipe Contepomi looks to referee Joël Jutge after Gonzalo Longo gathers his own charge-down of Dan Parks's kick to touch down for Argentina.

QUARTER-FINAL

ARGENTINA v SCOTLAND

ANDREW COTTER

Perhaps it was asking too much to hope that the last of the quarter-finals of RWC 2007 could live up to the three classics which had gone before.

The trend of the weekend had been for upsets, the fashion for exhilarating rugby; but Paris, as we all know, follows its own fashion, and the style on the night of Sunday 7 October was very different as Scotland and Argentina met in a World Cup for the first time. This was grim and gritty rugby – more boiler suits and dungarees than haute couture.

At least in its atmosphere this game could match its predecessors. Paris may have been rather reluctant to rise from its post-celebratory slumber following events in Cardiff, but it is remarkable what a day in the warm autumn sunshine – the French capital wearing its Sunday best – can do for flagging energy levels. South Africa's victory over Fiji was rugby's equivalent of the hair of the dog, and by the time the rugby circus had reached the stark surroundings of the Stade de France late in the evening, the party was once again in full swing.

It was difficult to overstate the importance of this game to both countries: Scotland were looking to reach the semi-finals for the first time in 16 years; Argentina simply for the first time. And oh, how it mattered not only in Paris but also on the Pampas – so much so that kick-off in the football derby to end all derbies, Boca Juniors against River Plate, had been moved to accommodate the rugby. Remarkable. There had even been a message of support from a former Boca Juniors player called Maradona – he of the most infamous knock-on in history.

This was, of course, supposed to be a French night at the Stade de France (although by now everyone knew that their defeat against Argentina had merely been part of a crafty grand plan to take the scenic route and enjoy victory over the All Blacks along the way), so a fair number of natives were to be found among the kilts and the striped shirts of the Pumas. Indeed, some of the loudest singing of the evening came when the Marseillaise filled the ground, and some of the

ABOVE Flag bearers lead out the Argentina and Scotland teams at the Stade de France ahead of the match. **FACING PAGE** Pumas captain Agustín Pichot rallies his troops one final time as they line up for the anthems.

biggest cheers were reserved for when the giant screens replayed Yannick Jauzion's try against the All Blacks in Cardiff from the previous day. But it was also clear in their support that those 'neutrals' harboured no grudge whatsoever against the Argentinians for that upset on the opening night exactly a month before. All had been forgiven and forgotten, and the players in the light-blue and white stripes seemed to be enjoying the greater local support.

But neither neutrals, Scots nor Pumas were entirely enamoured of the rugby which both sides produced in the first half. True, a less than free-flowing game had been widely predicted, but it was still rather disappointing when it came to pass (or rather not pass). The first 40 minutes were often tense and ugly, dominated by the touch-finding kicks and towering garryowens of Dan Parks for Scotland and Argentina's Stade

Français fly half Juan Martín Hernández. One particular missile from Hernández rose high enough to strike the cable carrying the camera that provided the shots from above the pitch.

Little surprise then that the first points came courtesy of a penalty. Scotland's Mike Blair took a high ball and was himself taken by offside Pumas. Just a pace inside the Argentine half was thought to be beyond the range of the hitherto perfect Chris Paterson, so it was Parks who stepped forward and protected his own pristine record with the boot by a matter of inches.

That, though, had come against the run of play, which flowed almost constantly in Argentina's favour, and the Pumas' own impressive points machine, Felipe Contepomi, made up for a miss with his first effort of the evening by knocking over his next two to put Argentina in front.

Sprinkled liberally here and there were dropped-goal attempts by the nonchalant Hernández, with his kicking from hand also keeping Scotland pegged back. And it was deep inside the Scotland 22 that the key moment of the first half occurred

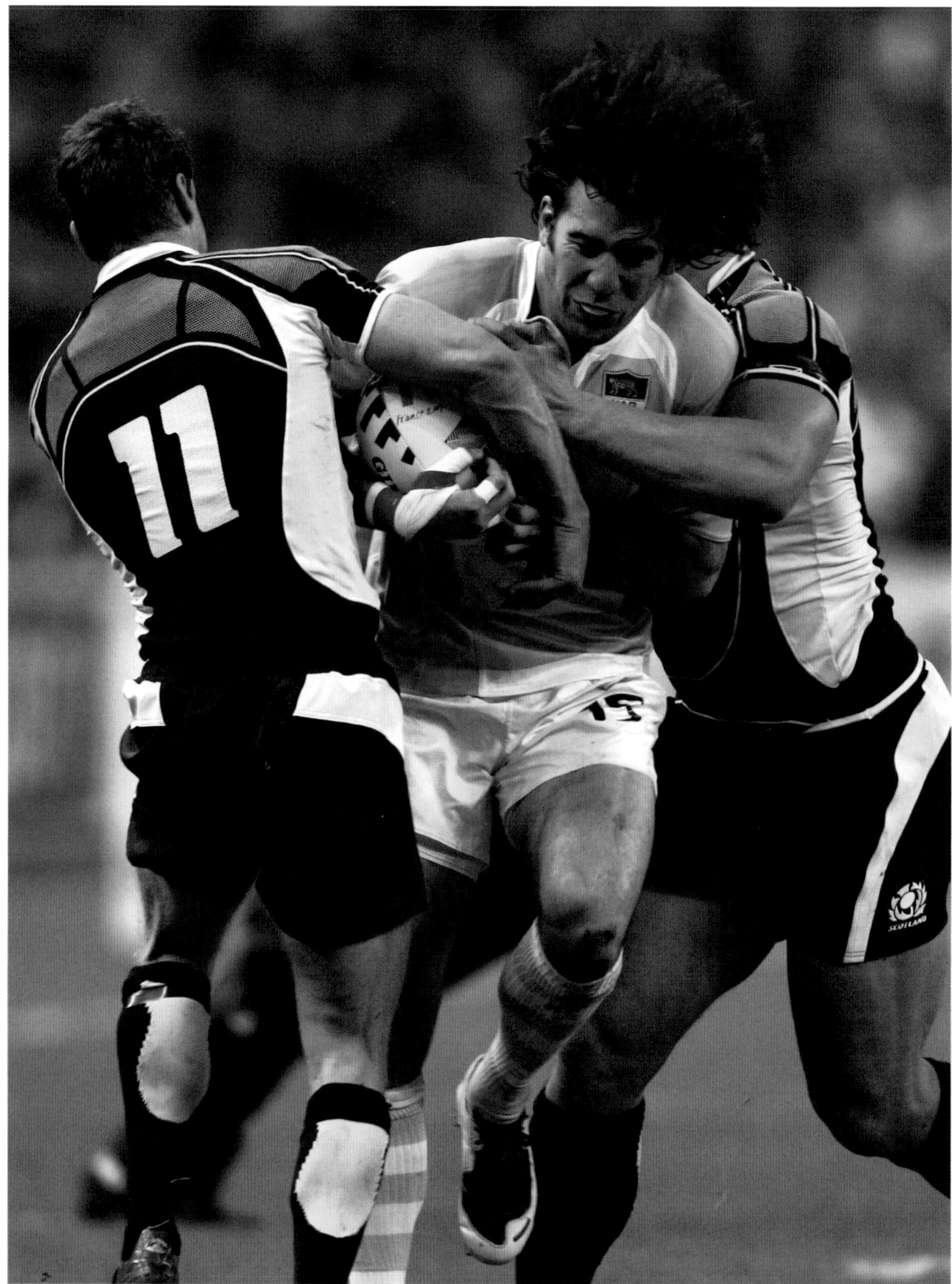
11
SCOTLAND

as Argentina took a grip on the game. For once, Parks fluffed his lines as his attempted clearance was charged down by the ever lively Pumas No. 8, Gonzalo Longo. Sean Lamont appeared to have things covered, but for just a moment he was hypnotised by the ball bouncing in front of him on the Scottish line, and his hesitation let in the diving Longo to touch down. Contepomi's conversion gave Argentina a ten-point lead.

But what would a game involving Scotland be without a penalty or two from Chris Paterson? The sharpest shooter in the game got his first chance of the evening when the Pumas infringed in the ruck, and from 30 metres Paterson made it 16 out of 16 at this World Cup and gave Scotland far greater hope at the break, at which they were trailing by just seven points.

For spectators gorged on the three previous epics of the weekend, this was a stodgy affair, and the crowd occasionally lapsed into boos with another boot of the ball. Yet all the while the atmosphere remained fully charged, in the knowledge that the winners would at least boldly go where no Australians or New Zealanders were going this year.

BELOW He's given the ball an almighty thump... Fly half Dan Parks converts a penalty from pretty well halfway to open the scoring after 16 minutes. At this point, Scotland had not missed with a shot at goal in the tournament. **FACING PAGE** Oof! Argentina full back Ignacio Corleto runs into a crunching tackle from Chris Paterson and colleague.

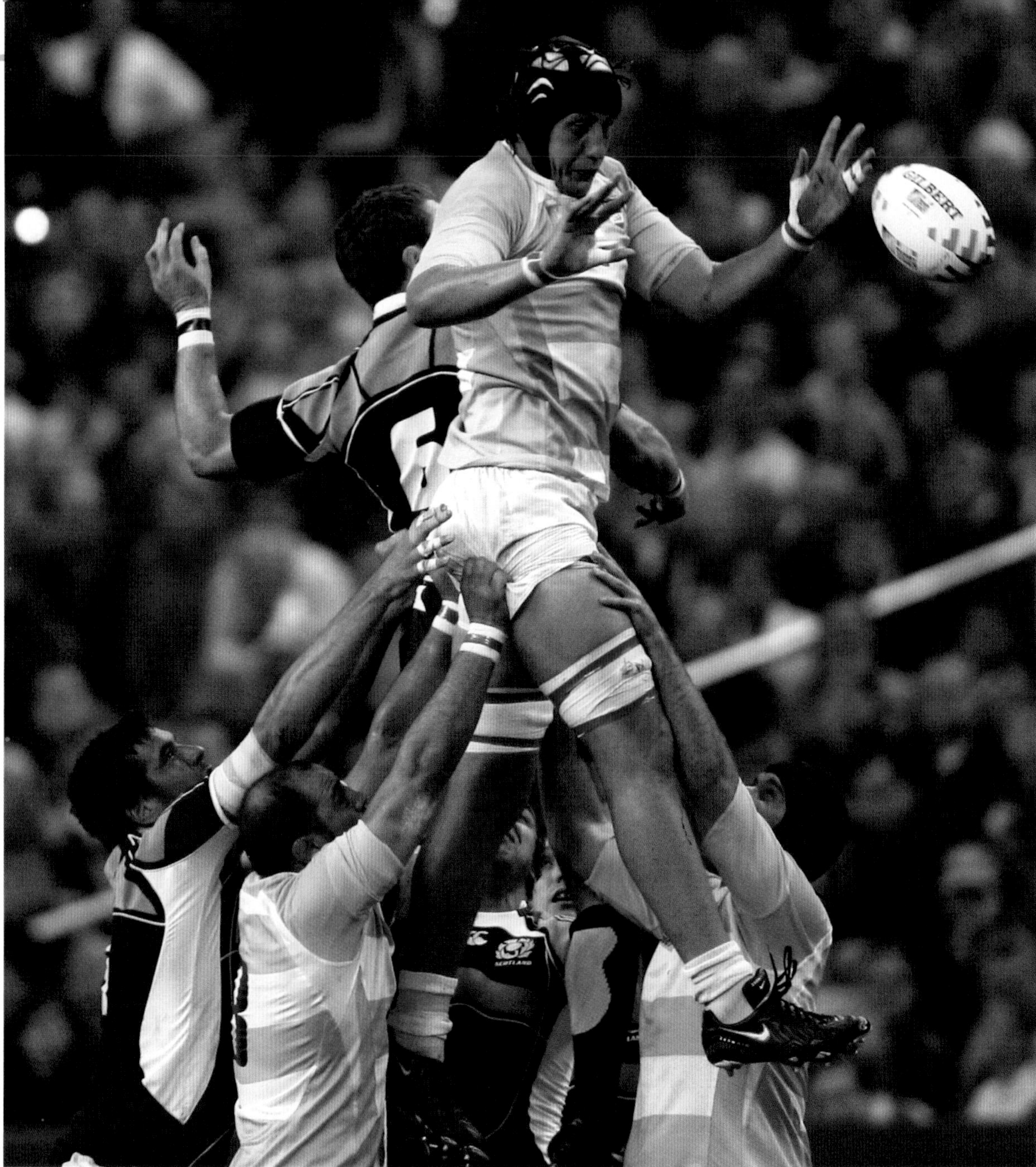

ABOVE Argentine lock Patricio Albacete collects and despatches at a line out. **FACING PAGE** Sean Lamont cannot prevent Gonzalo Longo from claiming the first try of the match for Argentina after the No. 8 charged down Dan Parks's attempted clearance inside the Scottish 22.

Still, though, Scotland were fumbling and uncertain. A desperate clamour from the supporters for more expansive rugby in the second half went unanswered as the game restarted in familiar fashion. The boot of Contepomi re-established a ten-point lead and then Parks, from fully 45 metres, recorded Scotland's first missed kick at goal of the tournament.

When Hernández finally found his target after 55 minutes with one of his dropped-goal attempts, the Pumas led 19-6 and the game appeared to be slipping away from Scotland. Eventually, though, came the change of pace and plan from Frank Hadden's side.

Andrew Henderson had already come on in the centre for Rob Dewey and now the other members of the supporting cast took their cue. Chris Cusiter, Scott Macleod, Craig Smith and Kelly Brown all trooped on, and all would play key roles in revitalising the Scottish challenge.

It was some rampaging from replacement prop Smith that made the first real progress towards Argentina's line, through a

'07

defence which had so far conceded only two tries in the entire tournament. MacLeod, on for Jim Hamilton, also played his part and the final scoring pass was given by flanker Kelly Brown to Chris Cusiter, the scrum-half appearing on hand a couple of yards out to go over in the corner and score Scotland's first try since their pool game rout of Romania. This try, though, was far more precious and when Paterson's conversion from the touch line sneaked in off the left-hand post (make that 17 from 17), Scotland were within a converted try of victory.

By now the game, the stadium and Scotland's players had all come to life, and whether it was through greater fitness or simply sheer desperation at finding themselves on the edge of the World Cup abyss, Scotland spent the last ten minutes involved in various assaults on the Pumas' line.

The best chance came from a five-metre line out, but Argentina's defence repelled several phases of Scottish forward endeavour, and Parks's eventual cross-kick for Sean Lamont in the corner was too strong. The score remained at 19-13.

Scotland's last breath came with a scrum just inside Argentina's half. 'This is the game,' said referee Joël Jutge with only ten seconds remaining … and Scotland knocked on.

And that *was* the game, summed up in a moment: in a Scottish mistake as Argentine celebrations began; celebrations which would continue long into the Parisian night.

For Scotland there was a crumb of consolation that a young, still inexperienced side offered some hope for the future. Far greater, though, was the numbing thought of a golden chance which had got away. 'That's the hardest thing to take,' said Scotland coach Frank Hadden. 'We had an opportunity which we didn't convert, but I've said to the players let's have no regrets and let's learn from it. It's a young group and I expect us to be a serious threat in the next two or three Six Nations.'

A tournament and a goal, of course, which Argentina did not have. But that only seemed to intensify their joy at continuing this World Cup run and picking off another of the old guard along the way. All the more satisfying for a 'golden generation' of Pumas, who knew that this would be a final World Cup, among them captain Agustín Pichot: 'We don't know how far we can go here or what the future holds, but right now we do know that we are one of the four best teams in the world.'

The next challenge would be the tougher prospect of South Africa; a thought not immediately on the mind of giant Pumas prop Juan Martín Scelzo as he marched down the Stade de France tunnel, disrupting several television interviews as he beat a drum almost as large as himself. On and off the pitch, Argentina continued to make a big noise at the World Cup.

FACING PAGE, TOP Scotland replacement prop Craig Smith charges upfield. **FACING PAGE, BOTTOM** Juan Martín Hernández drops a goal off his left foot to put Argentina 19-6 up. **BELOW** Chris Cusiter goes over in the corner to give Scotland a lifeline at 19-13 after the conversion. **FOLLOWING PAGE** No-side, and the celebrations begin for Argentina.

'07

The twins Contepomi after the Pumas' win v Scotland.

What they said...

ABOVE Argentine full back Ignacio Corleto and Scotland No. 8 Simon Taylor shake on it at no-side. **RIGHT** Scotland coach Frank Hadden watches his players warm-up at the Stade de France ahead of the match.

Argentina: Marcelo Loffreda (coach)

“We have made history and achieved something unique for our nation and shown that we are worthy of more recognition. Many players through the story of Los Pumas rugby have contributed to this.”

Argentina: Agustín Pichot (captain)

“We are a family. Perhaps technically we are not the best team but we did everything possible to leave our mark on the pitch. We wanted to make history.”

Scotland: Frank Hadden (coach)

“They had a bit of a stranglehold for threequarters of the match and it was very difficult for us to do anything. Some of our decision-making lacked maturity. Argentina were streetwise and smart.”

Scotland: Chris Paterson (wing)

“I come away buoyed but disappointed because I genuinely thought we could have scored at the end. Two or three feet could have been the difference between staying here for the next fortnight. I don't want to go home. I think maybe we should have played more rugby, less kicking.”

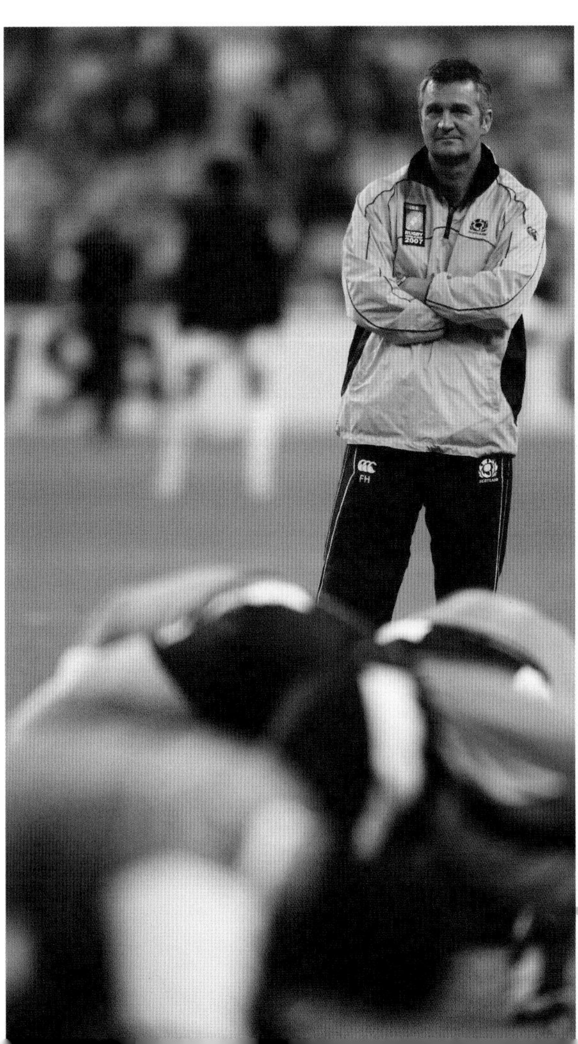

The nightmare returns to haunt France and their fans. Jonny Wilkinson, from in front of the posts, prepares to slot a penalty.

SEMI-FINAL

ENGLAND v FRANCE

MICK CLEARY

The Rugby World Cup caravan swung out of Marseilles and headed north. The England squad could have floated all the way to Paris on a cloud of euphoria.

Either that or they could have found 100,000 white-shirted slaves to bear their garlanded heroes all the way to the city. They were a hot item.

It was a hell of a story. The squad had little real idea just quite what they had unleashed. It had been the same in 2003. The distance makes little difference. You exist inside a bubble whether it's 12,000 miles away or a short train ride away.

You can always gauge the popularity of a story by just how wide-ranging the media coverage is. The regular correspondents will file their stuff as normal. Well, not quite as normal. Multiply that workload by ten and you'll get some idea of how much they were filing. No, the real barometer is in the number of news reporters sent to an event, with their offbeat ideas and stunts.

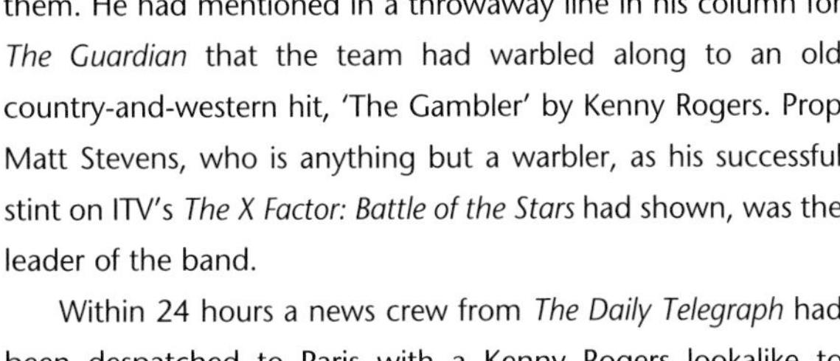

Back-row forward Martin Corry was to blame for one of them. He had mentioned in a throwaway line in his column for *The Guardian* that the team had warbled along to an old country-and-western hit, 'The Gambler' by Kenny Rogers. Prop Matt Stevens, who is anything but a warbler, as his successful stint on ITV's *The X Factor: Battle of the Stars* had shown, was the leader of the band.

Within 24 hours a news crew from *The Daily Telegraph* had been despatched to Paris with a Kenny Rogers lookalike to serenade the boys. Meanwhile, somewhere in America, a rather bemused but very grateful Rogers was being persuaded to don an England shirt to send a good luck message to the lads. And rather funny it was too.

England were big news. It's rare that rugby gets a chance to give football a dig in the ribs on the sports pages. Its big sporting brother rarely cedes an inch of space. The back pages are his turf. For once, though, football had to take second billing, even though there were important Euro 2008 qualifiers being played.

Small wonder that there was an air of incredulity about things. A few days earlier England had been no-hopers, seemingly coming to the end of what had been a troubled tournament. They had been challenged, found wanting, and recovered. But that, as it appeared, was about to be that. It wasn't. Only sport can do this – swing crazily from one state of being to another.

Wonderful as the moment, uplifting as the whole experience had been, it was important that England kept feet firmly on the floor. They had achieved something very significant in beating the Wallabies. But if they truly wanted it to become an experience to treasure then they had to follow it up. And whom better to follow it up against than the host nation?

France in a World Cup semi-final at the Stade de France. It was a fantastic billing, a re-run of 2003.

England could still lay claim to their underdog status and that suited them just fine. France had also suffered a considerable setback earlier in the World Cup, flopping badly on the opening night of the tournament against Argentina. Given that the Pumas had battled their way through to the other semi-final, that result didn't look to be quite as damning as it had to some people at the time.

France, though, had not played with any punch or soul. They had been limp and jittery. Like England in the wake of the South African drubbing, France were on the brink. Either they pulled together or they were out, an unimaginable scenario for the entire country. They had come through. And here they were, full of enthusiasm and confidence after their own splendid bit of work in Cardiff.

They faced the prospect of playing England with a good degree of optimism. They had played them twice in August and prevailed both times. The first game at Twickenham had been a hard-fought encounter, France coming through at the death, with Sébastien Chabal doing the damage in the closing stages. England felt that they ought to have won that game. But they didn't. Their finishing and their composure let them down. There were no such excuses to be had in Marseilles a week later. England were roundly beaten, a sobering end to their warm-up programme and a portent of things to come.

England and France knew each other well, by dint of those games as well as through the crossover of talent between the countries, notably reflected in the respective captains, Phil Vickery and Raphaël Ibanez. Front-row brothers in arms at Wasps; adversaries-to-be at the Stade de France.

The two men were cut from similar stone: quiet, unassuming men with great solidity of character. Both were charged with leading their men to a World Cup final. Big task. Neither was to shirk the responsibility.

England had little intention of changing their approach. They were determined to be as grounded and down-to-earth as they could. And why not? It had served them well. 'We were grumpy and horrible in Marseilles and we won, so I want us to be grumpy and horrible again,' said forwards coach John Wells.

The forward effort was once again going to be central to just how England would fare. France, though, were not Australia. They would not fold. 'The scrum has got to be a big focus for us again,' said scrummaging coach Graham Rowntree. 'If you're going to beat any French side you've got to be able to take the energy from them in the scrum because they build from there. They've got a wily old pack.'

Rowntree had managed to draw significant performances from the two props, Vickery and Andrew Sheridan. Sheridan had attracted most of the attention for the exploits in Marseilles. But the performance of Vickery, who had been plagued by injury and then missed two games through suspension, was just as remarkable. 'That was one of his best games at any level for a long time,' said Rowntree. 'His work rate, his tackle and his scrummaging were all right up there. He led from the front.'

England had also managed to get the best from Sheridan. 'Sheri has played well for England before but not to that level,' said Rowntree. 'He's an incredibly strong bloke and has always had that physical durability. But the mark of a great player is the ability to do it week in, week out. Let's see if he can do it again. If he can, and again the following week, then he's world class.'

The same was true of the entire England pack of forwards. 'There had been a lot of angst and unhappiness in there about how they'd been playing and it all came out against Australia,' explained Rowntree.

BELOW John Wells (right) with Graham Rowntree and Brian Ashton at a training session. Wells declared that 'grumpy and horrible' would do for him. **FACING PAGE** Bernard Laporte, flanked by Jo Maso (left) and Raphaël Ibanez, selected his heavy kickers Traille and Beauxis once again.

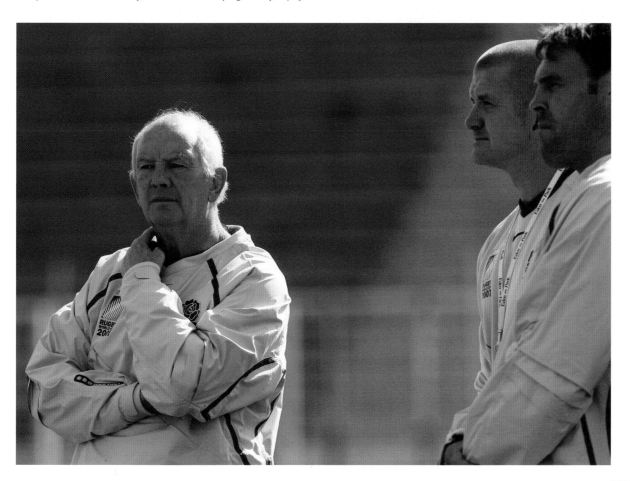

They would have the chance to bring it all out again against France. Brian Ashton went with the same 22, the first time that he'd felt able to do that in his reign as head coach. It was the first time in 28 matches that England were to field an unchanged starting XV. France, too, kept with those who had done them so proud at the Millennium Stadium. Both sides must have been doing something right.

Bernard Laporte's selection, with Lionel Beauxis at fly half and Damien Traille at full back, clearly indicated that France

RIGHT Within moments of kick-off Josh Lewsey collects a kick-ahead and smashes through and over Damien Traille to score the game's only try. **BELOW** Mike Catt and Andy Gomarsall rush to congratulate Lewsey, who would later incur a hamstring injury that would put him out of the final.

were once again going to play a kicking game. Play for territory. And keep the pressure on. It was not the French way. But it had become the Laporte way.

England had their own kicker, of course, one who haunted the dreams of most French rugby supporters – Jonny Wilkinson. He had done for them in Sydney four years earlier, scoring all the points in that 24-7 victory. Would he do for them again? Well, Wilkinson was not having things all his own way.

By his own high standards Wilkinson had been misfiring throughout the tournament. The leading points scorer in Rugby

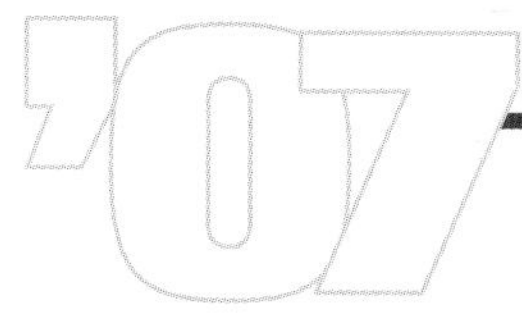

World Cup history with 234 points at the juncture, he had missed 9 of 24 attempts at goal, way beneath his normal return of around 80 per cent.

There had been perceived difficulties with the ball, although other kickers seemed to have no such problems. Two days before the semi-final, Wilkinson was to be found at the Stade de France going through a two-hour kicking session. He was delighted to have had a full complement of six match balls with which to practise. Previously, teams had been allowed only two of the dedicated balls prior to a game. Wilkinson was not looking for excuses. 'The confidence doesn't change,' he said. 'You've just to get on with these things.'

The clock was ticking. The last couple of days, the last few hours before a big match are testing times for players. All the work has been done. They just want to get on with it. Brian Ashton doesn't believe in burdening players with too much. Through Friday and Saturday he gradually removed himself from the scene. 'It's their game,' he said.

The senior players come to the fore. The captain comes to the fore. At 7 pm on Friday evening at the team hotel in Neuilly-

sur-Seine, on the outskirts of Paris, Vickery addressed the team. It was only a five minute speech. But it was heartfelt. Earlier that day, Vickery had addressed the media. Normally these eve-of-game press conferences are pretty flat affairs. No one wants to give away anything, so they clam up. Not Vickery. Not on this occasion. He wanted to tell it as it was.

'If my players are not prepared to sacrifice body and soul for the cause on Saturday night, reach down and find a performance within themselves that they might not thought that they had, then you can forget all about game plans for this and that because it won't work without that aggression and passion,' said Vickery.

'That's got to come first. And it's got to be full-on from minute one. Our squad, from number one to 22, has got to stand up and be counted, that's for sure. I don't want to go home, with pats on the back for giving it a good go, and people saying, "well done, old boy, you nearly got there." I want to be remembered for achieving something, for really doing something. This is a once-in-a-lifetime opportunity. None of us is going to let it go by just like that. It would be such a waste. If we lose on Saturday night, then last weekend means nothing. We might as well not have bothered. I've got some bloody heroes in my team and they will be giving it a real go. We all know we've got to perform better or we'll get beaten, and beaten convincingly. It's mental toughness we need now, not game plans galore. It's about physicality, about bravery, about guts.'

Some rallying cry. It worked. England were on their mettle.

Even the most one-eyed England optimist, though, could not have anticipated the start England were to get. Within 80 seconds there were five points on the board, scored by Josh Lewsey, who took advantage of Traille's dithering at the rear to pounce on the kick-through from Andy Gomarsall. Disaster for France. Delirium for England.

That shock score stung France into action. They played some rugby in that opening quarter. And very little in the remaining hour. They retreated back into kicking mode, banging the ball long at every turn.

They got some return for their limited tactics, inducing errors which led to penalties. Beauxis knocked over a couple in that opening quarter, scores that would take France into the half-time interval with a slender 6-5 lead. Four minutes after the restart the Beauxis boot had done it again, banging one over from 40 metres.

Wilkinson, meanwhile, was having his usual difficulties. The conversion had missed, as had a penalty and dropped-goal attempts. He was back on the mark with a penalty goal in the 47th minute, though. 9-8. Tight, tense, all to play for.

A Wilkinson dropped-goal attempt in the 59th minute thudded into an upright. Nerves were beginning to fray. Up in

FACING PAGE The weight of responsibility seems to lie heavily on 21-year-old Lionel Beauxis as he lines up a goal kick. **BELOW** Dimitri Szarzewski goes high on Jason Robinson, conceding a kickable penalty.

the stands the French fans got edgy. Surely their men would pull clear to make the dream come true?

The nightmare returned to haunt them. In the 75th minute, substitute hooker Dimitri Szarzewski hung out a lazy arm as Jason Robinson cut in to the 22. Penalty. It was a strict call, but in the context of the World Cup, the right call. Wilkinson lined it up. And over it went. Two minutes later the England pack went churning downfield. Phase after phase. Working for position. Back to Jonny. And over the dropped goal went. 14-9.

Victory was in sight. France stirred themselves from their torpor and launched a desperate, last-ditch attack.

Too little. Too late. England were through to the World Cup final. Who would have thought it?

ABOVE The final nail. Jonny Wilkinson drops a goal to leave England 14-9 up and heading for the final. **LEFT** England skipper Phil Vickery and Man of the Match Mike Catt enjoy the moment.

Brian Ashton applauds England's hard-fought victory.

What they said...

England: Brian Ashton (coach)

“It would be a blatant lie if, hand on heart, I said that I believed we could be finalists after a disappointing first two weeks. But they're bright lads. They've been through it before. You can't beat experience.”

England: Phil Vickery (captain)

“Sometimes in sport things don't make sense. It's mind-blowing compared with where we were four weeks ago. I never expected to get to the last two. It's a huge effort. We've worked, kept digging in, made the opposition struggle and never gave up.”

England: Joe Worsley (repl)

“I got on my bike. Clerc is a bit sharp and would get clear if I didn't tackle him straightaway, and I just managed to get a hand on him.”

England: Jonny Wilkinson (fly half)

“Catty said to me before the start: 'This is Jonny Wilkinson time.' But I was still thinking before the last penalty: 'If you miss this you have stuffed up in big style'.”

England: Mike Catt (centre)

“Four weeks ago we were going home early. We've had some lows.”

France: Bernard Laporte (coach)

“The England team were strong. We were not. There were a lot of opportunities taken by England and not enough by our side. We were unable to score later on. We wanted to be champions. We failed.”

France: Raphaël Ibanez (captain)

“We knew it would be tough for us. England did exactly what they had to do. We didn't have the tempo. We worked really hard after a bad start to the tournament.”

France: Fabien Pelous (lock)

“We were certainly missing a bit of punch to find a way through the England defence.”

France: Damien Traille (full back)

“I slipped as I went for the ball. I was trying to avoid a line out.”

BELOW Elation, relief, despair and utter exhaustion at the final whistle, as England keep alive their hopes of retaining the World Cup.

Interception number one. Fourie du Preez scampers away to score the first South African try after snaffling a pass by Argentine centre Felipe Contepomi.

SEMI-FINAL

SOUTH AFRICA v ARGENTINA

STEPHEN JONES

Suddenly, the energy had gone. The passion and the intent were still there, but these marvellous Pumas, whose heroics had been the story of the whole event, found that on their biggest day there was nothing left in the tank.

It was understandable. Many of the top Test teams are well used to playing massive matches on a weekly basis, as the autumn and spring windows give them the opportunity. But for the Pumas, starved of competition, this was a whole new scenario. They had given everything in their previous games, with four tough pool matches in the 'pool of death' followed by another sapping match against Scotland in the quarter-finals. Significantly, they had also played many of their front-line players in the matches against Namibia and Georgia.

This error-ridden effort – with every one of the four Springbok tries coming from a horrible turnover mistake by the Pumas, and which featured a string of simple handling and other errors – was surely caused by the exhaustion, which sapped minds and bodies.

There were other technical matters in this rather poor game. The South African line out was absolutely dominant, with the superb Victor Matfield and company not only winning all bar one of the 19 Bok line outs but also stealing eight of the 19 Argentina throws. That was a crippling deficit. It meant that when Juan Martín Hernández was kicking long out of hand, he could not afford for the ball to go into touch, because his team were never going to recover it. There was also the bewildering refereeing of Steve Walsh, who caned the Pumas unmercifully.

All this meant that the South Africans had to do very little more than absorb the superior Argentina scrum, absorb the meaty Argentina driving maul and sit back and feast on the errors. They were no great shakes in attack themselves because the midfield hinge of Butch James and Francois Steyn worked only fitfully, Fourie du Preez was not at his best at scrum half and the Springboks' own driving maul was reasonably well held.

Percy Montgomery at full back was never under pressure, so his defensive game and his kicking were on song. Bryan Habana, the devastating poacher on the left wing, was in deadly form with two more tries to add to the long list. John Smit, so important for the team, was also prominent, and although Schalk Burger was well held by the Pumas' back row, Juan Smith was influential on the open side and he warmed up to mark Jonny Wilkinson in the final.

However, at the semi-final stage the only thing that matters is winning, and South African were never headed. Argentina did come back to 24-13 in the second half, but the Pumas were simply not composed enough on the ball to take it any further, and any attacking platforms they did set up quickly crumbled when the basics let them down or the line out coughed up another ball.

For the Pumas, Juan Martín Fernandez Lobbe had a brilliant game on the flank and the tough Puma tight five was almost as good as ever. But Gus Pichot at scrum half had a poor day with his service, Felipe Contepomi was fractious and off form, and it was left to the splendid Hernández, with the odd run from Horacio Agulla, to pose a threat. Hope for England was fanned by the sight of the Springbok pack retreating in the scrum, even

BELOW Francois Steyn manages to get the ball away as the Contepomi brothers arrive. **FACING PAGE** Pumas flanker Juan Martín Fernandez Lobbe and Springbok lock Victor Matfield both put in magnificent performances.

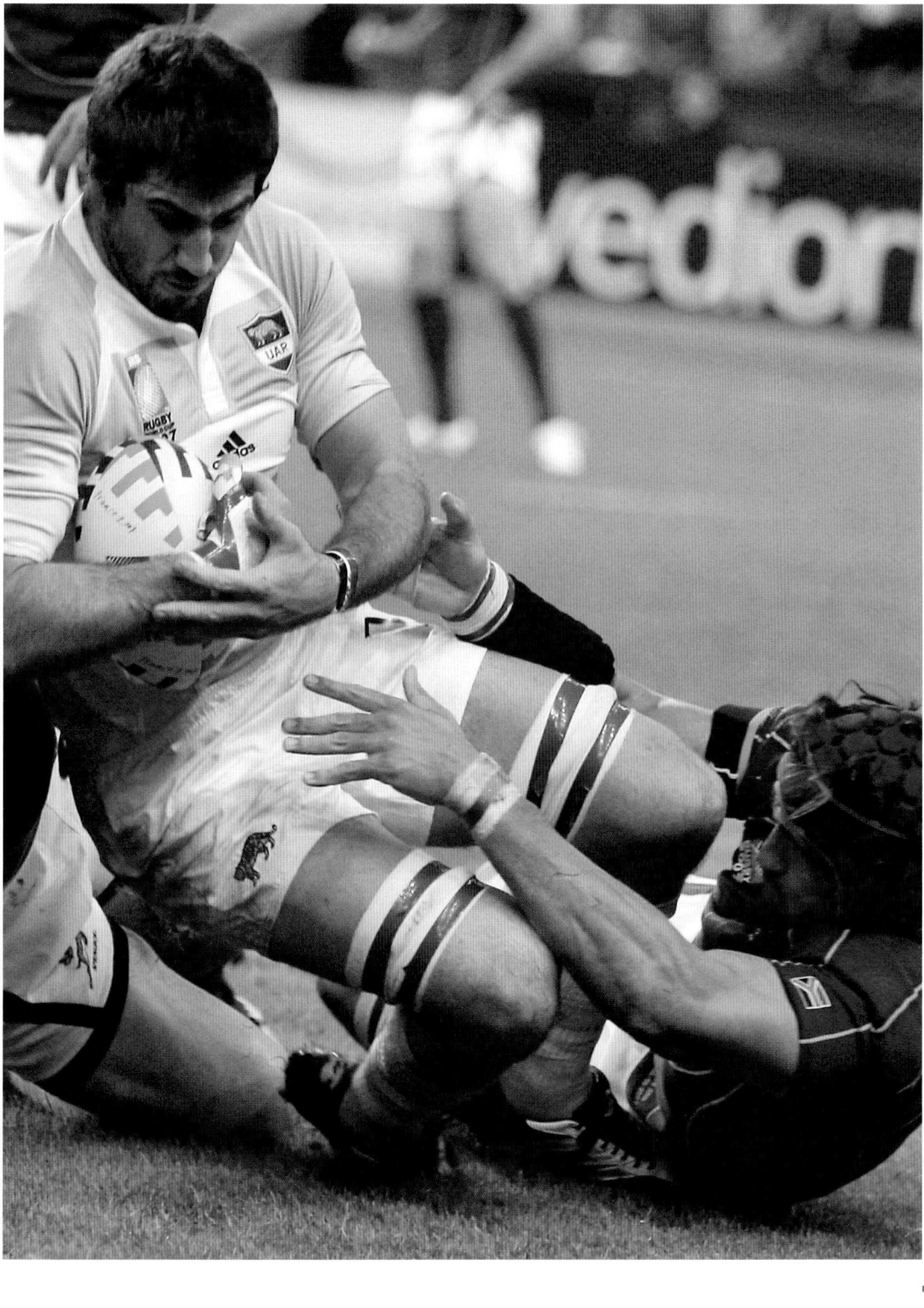

after Martín Scelzo on the tight head was replaced by Omar Hasan, admittedly as redoubtable a reserve prop as there was in the whole tournament.

It was just a tiny bit flat. As ever, there was a splendid crowd at the Stade de France, including banks of blue-and-white-striped Pumas fans with banners and streamers. There had been a massive build-up, with Argentina itself alive with the possibilities for its rugby heroes. It was also slightly devalued because we had here two teams so gripped with the enormity of the occasion that they preferred to exist, to absorb rather than to go out and claim victory. In that sense it was not unlike the first semi-final the night before.

The opening passage of play typified what was to come. It was Argentina who clearly settled better. They managed to flatter to deceive by looking secure on their early line outs and they made a few dents with their driving. However, just as they were pushing for the score that would put them into the lead and as they were launching an attack, a long pass from Felipe Contepomi in the general direction of two of his forwards was anticipated and picked off by Fourie du Preez, who had the pace to hold off the chasers and run all the way to score. Montgomery converted and it was a cruel blow.

Montgomery, striking the ball cleanly, restored a seven-point lead for South Africa with a penalty after 17 minutes, just two minutes after Felipe Contepomi had put Argentina on the board, also with a penalty. The Pumas were trying anxiously to set themselves up with the traditional power running of Gonzalo Longo at No. 8 and they had some success. But the energy was not quite there and the errors were frequent and maddening. Contepomi gave them hope with his second penalty, and after 30 minutes' play it was 10-6 to South Africa.

But then came another ghastly error. Longo, of all people, turned the ball over to South Africa and it was quickly moved to Habana with the defence out of position. Habana chipped ahead, chased, regathered and scored. It looked simple, but it was a deadly piece of finishing, and the conversion by Montgomery gave South Africa a heady 17-6 lead.

On half-time, a poor pass from Pichot died at the feet of Hernández, who knocked on. From that position, South Africa attacked hard, and Danie Rossouw strode his way over, the conversion by the steady Montgomery sending the South Africans in at the interval 24-6 up.

RIGHT Flying machine Bryan Habana sets off after his own kick to score the first of his two tries. The second was his eighth of the tournament, equalling Jonah Lomu's record for a single RWC, set in 1999.

UAR
adidas
UAR
RUGBY
2007
adidas
2007
adidas
UAR
adidas

Argentina had to score next. They still looked leaden-footed, they still made errors, they still kept losing their own line out and they were still being pinged by Walsh. But to their great credit, they did score next. They seized on a South African mistake, the heavy forwards driving the ball to the line, and with the defence sucked in, Hernández went wide and Manuel Contepomi scored. At first it seemed that the ball had not been grounded properly, but Tony Spreadbury, the Television Match Official, awarded the score, and the conversion by Felipe Contepomi made it 24-13. At that point, Argentina needed to dig deep and come up with one more score. There was a definite lack of bite about South Africa at this stage of the game. If only there had been a little more freshness in the legs and minds. Certainly, attempts by South Africa to create much themselves were sporadic in the extreme.

However, they persisted. Montgomery kicked penalties for the Springboks in the 71st and 75th minutes to take it to 30-13,

ABOVE Manuel Contepomi beats Percy Montgomery and JP Pietersen to score Argentina's try. **LEFT** Argentina coach Marcelo Loffreda congratulates his opposite number Jake White after the match. **FACING PAGE** Percy Montgomery put in a faultless goal-kicking performance, booting three penalties and four conversions. **FOLLOWING PAGE** Gather round lads! Jake White speaks to his team after their 37-13 win.

and that was about it. Argentina attacked in desperation towards the end, but in some ways the outcome was inevitable. Hernández sent out a long pass to try to get outside the South African midfield defence, Habana snaffled it with some ease and ran around 80 metres to score with a triumphant dive. The conversion by Montgomery ended the scoring at 37-13.

The closing stages were fractious, with both Juan Smith and Felipe Contepomi sent to the bin for separate offences, but harmony reigned at the end. The Pumas took a leisurely lap of honour to thank their supporters, obviously using up the last reserves and realising to their horror that they had to play the bronze-medal match against France at the end of the week.

It was a shame that they could not bring their proper game to the semi-final, but their epic win over France in the opening match and their destruction of Ireland and Scotland placed them squarely amongst the best four teams in France 2007. Forwards like Longo, Rodrigo Roncero and Patricio Albacete had been wonderful, Pichot was a commanding figure on and off the field, and Hernández, a tough character as well as a rare talent, was one of the players of the tournament. South Africa strode on to their final confrontation with England, with a day less to prepare, with definite strengths in their team and yet with concerns, too. This semi-final may not have been vintage, but endless talking points were thrown up and carried into the last week.

Danie Rossouw – a try and Man of the Match v Argentina.

What they said...

South Africa: Jake White (coach)

“At times we got a bit nervous and made mistakes.”

“They are all special players, but Habana has the killer instinct given to few players. In a few years his achievements will stand out in the records. Percy Montgomery is our most capped – he holds something like 80 records in South Africa, and he's proved why he is such a talent again in this cup.”

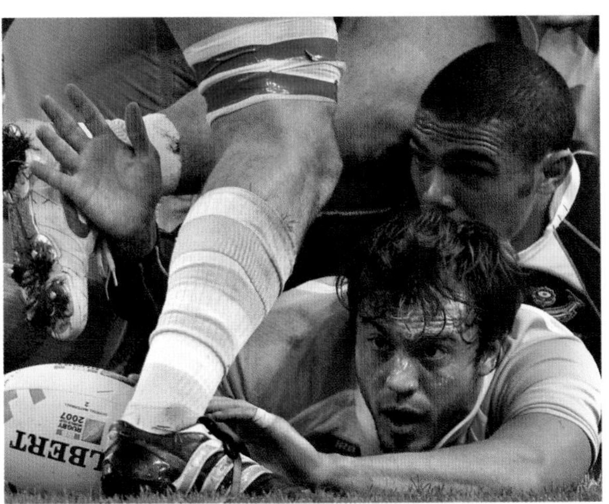

ABOVE Juan Martín Hernández and Bryan Habana find themselves at the bottom of a ruck. **RIGHT** South African fans celebrate in Paris after watching the match on a giant screen in the shadow of the Eiffel Tower.

South Africa: John Smit (captain)

“For the first 40 minutes, technically we were receiving kicks well and stuck to our guns, which showed on the scoreboard. Argentina's try forced us to regain our concentration.”

“None of my 70 Tests compares with a World Cup semi-final.”

South Africa: Bryan Habana (wing)

“All credit to Argentina, they came out fighting. They are so full of passion.”

Argentina: Marcelo Loffreda (coach)

“It was a really tough game. South Africa were very consistent. We paid a high price for lots of errors.”

“I thought maybe we could come back but the score stayed with that 11 points difference.”

Argentina: Agustín Pichot (captain)

“South Africa were the better team. We did everything in our power, we gave everything we had.”

Argentina: Felipe Contepomi (centre)

“There will be many players who leave this squad. The good thing is that a great group was created. This team showed that you can go very far with very little.”

Juan Martín Fernandez Lobbe (left), Juan Manuel Leguizamón (right) and Horacio Agulla let themselves go after the Pumas' bronze final victory over France.

THIRD-PLACE PLAY-OFF

FRANCE v ARGENTINA

DAVID HANDS

They finished as they started and their joy was unconfined. In many ways Argentina defined this World Cup – by breaking the mould, by overcoming the world's traditional rugby powers to finish third, by playing ugly but effective rugby, by showing that they could also play a beautiful game, by being unpredictable.

A week before, they had been so cast down. They had frozen on the big stage against South Africa, they had produced their most error-ridden display of the tournament and so they wound up against France in the bronze final, the match that no one really wants to play.

Except that Argentina did. Third place meant so much to them, far more than to France, whose aspirations had been the winning of their own tournament. That is not to say that France did not come to the Parc des Princes to play. They had reasons of their own: to say farewell to two legends of the game, Raphaël Ibanez and Christophe Dominici, who, along with the likes of Fabien Pelous, Pieter de Villiers and Serge Betsen, will not be seen again at international level.

Indeed France dominated the first half-hour and found themselves 17-3 down after Argentina scored two tries in four minutes. Not only that, French composure was leaking away; their record against Argentina has not been good in recent years and this was their sixth defeat in the last seven matches between the two countries.

That sequence includes, of course, the opening match of the World Cup, which Argentina won 17-12, setting in train a chain of events which sent France to play New Zealand in a quarter-final in Cardiff and spared England the prospect of meeting the All Blacks in the semi-finals. But here, try as they might, France could not breach the Argentine

defence and they became increasingly frustrated at perceived offside play.

There may be romance in the Argentine soul, but there is also a thoroughgoing pragmatism which includes the ability to get under the skin of the opposition. Agustín Pichot and Felipe Contepomi are past masters at the art of niggling, while forwards like Gonzalo Longo just tend to keep coming at you; they never go away.

'Argentina is not just a rugby team, it's a whole lot of things, with heart, with soul,' Pichot, the scrum half whose clubs have included Richmond and Bristol, said. He has been the heartbeat of the team for so many years, though this was his last international in Europe – one more for the road, perhaps, at home in Buenos Aires to make his farewells, and then retirement.

'You have to look inside yourself and that's what the team did,' he added. 'We were very tired, like the French, after a very

ABOVE Martín Durand and Thierry Dusautoir clash in what was at times a fractious match that produced three yellow cards. **LEFT** Yannick Nyanga is held up right on the Argentine line and lets slip the ball before he can ground it as France push for a score before half-time.

ABOVE Federico Martin Aramburu escapes the clutches of France lock Jérôme Thion to score Argentina's third try. **FACING PAGE** Thank you and goodnight! Felipe Contepomi takes a bow after scoring his second, and his side's fifth, try, which he also converted for a 34-10 scoreline.

stern World Cup but Argentina searched for this mentality. This was the end of the best team I have ever been part of in sport.'

There was a handshake between Pichot and Dominici, club colleagues at Stade Français, in the first five minutes, but nothing else was shared. The goal-kickers, Jean-Baptiste Elissalde and Contepomi, exchanged penalty goals, Argentina played their long-ball game and France tried to run, to find some rhythm through Frédéric Michalak, who, earlier in the week, had been so critical of the game imposed on France by the retiring coach, Bernard Laporte.

Instead Argentina struck twice. They recovered a high ball, established two rucks and Pichot sent Contepomi into the corner for a try the centre converted from the touch line. Then Juan Martín Hernández spiralled a long penalty close to the French

'07

line, Argentina mauled their way from the line out and Omar Hasan plunged over beneath the posts.

Grimly France pounded away to try and recover ground before the interval, grinding out four penalties which should surely have meant an earlier yellow card than those finally awarded to Ibanez and Rimas Alvarez Kairelis. Ibanez' disgust at the refereeing of Paul Honiss, now the world's most experienced official, was clear as he flung away a water bottle and walked off, a sad end to so distinguished a career for the France captain.

The return of Kairelis came just in time for Argentina's third try, created by a wonderful break down the left by Ignacio Corleto and a glorious pass off his left hand by Hernández, which gave Federico Martin Aramburu the chance to skip over. Although there was a third yellow card, against Juan Manuel Leguizamón only three minutes after his appearance as a replacement, there was no coming back for France.

While Argentina were still down to 14 men, Horacio Agulla seized turnover ball and broke from his own 22 to send Corleto striding majestically through for the try. Clément Poitrenaud then finished off a sweeping French attack, but in the 77th minute Felipe Contepomi placed the final dart in the hosts' side. Leguizamón made a powerful surge down the centre of the field and the centre was there to finish, converting his own try once again to take the final score to 34-10.

It was as wonderful a conclusion for the South Americans as it was dire for the host nation. France deserved better for the

organisation of so splendid a tournament. They had raised national hopes to the sky by beating New Zealand, but on the way they have lost that traditional Gallic magic, and to see backs and forwards mistiming pass after pass here was ineffably sad.

But Argentina's credentials as a world power are there on the table for all to see. They lose a generation of players, too, as well as Marcelo Loffreda, their articulate coach, who is off to Leicester. The world must now decide what to do with the third-best team of this World Cup. They need tournament play and they cannot continually be excluded from either the Tri-Nations or the Six Nations. Their union must formulate what it believes to be best for them, and one or other of the hemispheres must give them house room, because they have already broken down the front door.

RIGHT Man of the Match Agustín Pichot consoles Stade Français clubmate Christophe Dominici, for whom this game brought down the curtain on a 67-match international career. **BELOW** Argentina's 'golden generation' of 2007. 'They finished as they started and their joy was unconfined.'

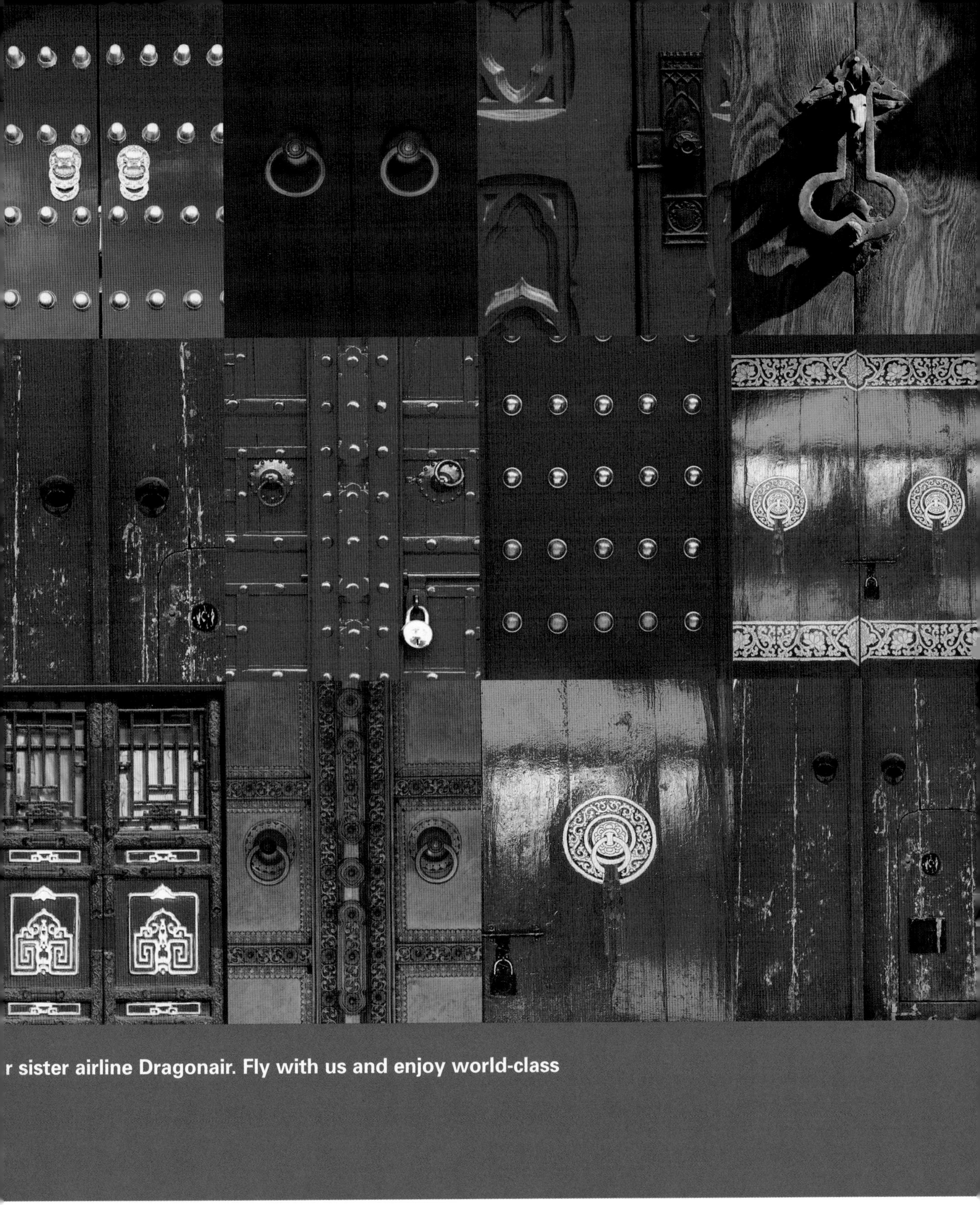

TOSHIBA
GMF
edf
PEUGEOT
RUGBY WORLD CUP 2007
SNCF
vediorbis
VISA
Fly Emirates

Back-row dynamos Schalk Burger and Lewis Moody scramble after loose ball during a hard-fought finale to RWC 2007 at the Stade de France.

FINAL

ENGLAND v SOUTH AFRICA

JOHN INVERDALE

You're reading this chapter at the end of the book, so let's not pretend you don't know who won. This is not an Agatha Christie novel where we're about to gather all the possible suspects in a room and systematically work our way through their alibis before finally nailing the guilty party.

Nonetheless. Try to pretend you don't know the outcome and the ensuing English disappointment, and cast your mind back to the week of the build-up to the final. The frantic scavenging for tickets on the Internet and offers from long-lost Kiwi cousins who didn't want to go a game that didn't feature the All Blacks and who fancied making a killing. Remember the even more frantic attempts by the hordes of England fans to find ways of getting to Paris. Every Eurostar train booked, every flight overbooked. There were thousands who drove through the night, mostly ticketless, who then slept in the backs of vans or on overpopulated hotel floors. They said that 60,000 made the journey, and less than half that number probably saw the match in the Stade de France. Some of those who did paid several thousand pounds for the privilege. England's sweet chariot, ridiculed for much of the preceding three years and humiliated by these same Springboks just a month earlier, had somehow refuelled, found an extra gear and was poised on the brink of history as Brian Ashton's side sought to retain the Webb Ellis Cup. Like so many things, the build-up was probably more fun than the event itself, but maybe that's said with the benefit of hindsight. You remember now. It really was an extraordinary week of pre-match tension.

Four years earlier, it had rained for most of the day in Sydney as Johnno and Jonny inspired England's narrow triumph over the Wallabies, but while Johnno was long gone, Jonny, despite all those injury setbacks, was still there. And in marked contrast to Australia, Paris on final day was like in the movies. Champagne air and crystal blue skies.

To walk past Notre Dame as it glistened in the autumn sunshine, and to eavesdrop on a hundred conversations, was to hear the name 'Wilkinson' over and over again. He may not have been playing that well, but the aura of that deadly, metronomic boot gave England hope, and cast fear into every South African heart.

As the 80,000 fans tried to overcome the transport chaos wrought by a highly convenient rail strike – which you suspect would have been called off had France made the final – Jonny was out there on the pitch, practising, practising. And he didn't have to wait too long until all that work paid off. After an early Percy Montgomery penalty had put the Boks ahead, England were awarded a penalty right on the touch line. Wilkinson struck the ball as sweetly as could be: 3-3. After the initial sparring, now the game could begin.

In the run-up, all the talk had been of how the South African front row would crumble under pressure from Vickery, Regan, Sheridan and the boys. However, there was to be no wholesale capitulation. The Boks had done their homework. In fact it was only in the line out, where Victor Matfield was a towering force and deservedly took Man of the Match, that there was a definitive winner. At key moments at the start of the first half, and towards the end of the second, it was a white hand that threw the ball in, but a green and gold one that stole it.

Montgomery kicked two more penalties, one needlessly given away by Lewis Moody, to give the South Africans a 9-3 half-time lead, but if anyone had expected the first 40 minutes to offer any Hollywood tries such as the Argentinians had provided in the third-place play-off the night before, they were disappointed and misguided. This after all was a final. So it was kick and chase and tackle and kick and chase and tackle. Two well-drilled teams who knew exactly how to nullify their opposition. If South Africa had planned to throw the ball around, they met a blitz England defence, and if they intended to kick long, they were faced by two and sometimes three England full backs, waiting to return their best efforts with interest.

One break from Francois Steyn promised much, and a late surge from the South African pack threatened the England line, but the half-time whistle signalled the end of a cagey first period, the only real debate being referee Alain Rolland's inconsistent interpretation of the crossing and obstruction laws, which England probably got the worst of. But surely this match wouldn't turn on a contentious call from an official...

RIGHT Percy Montgomery punishes another English indiscretion. The South Africa full back kicked four penalties in the match to end the tournament as the leading points scorer with 105.

And so to the abiding image of this match – and perhaps of the entire tournament from an England perspective. Half-time came and went in a blur. It may not have been a great game, but it was compelling and with less than a score in it, it threatened to be another nail-biting finish unless there was someone out there who could provide a moment of individual brilliance to turn the match. There was.

Until Paris, Mathew Tait's international rugby CV had been unfairly dominated by his debut upending by Gavin Henson in Cardiff. His blistering break in the early minutes of the second half banished all memories of that. He darted, he jinked, he made almost 50 yards, scything through the Springbok defence before being hauled down just short of the line.

The ball was spun left and wing Mark Cueto dived in at the corner. England had broken the deadlock through a supreme piece of attacking play. The score was 9-8. If Jonny kicked the conversion England were in front. South Africa would have to come out and play now. The giant screens showed Princes William and Harry wreathed in smiles. 'Swing Low' rang out around the Stade de France.

And then you realised that Alain Rolland had gone to the Television Match Official, Stuart Dickinson, for confirmation of the score. Cueto had grounded the ball perfectly, so surely it was just a question of rubber-stamping. He couldn't have put a foot in touch, could he? Angle after angle. Minute after minute. It must have been the longest piece of deliberation by a video official in history. Three cameras clearly showed Cueto's body in mid-air as the ball was touched down. But then the hammer blow for the England troops on and off the field. Another angle. And the tiniest split second before he'd scored, Cueto had put the tiniest sliver of toenail on the touch line. He had. You didn't want to believe it, but there it was. The camera never lies. No try. Even in Paris, you could hear the groan of disappointment from Cornwall to Cumbria.

Schalk Burger had been offside, so England got a penalty which Jonny knocked over to reduce the deficit, but his side were devastated. The game closed down again. One by one, England's forces became depleted. Vickery had left the field at half-time, and now Jason Robinson and Mike Catt departed to injury. Robinson's farewell from the rugby arena was with a right shoulder hanging limply to his side, while Catt, who'd been there in the England side 12 years earlier when South Africa had last won the trophy, limped off into international retirement. Both had made immeasurable contributions to the English game, but as their replacements Dan Hipkiss and Toby Flood turned the back division from wise to wide-eyed, you felt they were destined to ride into the sunset with runners-up medals round their necks.

FACING PAGE A determined Martin Corry stops Springbok skipper John Smit's drive for the line. **BELOW** Jonny Wilkinson closes in on Francois Steyn. The young South African centre had the last laugh, though, landing a long-range penalty to extend his side's lead to a winning 15-6.

Alain Rolland made another idiosyncratic decision about obstruction which presented Francois Steyn with a long-range opportunity that the prodigious kicker duly took, and even though there were 18 minutes to go, there was a nagging doubt that the chariot had finally run out of steam. Cueto's non-try had been the moment of destiny. South Africa knew exactly what to do. They kicked deep and challenged England to score from 60 yards or more. They were never going to do that. An optimistic Wilkinson tried a dropped goal from 45 yards, but it fell apologetically short. All the experts had said that if the game was tight going into the final quarter, then the experience of Sydney and the magic of Jonny would possibly see England home. But tight meant within one score, and the task of scoring more than once appeared ever more mountainous as the clock ticked on, and then Joe Worsley, himself a replacement for Lewis Moody, was replaced by scrum half Peter Richards in the back row.

The Springbok tackling was unwavering, ferocious, colossal. Pick any word you choose and you won't do it justice. Theirs was the ultimate embodiment of a triumph built on defence. Maybe they had been one of the most creative and expansive teams in the tournament, but not tonight. Bryan Habana barely touched the ball. Instead he spent his evening hammering into any white shirt that moved, driving them backwards. He'd been expected to be the Springbok match winner, but it was the unwavering lighthouse Matfield and the supreme full back Montgomery who saw them home. For those who'd thought Monty was a show pony more concerned with highlights in his hair than in his career, this was his final riposte.

The match didn't so much end as fizzle out. Down 15-6, England were never going to score twice, so when du Preez kicked the ball into the crowd to spark the final whistle, it brought delirium to the Springbok support, and a sense of resignation, albeit proud resignation, to the English army. Their team had achieved more than any had thought possible, but in the cold light of day, they also probably felt this was a chance that had slipped through their fingers. Vickery, Ashton and the rest of the side were magnanimous in defeat, but at the back of their minds they must have been thinking 'if only…'.

For the Springboks, it was a glorious occasion, perhaps even to rival their famous triumph of 1995. Nelson Mandela had sent a video message before the match, and as their president, Thabo

FACING PAGE Mathew Tait sets off on a scintillating run that took him almost to the line. **ABOVE AND RIGHT** Mark Cueto seemed to have scored, but his foot was adjudged to have been in touch before he touched down.

Mbeki, was paraded on the shoulders of captain John Smit on a lap of honour, there was a genuine sense of a sport at last beginning to be at ease with itself in the political maelstrom of South African society. Before the match, there had been talk that a defeat would have meant the name 'Springbok', with all its apartheid-era connotations, being banished to the history books. This triumph probably secured its future – in the short term at least. They were celebrating in Soweto like everywhere else, and one of the most fascinating aspects of the next World Cup in 2011 will be to see the composition of the South African squad – will it have been chosen by politicians or rugby men?

And what of Jonny? The Springbok discipline had meant the man with the golden boot had been reduced to the role of bit-part player. The image beamed on to the large screens inside the stadium, of a dejected superstar – the man 'whodunnit' four years earlier – head bowed, alone amid 80,000 people and all his team-mates, was as poignant as his irresistible smile had been in Sydney on that famous November night.

You knew before you began reading this how the story was going to end, and so you've doubtless discussed time and again the controversy over the disallowed try, and whether South Africa probably just about deserved their triumph. But there is still something that needs solving. As the last of the tons of green and gold confetti that had been showered on the victors was being cleared from the Stade de France pitch, the mystery remained. How do you retain the Webb Ellis Cup?

BELOW Bryan Habana acknowledges the final departure of Jason Robinson from a competitive rugby field. **FACING PAGE** Alain Rolland blows the final whistle and it's South Africa's World Cup. **FOLLOWING PAGES** President Thabo Mbeki joins his players in their celebrations.

'07

RUGBY
WORLD CUP
2007
Final
The Webb Ellis Cup

Jason Robinson bids farewell to club and Test rugby.

What they said...

South Africa: John Smit (captain)

"England gave us a good run. But we responded well to their tactical kicking. I want to hold the World Cup for the rest of my life. The dream has come true."

South Africa: Jake White (coach)

"It's an unbelievable experience. To see the president of our country holding the World Cup is something to be proud of."

"Danie Rossouw's try-saving tackle on Mark Cueto sums it up – a No. 8 on a wing. That's why we coach, because you want 15 guys who are all in it together."

South Africa: Os du Randt (prop)

"I don't remember the first one, it's too long ago, but I''m going to enjoy this."

ABOVE Os du Randt with his wife, Hannelie. The prop was a World Cup winner in 1995 and again in 2007. **LEFT** Springbok No. 8 Danie Rossouw, whose intervention at the line was instrumental in preventing an England try.

South Africa: Percy Montgomery (full back)

"We've been building and building and working towards winning."

South Africa: Bryan Habana (wing)

"It was cup final rugby at its best. We knew it would be a tactical battle. We managed to get the upper hand. I had a consoling word with Jason Robinson when he was injured because I have the utmost respect for the way he has conducted himself. He has been a master and a genius."

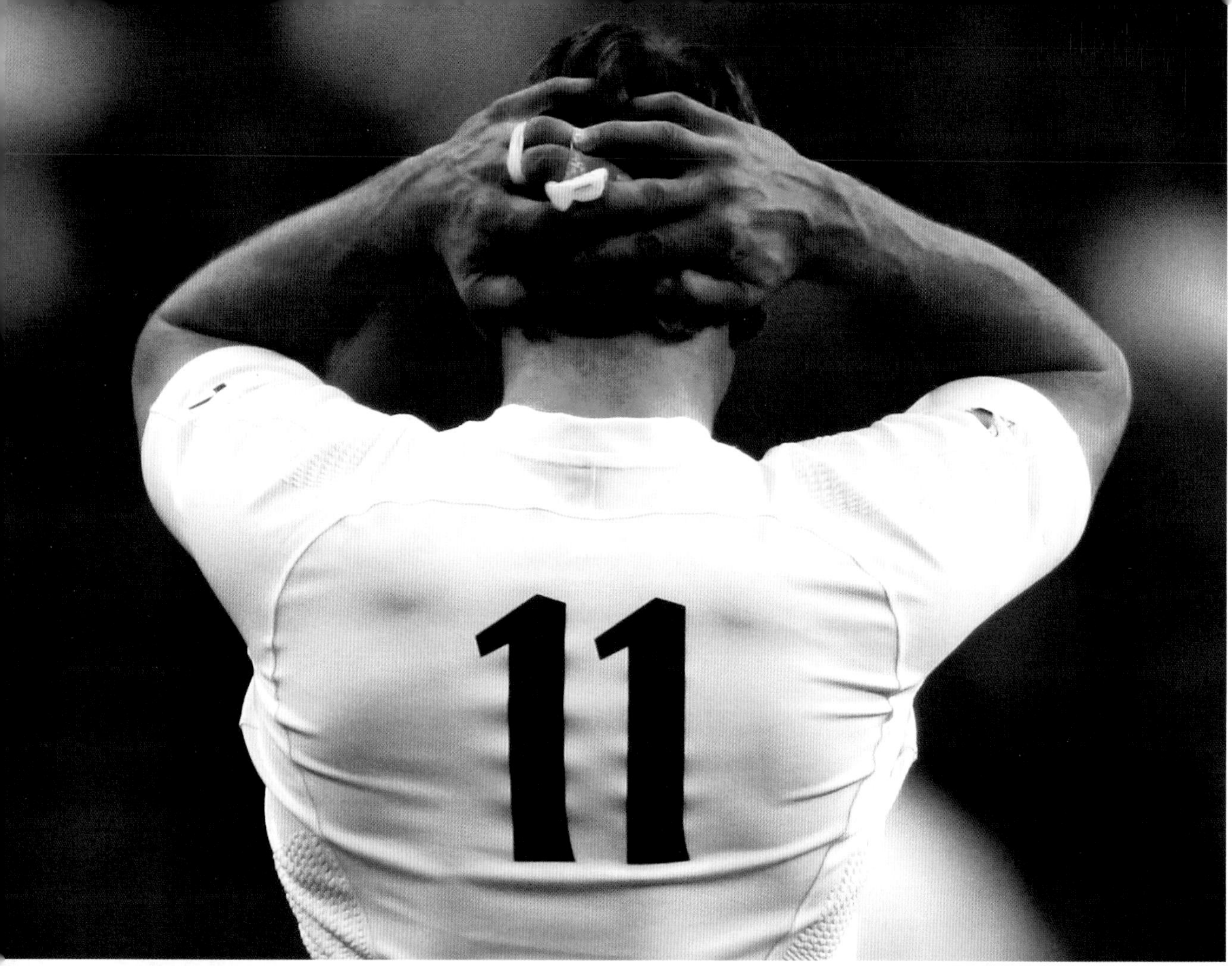

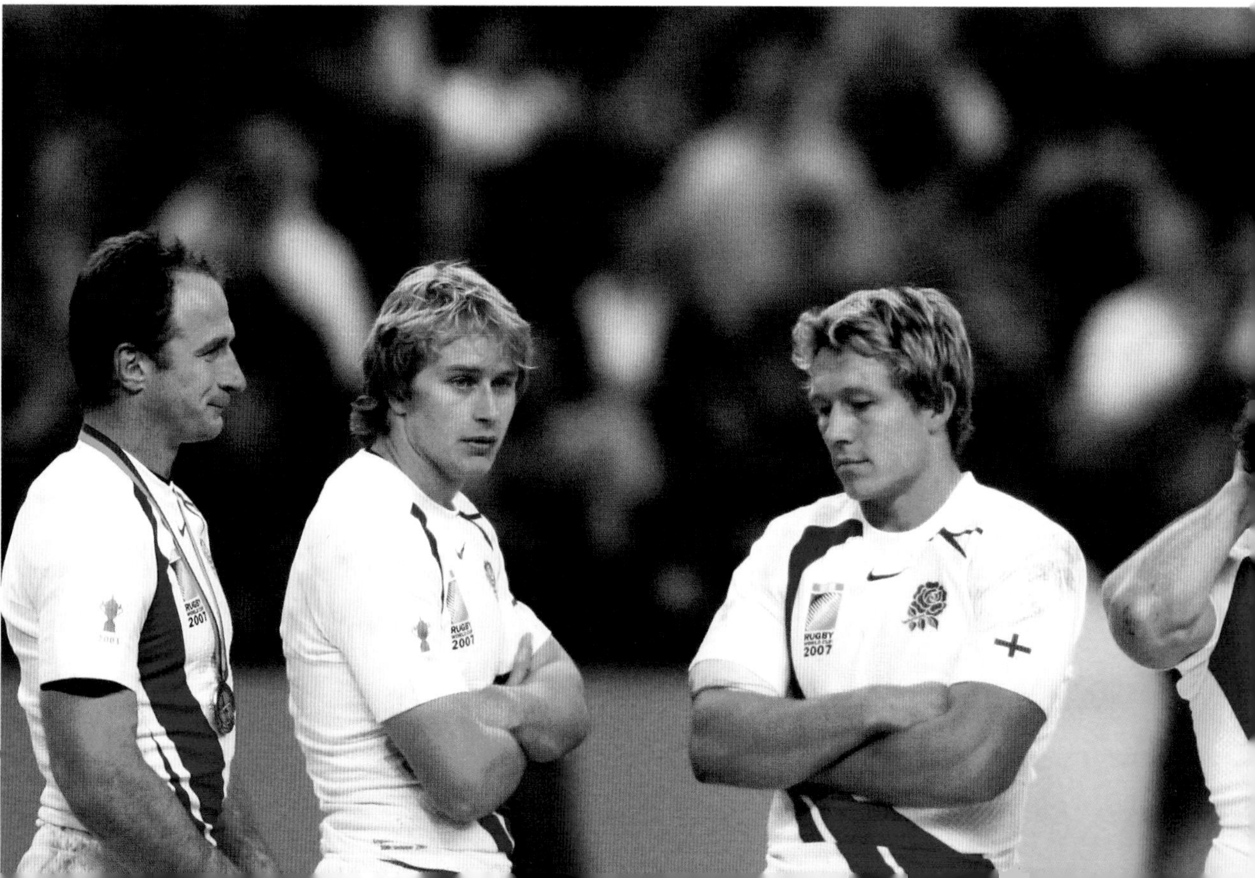
RUGBY
2007
RUGBY
2007
RUGBY
2007

England: Brian Ashton (coach)

“These seven weeks have been a great adventure and I am very proud of the players getting to the final and putting up such a fight. No one, outside our squad, thought we would do anything at all. We showed the world that if things had gone slightly differently we would have won. I told the players they have nothing to regret and many of them have a bright future.”

England: Phil Vickery (captain)

“I can't fault anyone. We've had a magical time here. We didn't take our opportunities and we put ourselves under pressure. I'm so proud of this team. We came in for a barrage of criticism at times but ultimately we've fallen at the final hurdle. We have had some real warriors at this World Cup. I've been on the pitch receiving a World Cup. To see another team receive it is like a shot in the heart. But we have given England rugby hope for the future.”

England: Mark Cueto (wing)

“My immediate reaction was that it was a try and that is why the rest of the team went back to the halfway line. I looked at the replays and still thought it was a try, and I will believe it was until the day I die.”

England: Jonny Wilkinson (fly half)

“We gave it the best we had and at times we got close. We didn't feel we were going to lose.”

England: Mathew Tait (centre)

“For players like me and Toby Flood it has given us a goal of 2011. Obviously, there are four Six Nations Championships to be won. But that is a European event. This is global.”

England: Jason Robinson (full back)

“I have achieved far more in rugby union than I ever believed possible seven years ago.”

FACING PAGE TOP: England wing Mark Cueto reacts as his try is disallowed. **BELOW LEFT** Disappointment and dejection on the runners-up podium. For Mike Catt, the end of a glittering career; for others such as Mathew Tait, a target to shoot for in 2011. **BELOW:** England captain Phil Vickery – proud of his troops.

JVC

Rocket man. Takudzwa Ngwenya of the USA fires up the afterburners and streaks past Bryan Habana on the outside in the Pool A clash in Montpellier.

LOOKING BACK

TALES OF THE UNEXPECTED

ALASTAIR HIGNELL

The biggest? Yes. The best? Possibly. The most unpredictable? Without a shadow of a doubt. As the song goes, two out of three ain't bad.

The dream scenario for organisers, broadcasters and hosts would have seen a French team contesting the final on French soil against pre-tournament favourites New Zealand – and beating them to earn everlasting fame, the adulation of millions and the undying gratitude of President Sarkozy. The reality was slightly different. France did beat New Zealand, albeit in Cardiff, and while the ensuing euphoria was genuine enough it evaporated in semi-final defeat by England. The transport strike in the week of the final was an early indication that the feel-good factor that Sarkozy had banked on was missing.

Nevertheless, targets were reached and even exceeded. Even before the final, the number crunchers reckoned that the tournament would realise a profit of £90 million, up by a quarter on Australia 2003. With TF1 and ITV posting record numbers of viewers, the total audience exceeded 4 billion for the first time, while record ticket sales of 2.27 million worked out at an average crowd of 47,000 spectators for each of the 48 matches.

And the paying customers certainly got value for their money. The opening match, with Argentina recording a totally unexpected victory over France, set the tone. The quarter-final Saturday, when England's against-the-form-book win over Australia was followed by France's epic victory over New Zealand, must rank as the most extraordinary day in RWC history. In between, Argentina, again, had upset the odds with a defeat of Ireland, while Fiji's scintillating win over Wales was the match of the tournament, perhaps of any tournament.

Two contrasting semi-finals – with England somehow edging past France, and South Africa comfortably seeing off the challenge of an at-last fallible Argentina – produced a final line-up that nobody in their right mind could have predicted; a final, moreover, that for the first time in World Cup history featured neither Australia nor New Zealand.

The final did, however, feature two sides who knew what it took to win the Webb Ellis Cup. England, of course, were defending champions, but they had looked anything but until their last two matches. While ten of their squad had picked up winners' medals in Sydney in 2003, South Africa, remarkably, still had 1995 World Cup winner Os du Randt in their starting line-up. That he was able to complete a remarkable double at the end of a predictably tense but never pretty final was testimony not just to his heroics in the face of England's front-row onslaught but also to his colleagues' unwavering commitment in defence of their line. The Boks had averaged 45 points and five tries a match in the run-up to the final, but it was their ability at the other end of the pitch that won them the World Cup. England were so much better than they had been five weeks earlier. They just weren't good enough.

With the next IRB meeting just weeks away, the tournament organisers had a lot to be proud of. Communication problems were not verbal, as expected, but they were visual. The sight of

Scotland and New Zealand turning out in the same shade of grey for their match at Murrayfield was as ridiculous as the explanations were pathetic; still, if the fact that neither side had thought to bring a spare set of jerseys from their bases in France served to highlight the folly of not playing the whole tournament in the host country, some good might have come of it. Elsewhere, the tiny numbering on the shirts of the England and South Africa teams and the unusual font on the backs of the Pumas contributed to confusion rather than clarity, while the row over the match balls produced more than the expected amount of hot air.

New Zealand's Dan Carter kicked less well than usual, and complained about the balls. Jonny Wilkinson kicked less well than usual, but didn't, though England let it be known that some match balls were overinflated, and Jonny was seen on more than one occasion asking for a different ball before an important kick. Meanwhile, Scotland's Chris Paterson achieved a 100 per cent success rate, Percy Montgomery kicked beautifully, and ball manufacturers Gilbert issued a press release claiming that these World Cup balls were the best ever!

Problems with ball pressures and shirt numbers could be dismissed as minor, fixable irritations; the proposal to reduce the number of competing teams at the next Rugby World Cup from 20 to 16 could not be dismissed quite so easily. After defending the 20-team concept in Sydney in 2003, the IRB had – despite pumping money into competitions for emerging rugby nations – performed a U-turn. As the 2007 tournament approached, it seemed to be arguing a case for a reduced tournament in New Zealand in 2011. If anything could make the board change its collective mind, it was the performance of these so-called lesser nations. Argentina, reaching the semi-finals for the first time ever, were the standard-bearers, but Fiji, reaching the last eight for the first time in 20 years, Georgia, who pushed Ireland to the wire in their pool match, and Tonga, who but for an unlucky bounce might have beaten South Africa in Lens, were not far behind. Romania, Canada and Japan all put in good performances, while the USA's effort will always be remembered for the way Eagles winger Takudzwa Ngwenya left the great Bryan Habana trailing in his slipstream on the way to the try line.

IRB delegates in Paris were left in no doubt that, given the right support, the emerging nations had the potential to offer a serious and credible challenge to the established order. They were also reminded of their moral obligations to spread the game as far and as wide as possible, and of the financial imperatives that would underpin that crusade. A 16-team tournament might exclude both the USA and the whole of Asia. It seemed, as the lights finally went out on a wonderful final and a magnificent tournament, that the game's governing body would see sense as they set about planning the details of RWC 2011 in New Zealand.

What's the French for 'If it ain't broke, don't fix it?'

LEFT Whose side are you on? Scotland and New Zealand battle it out in Edinburgh wearing confusingly similar strip. The 'All Blacks' won this Pool C encounter 40-0, running in six tries in the process.

GILBERT
RUGBY
2007

Victor Matfield provides ball on a plate for team-mate Juan Smith during South Africa's semi-final against Argentina at the Stade de France.

PLAYER OF THE TOURNAMENT

VICTOR MATFIELD

EDDIE BUTLER

It's not entirely unheard of that a second-row forward might play a more central role than mere provider of grunt and grind. After all, a certain Martin Johnson was a bit of a key figure in England's triumph in 2003.

But it is still a murky position. And if you get one, you tend to get two. Johnson and Ben Kay. These second-row blokes tend to travel in pairs. Twin-headed monsters. And you can't have Men of a Tournament. And how do you choose? Cagney or Lacey, Bill or Ben, bacon or eggs?

Victor Matfield did not travel alone. He had a partner by the name of Bakkies Botha, a contender in his own right. And dear old Bakkies was the enforcer, the bad cop, the cosh who could persuade most people to bend to his will. Bakkies certainly had his place. And without him, Victor might not have been Victor. So, to Bakkies, an acknowledgement of your worth in this tribute to your partner.

But even Botha – especially Botha – might acknowledge that Matfield had one hell of a World Cup. South Africa weren't so strong that they didn't go backwards at the odd scrum in France – and second-rows can be as wounded by reverse motion as any front-row forward. But at the line out, Matfield was king. And in rugby the line out is the number one jungle. The scrum is just any old game reserve on the outskirts of town. The line out is Kruger National Park.

And this is where Matfield let his mane down. Nobody was safer on his own ball. Nobody was more of a pest on the opposition throw. Nobody analysed the set piece with the same instinct and intelligence as Victor.

And that was not the end of it. He revealed hands that could thread clever passes when the rest of the world was admiring their feet. He tackled like a demon, too. Just when it seemed Mathew Tait was through in the World Cup final, it was Matfield who raced back to bring him down. Big cat Matfield. And just when it seemed that the final would contain nothing but the boot of Percy Montgomery, the boot of Butch

James and Fourie du Preez, Matfield gave them a lesson in how to probe delicately and effectively. A chip that sent England spinning towards the touch line. Matfield pushing England into the area where he could hurt them even more.

This wasn't a one-off by any means. Matfield has been at the top of his game for ages now. At the top of his soaring line-out arc. Every game he played at the World Cup added to his aura. He was majestic against England in the pool game, towering in the set-piece safety net that allowed the Springboks to rally against Samoa, when just for a moment it seemed trouble was looming. He was quite simply brilliant. In his pairing, in his team. All on his own.

BELOW Victor Matfield – second-row forward, Player of the Final, Player of the Tournament and, of course, World Cup winner.

Mario Ledesma on the rampage against South Africa in the semi-finals. The Argentine hooker narrowly lost out to John Smit in Matt Dawson's World XV.

RWC 2007: WORLD XV

MATT DAWSON

In a World Cup so full of surprise results, it is very hard to pick a composite team based entirely on form at the World Cup. Take the pre-tournament red-hot favourites New Zealand.

They faced no opposition in running up cricket scores against Italy, Portugal and Romania (269 points in total) and only scored 40 points against the Scotland 2nd XV. In their first real test they lost to France in their quarter-final. So on World Cup form, only one All Black makes my World XV – Richie McCaw. There are no representatives from Australia, nor from the remainder of the teams who failed to reach the knockout stages, which include Wales and Ireland. So my final selection comes exclusively from the eight sides who reached the quarter-finals and is based on how they played in the six weeks of Rugby World Cup 2007.

At full back I have gone for a shortlist of four: Jason Robinson (England), Percy Montgomery (South Africa), Chris Latham (Australia), and Ignacio Corleto (Argentina). Corleto was one of the stars in France, but in the end I have chosen Percy Montgomery.

The two wings were quite easy to choose. On the left wing, it just had to be the brilliant Bryan Habana, blisteringly fast, so elusive and a superb opportunist. On the right wing, I've picked Vilimoni

Delasau of Fiji. He is all power and pace with wonderful ball-playing skills.

In the centre I've opted for an interesting partnership of Mike Catt (England) and Jaque Fourie (South Africa). Catty had a remarkable World Cup and it was hard to believe that he was 36 years of age. He called all the shots for England in the big matches, and Jonny Wilkinson plays so much better when Catt is alongside him. Fourie is a forthright, ruthless centre. His defence was outstanding, and not only did he score four tries in the tournament but he helped to create some of the best passages of South African back play. Catt's nearest challengers at No. 12 were the talented 20-year-old South African Francois Steyn, who looks to have a great future ahead of him, and Matt Giteau (Australia), who looked very good until the quarter-final defeat against England. Challenging for Fourie's place at No. 13 would be Australia's captain Stirling Mortlock, who, alongside Giteau, provided most of the creativity in the Australian back division (and also got though the whole tournament without missing a tackle) and the Fijian centre Kameli Ratuvou, who scored and created some of the best tries in the wonderful Fijian attacking team.

At fly half there were several great performances, but a lack of consistency, from Dan Carter (New Zealand), Pierre Hola (Tonga) and Jonny Wilkinson (England). Ahead of these three was Butch James, who played a key role in South Africa winning the World Cup. But head and shoulders above all was Juan Martín Hernández of Argentina. He is an immensely gifted natural footballer who produced breathtakingly exciting running in attack and showed wonderful skills in every match, from elusive sidestepping to scissor-passing, and his tactical kicking was an object lesson in international fly-half play. He was also as good in defence as Jonny Wilkinson, and there can be no higher praise. The fabulous success of Argentina in finishing third in the World Cup owed an enormous amount to the skills of Hernández at No. 10.

At scrum half, the best individual game was played by Mosese Rauluni for Fiji with his brilliant running which lifted the spirits of Fiji in their heroic efforts against South Africa in the quarter-finals. Andy Gomarsall had a tremendous tournament from start to finish for England, and Jean-Baptiste Elissalde was in great form for France. George Gregan and Byron Kelleher disappointed for Australia and New Zealand. Best scrum half of all, without a doubt, was South Africa's Fourie du Preez. He was outstanding in every single match. He could pass, run, break, kick and tackle with the greatest of ease and he was even able to sprint 70 metres to score a dramatic try against Argentina. He was quite simply the complete scrum half.

The pack was surprisingly easy to pick. The outstanding loose-head prop was Andrew Sheridan (England), and although Tony Woodcock (New Zealand) and Rodrigo Roncero (Argentina) played consistently well, there was no doubt Sheridan made the biggest impact. Similarly with the tight-head prop, where though Phil Vickery (England) and Carl Hayman (New Zealand) performed well, the best player was Martín Scelzo (Argentina).

Hooker was not so simple. Raphaël Ibanez (France) and Mark Regan (England) both deserve creditable mentions for some great rugby, but the final choice rested between John Smit (South Africa) and Mario Ledesma (Argentina). Going into the final, I had Ledesma just ahead, but Smit not only had a great final as a player but he was also a tremendous captain. So Smit gets the vote.

The lock-forward combination was the easiest of all to pick. As individuals, Bakkies Botha and Victor Matfield were top class and as a partnership they were unbeatable. Several other second-row players enjoyed good World Cups and deserve a mention in despatches. England's Simon Shaw and Ben Kay – with a special pat on the back for Kay because he played right through every one of England's seven Tests – Ali Williams (New Zealand), Nathan Sharpe (Australia), Patricio Albacete (Argentina) and Mamuka Gorgodze (Georgia) all did well.

No. 8 had five main contenders: Julien Bonnaire (France), Danie Rossouw (South Africa), Finau Maka (Tonga), Gonzalo Longo (Argentina) and Nick Easter (England). I thought Easter had a particularly big influence on England's improved forward efforts in their final five matches, but I give the vote to Julien Bonnaire. The selection at open-side flanker has turned out to be the only All Black to make the composite team. Richie McCaw still looked a player of the highest class, even as many of those around him slipped off their pedestals. Several other players were not all that far behind McCaw and stayed in the tournament a little longer. I'm thinking of Lewis Moody (England), Thierry Dusautoir (France), Akapusi Qera (Fiji) and Juan Smith (South Africa).

I narrowed the choice at blind-side flanker down to just two players: Schalk Burger (South Africa) and Martin Corry (England). It would have been easy to make a good case for either player, but in the final analysis I have gone for Schalk Burger. He kept his discipline under control in the final and made a major contribution to South Africa's success.

The goal-kicker is obviously Percy Montgomery, and the captaincy is also pretty obvious. The only two regular captains in this XV are John Smit and Richie McCaw, and with eight South Africans in the side it would make sense to choose John Smit.

RUGBY WORLD CUP 2007: WORLD XV

Percy Montgomery

15

Bryan Habana

11

Vilimoni Delasau

14

Mike Catt

12

Jaque Fourie

13

Juan Martín Hernández

10

Fourie du Preez

9

Andrew Sheridan

1

John Smit

2

Martín Scelzo

3

Bakkies Botha

4

Victor Matfield

5

Schalk Burger

Julien Bonnaire

Richie McCaw

A's

No green hair here! Epi Taione (aka 'Paddy Power'?) of Tonga bursts through the England midfield during the Pool A game at the Parc des Princes.

THE HIGHS AND THE LOWS

CHRIS JONES

What a difference five days makes! After seeing their World Cup dreams vanish at the Stade de France against South Africa, Argentina's Agustín Pichot and Juan Martín Hernández sat on a pitch-side bench, arms around each other's shoulders, crying their hearts out.

It was a picture of absolute desolation, a unique opportunity missed to put a country that has been so badly treated by the international game into the showpiece final of the sport.

On a balmy night five days later at the Parc des Princes – still the best rugby stadium in Paris – Pichot and Hernández are arm in arm again, but this time jumping for joy after a staggeringly brilliant 34-10 destruction of hosts France to claim third place in the tournament. The small but hugely vocal contingent of Pumas fans had started their songs of triumph long before the final whistle, and the players who had been replaced jumped in unison on the touch line, knowing they had given Argentina its greatest rugby day. Let the International Rugby Board try and marginalise these true rugby warriors now!

The manner of the Pumas' victory, based on slick handling and brilliant support running, contrasted starkly with the up-and-under rugby that had got them into the semi-finals. As Pichot had said after their brilliant opening-match win over France at the Stade de France, 'it's boring but we love it'. Ironically, their love of putting boot to ball probably cost them a place in the final, as South Africa punished the Pumas every time they let their normally high standards drop.

In many ways, Argentina carried the flag for the put-upon nations of the rugby world. This was supposed to be a cup that proved there was still a massive gulf between the 'haves' and 'have nots', but it turned out to be something very different, suggesting a move to downsize the tournament from 20 teams to 16 was based on host New Zealand's financial projections for 2011 rather than building the game in countries like Portugal and Georgia.

Who would have thought more than 45,000 fans would turn up at the Parc des Princes for Italy's match with Portgual? And who would have imagined the Portuguese, unknown and unheralded on such a big stage, would be more impressive at half back, play with such passion and desire and reveal how well organised their defensive system had become? Portuguese fans matched the size of the Italian following, and the neutrals also recognised that in Portugal here was a team worth backing.

BELOW Simon Easterby feels the force of lock Mamuka Gorgodze as Georgia run Ireland too close for comfort in their Pool D match in Bordeaux. An out-of-sorts Ireland struggled to a 14-10 win against a side that were later to seal a maiden RWC victory, against Namibia.

For Georgia the World Cup was even more important, because the way the international fixture schedule works, countries from their tier-two level only get to face the big boys like Ireland every four years – if they end up in the same World Cup pool. It is an absolute travesty, and how can we truly grow the game if a self-serving cartel operates at the top end of the sport and entry is barred to so many? That is why every non-Irish rugby fan was cheering for Georgia when the teams met in one of the most enjoyable matches of the tournament.

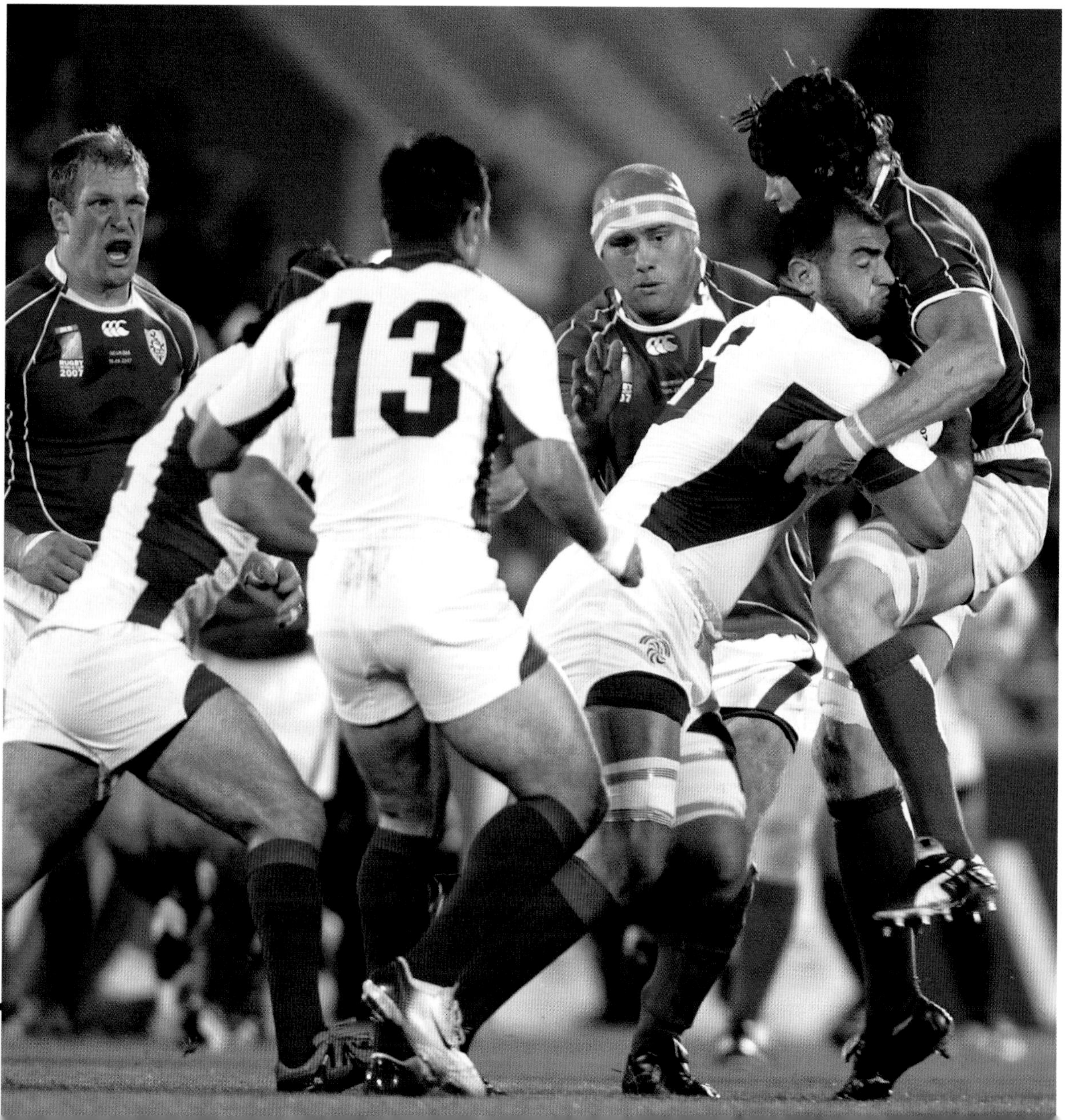

Ireland, so out of sorts it was almost laughable, were one moment of madness away from handing Georgia a victory that would have been the greatest rugby upset of all time: the second best team in Europe beaten by a country that had absolutely nothing and had to send its best players – a small but

wonderfully talented and committed bunch – all across Europe in search of a living from the game. Ireland had all the money, the big sponsorship backing and a lifestyle the Georgians could only dream about, but that counted for nothing on a night of triumph for the little countries at the tournament.

It was almost as if Tonga had taken inspiration from a country none of their players will have ever visited and that they probably couldn't find on a map. Tonga could and probably should have beaten South Africa in their pool match in Lens, and this island nation was to give the World Cup two of its most ridiculously silly stories, to prove that despite the dead hand of Rugby World Cup organisers, you can still show a little bit of ingenuity in the tournament.

Epi Taione, the Tonga and former Newcastle and Sale centre, tried to change his name to 'Paddy Power' by deed poll to thank the betting company for giving the team £10,000 to enable the Islanders to have a proper training camp before the tournament started. When this was blocked, he came up with the idea of dyeing everyone's hair green before their final pool match with England – a game that could have put them into a first quarter-final appearance.

They were ordered to 'wash that dye right out of your hair', which ruined what would have been an amazing picture on the night of the match: England all pristine and in white while standing alongside them waiting to belt out their national anthem would have been large, red-shirted men with fluorescent green hair. Come on RWC organisers, where was your sense of fun?

Of course it wasn't all about fun and potential giant-killing acts to embarrass the rich and famous in the sport. There were also moments of madness that did the sport no favours. England captain Phil Vickery's swinging leg tripped up American centre Paul Emerick and earned the prop a two-match ban. It was to set the scene for a rash of banning orders as the RWC disciplinary officers cracked down on foul play – particularly incidents not given the correct punishment at the time.

Schalk Burger was also banned on video evidence after he used a swinging arm on a Samoan player, and high tackles were to be a recurring theme throughout the tournament. This form of attack is potentially very damaging as it targets the jaw, cheekbone and nose area, which is totally unprotected. Quite rightly, referees did not tolerate the incidents they saw, while the video refs tried to pick up any that got away.

It is vital for the development of the sport that this form of illegal tackling is outlawed completely, although, as we saw with incidents of spear-tackling (most notably by Emerick against England and by Georgia's Otar Eloshvili on Rémy Martin during the France match), players are still picking up opponents and not releasing at the top of the tackle. Some continue to drive their opponent into the ground – head first – even though they must realise the possible life-changing injuries to necks and spines this would cause.

Global television audiences broke all records for the 2007 tournament, and the game cannot afford to put such incidents before a wider public that has yet to fully embrace the sport. Why would a parent in the USA or China want their son or daughter to play rugby if spear tackles and swinging arms in the face are allowed to continue to feature at the very highest level?

Of course, the majority of matches were completed without anything to worry potential converts, and the highs far outnumbered the lows in the most remarkable World Cup ever staged. Only the decision – for political reasons and revolving around votes that allowed France to stage the event – to play some matches in Scotland and Wales grated. Why drag Fiji and Canada out of their French bases to play a game in Cardiff and then bring them all the way back to France again in such a short space of time? It was telling that the organisers didn't make two of the big nations face each other in front of empty seats after a similar travelling nightmare!

But, as we have already noted, the World Cup is still about the major nations and the control they have on the sport, and as Pichot warned: 'Either we can have a World Cup for six or eight nations or we can make it for the entire world by supporting countries like Argentina between tournaments.' Yet again, Pichot was spot on.

Let's finish on a high that must have been a bit of a major low for the owner of the yacht concerned. The two quarter-finals staged in Marseilles (why, oh why was one in Cardiff?) brought four teams and four sets of supporters to the second city of France for a weekend no one who was there will ever forget. First, we had England beating Australia in a World Cup final rematch and later France accounted for New Zealand in Cardiff. The Old Port of Marseilles went bonkers, English and French supporters danced arm in arm, and sirens (why do bar owners have them in Marseilles?) were sounded all night.

There was even singing and dancing on the enormous yacht moored in the Old Port, which grabbed your attention because it was flying the biggest Welsh flag ever seen. Wales hadn't made the last eight because Fiji had produced a stunning 38-34 win, but the Welsh fans still turned up – to support Fiji against South Africa in the quarter-finals. What a marvellous moment in a truly all-embracing cup that proved France could have staged the whole thing without any help and that rugby fans are still the best bunch of party animals on the planet!

IRB
RUGBY WORLD CUP 2007
Final
The Webb Ellis Cup
SPRINGBOK

STATISTICS

Rugby World Cup 1987-2007

Highest scores:

145 New Zealand v Japan (Bloemfontein, 1995)
142 Australia v Namibia (Adelaide, 2003)
111 England v Uruguay (Brisbane, 2003)

Biggest winning margin:

142 Australia v Namibia (Adelaide, 2003)
128 New Zealand v Japan (Bloemfontein, 1995)
98 England v Uruguay (Brisbane, 2003)
98 New Zealand v Italy (Huddersfield, 1999)

Most points by a player in a match:

45 Simon Culhane (New Zealand v Japan, 1995)
44 Gavin Hastings (Scotland v Ivory Coast, 1995)
42 Mat Rogers (Australia v Namibia, 2003)

Most tries by a player in a match:

6 Marc Ellis (New Zealand v Japan, 1995)
5 Chris Latham (Australia v Namibia, 2003)
5 Josh Lewsey (England v Uruguay, 2003)

Most points in one tournament:

126 Grant Fox (New Zealand, 1987)
113 Jonny Wilkinson (England, 2003)
112 Thierry Lacroix (France, 1995)

Leading aggregate World Cup scorers:

249 Jonny Wilkinson (England, 1999, 2003, 2007)
227 Gavin Hastings (Scotland, 1987, 1991, 1995)
195 Michael Lynagh (Australia, 1987, 1991, 1995)

Most tries in World Cups:

15 Jonah Lomu (New Zealand, 1995, 1999)
11 Rory Underwood (England, 1987, 1991, 1995)
10 David Campese (Australia, 1987, 1991, 1995)

Most tries in one tournament:

8 Jonah Lomu (New Zealand, 1999)
Bryan Habana (South Africa, 2007)
7 Marc Ellis (New Zealand, 1995)
Jonah Lomu (New Zealand, 1995)
Doug Howlett (New Zealand, 2003)
Mils Muliaina (New Zealand, 2003)
Drew Mitchell (Australia, 2007)

Most tries in a match by a team:

22 Australia v Namibia (Adelaide, 2003)
21 New Zealand v Japan (Bloemfontein, 1995)

Most penalty goals in World Cups:

53 Jonny Wilkinson (England, 1999, 2003, 2007)
35 Gonzalo Quesada (Argentina, 1999, 2003)
33 Andrew Mehrtens (New Zealand, 1995, 1999)

Most penalty goals in one tournament:

31 Gonzalo Quesada (Argentina, 1999)
26 Thierry Lacroix (France, 1995)
23 Jonny Wilkinson (England, 2003)

Most conversions in World Cups:

39 Gavin Hastings (Scotland, 1987, 1991, 1995)
37 Grant Fox (New Zealand, 1987, 1991)
36 Michael Lynagh (Australia, 1987, 1991, 1995)

Most conversions in one tournament:

30 Grant Fox (New Zealand, 1987)
22 Percy Montgomery (South Africa, 2007)
20 Michael Lynagh (Australia, 1987)
Simon Culhane (New Zealand, 1995)
Leon MacDonald (New Zealand, 2003)
Nick Evans (New Zealand, 2007)

Most dropped goals in World Cups:

13 Jonny Wilkinson (England, 1999, 2003, 2007)
6 Jannie de Beer (South Africa, 1999)
5 Rob Andrew (England, 1987, 1991, 1995)
Gareth Rees (Canada, 1987, 1991, 1995, 1999)

Most dropped goals in one tournament:

8 Jonny Wilkinson (England, 2003)
6 Jannie de Beer (South Africa, 1999)

Rugby World Cup 2007

Leading point scorers

Player	Team	Points	Tries	Cons	Pens	DG
Percy Montgomery	South Africa	105	2	22	17	0
Felipe Contepomi	Argentina	91	3	11	18	0
Jonny Wilkinson	England	67	0	5	14	5
Nick Evans	New Zealand	50	2	20	0	0
Jean-Baptiste Elissalde	France	47	1	12	6	0
Chris Paterson	Scotland	46	1	10	7	0
Pierre Hola	Tonga	44	0	7	10	0
Lionel Beauxis	France	43	1	7	8	0
Nicky Little	Fiji	42	0	9	8	0
Matt Giteau	Australia	40	3	8	3	0
Dan Carter	New Zealand	40	1	10	5	0
Bryan Habana	South Africa	40	8	0	0	0
Stirling Mortlock	Australia	37	1	10	4	0
Drew Mitchell	Australia	35	7	0	0	0
David Bortolussi	Italy	32	0	4	8	0
Stephen Jones	Wales	31	0	11	3	0
Shane Williams	Wales	30	6	0	0	0
Doug Howlett	New Zealand	30	6	0	0	0
Loki Crichton	Samoa	27	0	3	7	0
Mike Hercus	USA	26	0	4	6	0
Vincent Clerc	France	25	5	0	0	0
Joe Rokocoko	New Zealand	25	5	0	0	0
Chris Latham	Australia	25	5	0	0	0
Shotaro Onishi	Japan	24	0	3	6	0
James Hook	Wales	23	1	3	4	0
Merab Kvirikashvili	Georgia	23	0	4	5	0
Gavin Williams	Samoa	22	1	1	5	0
James Pritchard	Canada	21	0	3	5	0
Jaque Fourie	South Africa	20	4	0	0	0
Rory Lamont	Scotland	20	4	0	0	0
Juan Smith	South Africa	20	4	0	0	0
JP Pietersen	South Africa	20	4	0	0	0
Sitiveni Sivivatu	New Zealand	20	4	0	0	0
Paul Sackey	England	20	4	0	0	0

Most tries

Player	Team	Tries
Bryan Habana	South Africa	8
Drew Mitchell	Australia	7
Doug Howlett	New Zealand	6
Shane Williams	Wales	6
Vincent Clerc	France	5
Joe Rokocoko	New Zealand	5
Chris Latham	Australia	5
Jaque Fourie	South Africa	4
JP Pietersen	South Africa	4
Sitiveni Sivivatu	New Zealand	4
Paul Sackey	England	4
Juan Smith	South Africa	4
Rory Lamont	Scotland	4

Most conversions

Player	Team	Conversions
Percy Montgomery	South Africa	22
Nick Evans	New Zealand	20
Jean-Baptiste Elissalde	France	12
Stephen Jones	Wales	11
Felipe Contepomi	Argentina	11
Chris Paterson	Scotland	10
Dan Carter	New Zealand	10
Stirling Mortlock	Australia	10
Nicky Little	Fiji	9
Matt Giteau	Australia	8
Lionel Beauxis	France	7
Pierre Hola	Tonga	7
Luke McAlister	New Zealand	6

Most penalty goals

Player	Team	Penalties
Felipe Contepomi	Argentina	18
Percy Montgomery	South Africa	17
Jonny Wilkinson	England	14
Pierre Hola	Tonga	10
David Bortolussi	Italy	8
Nicky Little	Fiji	8
Lionel Beauxis	France	8
Loki Crichton	Samoa	7
Chris Paterson	Scotland	7
Shotaro Onishi	Japan	6
Mike Hercus	USA	6
Jean-Baptiste Elissalde	France	6
Merab Kvirikashvili	Georgia	5
Gavin Williams	Samoa	5
James Pritchard	Canada	5
Dan Carter	New Zealand	5
James Hook	Wales	4
Stirling Mortlock	Australia	4
David Skrela	France	4
Francois Steyn	South Africa	4

Dropped goals

Player	Team	Dropped goals
Jonny Wilkinson	England	5
Juan Martín Hernández	Argentina	4
Berrick Barnes	Australia	2
Ronan O'Gara	Ireland	1
Emile Wessels	Namibia	1
Gonçalo Malheiro	Portugal	1

Tries by country

New Zealand	48	Tonga	9
South Africa	33	Italy	8
Australia	31	Japan	7
France	27	USA	7
Argentina	23	Canada	6
Wales	23	Romania	5
Fiji	16	Samoa	5
Scotland	15	Georgia	5
England	12	Portugal	4
Ireland	9	Namibia	3

POOL **A**

8/9/2007 Lens

England: 28
Tries: Robinson, Barkley, Rees
Cons: Barkley (2)
Pens: Barkley (3)

15 Mark Cueto
14 Josh Lewsey
13 Jamie Noon
12 Mike Catt
11 Jason Robinson
10 Olly Barkley
9 Shaun Perry
1 Andrew Sheridan
2 Mark Regan
3 Phil Vickery
4 Simon Shaw
5 Ben Kay
6 Joe Worsley
7 Tom Rees
8 Lawrence Dallaglio

16 George Chuter*
17 Matt Stevens*
18 Martin Corry*
19 Lewis Moody*
20 Peter Richards*
21 Andy Farrell*
22 Mathew Tait*

USA: 10
Try: Moeakiola
Con: Hercus
Pen: Hercus

15 Chris Wyles
14 Salesi Sika
13 Paul Emerick
12 Vahafolau Esikia
11 Takudzwa Ngwenya
10 Mike Hercus
9 Chad Erskine
1 Mike MacDonald
2 Owen Lentz
3 Chris Osentowski
4 Alec Parker
5 Mike Mangan
6 Louis Stanfill
7 Todd Clever
8 Henry Bloomfield

16 Blake Burdette*
17 Matekitonga Moeakiola*
18 Hayden Mexted*
19 Inaki Basauri*
20 Mike Petri
21 Valenese Malifa*
22 Albert Tuipulotu

Referee Jonathan Kaplan

9/9/2007 Parc des Princes, Paris

South Africa 59
Tries: Habana (4), Montgomery (2), Fourie, Pietersen
Cons: Montgomery (5)
Pens: Montgomery (3)

15 Percy Montgomery
14 JP Pietersen
13 Jaque Fourie
12 Jean de Villiers
11 Bryan Habana
10 Butch James
9 Fourie du Preez
1 Os du Randt
2 John Smit
3 CJ van der Linde
4 Bakkies Botha
5 Victor Matfield
6 Schalk Burger
7 Juan Smith
8 Danie Rossouw

16 Bismarck du Plessis*
17 BJ Botha*
18 Johannes Muller*
19 Wickus van Heerden*
20 Enrico Januarie*
21 Andre Pretorius*
22 Francois Steyn*

Samoa 7
Try: Williams
Con: Williams

15 David Lemi
14 Lome Fa'atau
13 Gavin Williams
12 Jerry Meafou
11 Alesana Tuilagi
10 Eliota Fuimaono-Sapolu
9 Junior Polu
1 Justin Va'a
2 Mahonri Schwalger
3 Census Johnston
4 Joe Tekori
5 Kane Thompson
6 Daniel Leo
7 Semo Sititi
8 Henry Tuilagi

16 Tanielu Fuga*
17 Kas Lealamanua*
18 Alfie Vaeluaga*
19 Justin Purdie*
20 Elvis Seveali'I*
21 Loki Crichton*
22 Brian Lima*

Referee Paul Honiss

12/9/2007 Montpellier

United States 15
Tries: Stanfill, MacDonald
Con: Hercus
Pen: Hercus

15 Chris Wyles
14 Salesi Sika
13 Albert Tuipulotu
12 Vahafolau Esikia
11 Takudzwa Ngwenya
10 Mike Hercus
9 Chad Erskine
1 Mike MacDonald
2 Owen Lentz
3 Chris Osentowski
4 Alec Parker
5 Mike Mangan
6 Louis Stanfill
7 Todd Clever
8 Henry Bloomfield

16 Blake Burdette*
17 Matekitonga Moeakiola*
18 Hayden Mexted
19 Inaki Basauri*
20 Mike Petri
21 Valenese Malifa
22 Philip Eloff*

Tonga 25
Tries: Maka, Vaka, Vaki
Cons: Hola (2)
Pens: Hola (2)

15 Vungakoto Lilo
14 Tevita Tu'ifua
13 Sukanaivalu Hufanga
12 Epeli Taione
11 Joseph Vaka
10 Pierre Hola
9 Soane Havea
1 Soane Tonga'uiha
2 Aleki Lutui
3 Kisi Pulu
4 Lisiate Fa'aoso
5 Paino Hehea
6 Hale T Pole
7 Nili Latu
8 Finau Maka

16 Ephraim Taukafa*
17 Toma Toke*
18 Viliami Vaki*
19 Lotu Filipine*
20 Sione Tu'ipulotu*
21 Isileli Tupou*
22 Aisea Havili*

Referee Stuart Dickinson

14/9/2007 Stade de France, Paris

England 0

15 Jason Robinson
14 Josh Lewsey
13 Jamie Noon
12 Andy Farrell
11 Paul Sackey
10 Mike Catt
9 Shaun Perry
1 Andrew Sheridan
2 Mark Regan
3 Matt Stevens
4 Simon Shaw
5 Ben Kay
6 Martin Corry
7 Tom Rees
8 Nick Easter

16 George Chuter*
17 Perry Freshwater
18 Steve Borthwick*
19 Lewis Moody*
20 Andy Gomarsall*
21 Peter Richards*
22 Mathew Tait*

South Africa 36
Tries: Pietersen (2), Smith
Cons: Montgomery (3)
Pens: Steyn, Montgomery (4)

15 Percy Montgomery
14 JP Pietersen
13 Jaque Fourie
12 Francois Steyn
11 Bryan Habana
10 Butch James
9 Fourie du Preez
1 Os du Randt
2 John Smit
3 BJ Botha
4 Bakkies Botha
5 Victor Matfield
6 Wickus van Heerden
7 Juan Smith
8 Danie Rossouw

16 Bismarck du Plessis*
17 CJ van der Linde*
18 Johannes Muller*
19 Bobby Skinstad*
20 Ruan Pienaar*
21 Andre Pretorius*
22 Wynand Olivier*

Referee Joël Jutge

16/9/2007 Montpellier

Samoa 15
Pens: Williams (5)

115 Gavin Williams
14 Sailosi Tagicakibau
13 Elvis Seveali'I
12 Seilala Mapusua
11 Alesana Tuilagi
10 Loki Crichton
9 Steve So'oialo
1 Kas Lealamanua
2 Mahonri Schwalger
3 Census Johnston
4 Joe Tekori
5 Kane Thompson
6 Daniel Leo
7 Ulia Ulia
8 Semo Sititi

16 Tanielu Fuga
17 Muliufi Salanoa*
18 Leo Lafaiali'I*
19 Justin Purdie*
20 Junior Polu*
21 Lolo Lui*
22 David Lemi*

Tonga 19
Try: Taione
Con: Hola
Pens: Hola (4)

15 Vungakoto Lilo
14 Tevita Tu'ifua
13 Sukanaivalu Hufanga
12 Epeli Taione
11 Joseph Vaka
10 Pierre Hola
9 Enele Taufa
1 Soane Tonga'uiha
2 Ephraim Taukafa
3 Kisi Pulu
4 Inoke Afeaki
5 Paino Hehea
6 Hale T Pole
7 Nili Latu
8 Finau Maka

16 Aleki Lutui*
17 Toma Toke*
18 Viliami Vaki*
19 'Emosi Kauhenga
20 Sione Tu'ipulotu*
21 Isileli Tupou*
22 Hudson Tonga'uiha*

Referee Jonathan Kaplan

22/9/2007 Lens

South Africa 30
Tries: Pienaar (2), Smith, Skinstad
Cons: Pretorius, Montgomery
Pens: Steyn, Montgomery

15 Ruan Pienaar
14 Ashwin Willemse
13 Wynand Olivier
12 Wayne Julies
11 JP Pietersen
10 Andre Pretorius
9 Enrico Januarie
1 Gurthro Steenkamp
2 Gary Botha
3 CJ van der Linde
4 Bakkies Botha
5 Albert van den Berg
6 Wickus van Heerden
7 Danie Rossouw
8 Bobby Skinstad

16 John Smit*
17 BJ Botha*
18 Victor Matfield*
19 Juan Smith*
20 Bryan Habana*
21 Francois Steyn*
22 Percy Montgomery*

Tonga 25
Tries: Pulu, Hufanga, Vaki
Cons: Hola (2)
Pens: Hola (2)

15 Vungakoto Lilo
14 Tevita Tu'ifua
13 Sukanaivalu Hufanga
12 Epeli Taione
11 Joseph Vaka
10 Pierre Hola
9 Sione Tu'ipulotu
1 Soane Tonga'uiha
2 Aleki Lutui
3 Kisi Pulu
4 Paino Hehea
5 'Emosi Kauhenga
6 Viliami Vaki
7 Nili Latu
8 Finau Maka

16 Ephraim Taukafa*
17 Toma Toke
18 Inoke Afeaki*
19 Lotu Filipine*
20 Soane Havea*
21 Isileli Tupou*
22 Aisea Havili

Referee Wayne Barnes

22/9/2007 Nantes

England 44
Tries: Corry (2), Sackey (2)
Cons: Wilkinson (3)
Pens: Wilkinson (4)
Drops: Wilkinson (2)

15 Josh Lewsey
14 Paul Sackey
13 Mathew Tait
12 Olly Barkley
11 Mark Cueto
10 Jonny Wilkinson
9 Andy Gomarsall
1 Andrew Sheridan
2 George Chuter
3 Matt Stevens
4 Simon Shaw
5 Ben Kay
6 Martin Corry
7 Joe Worsley
8 Nick Easter

16 Mark Regan
17 Perry Freshwater*
18 Steve Borthwick*
19 Lewis Moody*
20 Peter Richards
21 Andy Farrell
22 Dan Hipkiss*

Samoa 22
Try: Polu
Con: Crichton
Pens: Crichton (5)

15 Loki Crichton
14 David Lemi
13 Seilala Mapusua
12 Brian Lima
11 Alesana Tuilagi
10 Eliota Fuimaono-Sapolu
9 Junior Polu
1 Kas Lealamanua
2 Mahonri Schwalger
3 Census Johnston
4 Joe Tekori
5 Kane Thompson
6 Daniel Leo
7 Semo Sititi
8 Henry Tuilagi

16 Tanielu Fuga
17 Fosi Palaamo*
18 Justin Purdie*
19 Alfie Vaeluaga*
20 Steve So'oialo*
21 Jerry Meafou*
22 Lolo Lui*

Referee Alan Lewis

26/9/2007 Saint-Etienne

Samoa 25
Tries: Fa'atau, A Tuilagi, Thompson
Cons: Crichton (2)
Pens: Crichton (2)

15 Loki Crichton
14 Lome Fa'atau
13 Elvis Seveali'I
12 Seilala Mapusua
11 Alesana Tuilagi
10 Eliota Fuimaono-Sapolu
9 Junior Polu
1 Kas Lealamanua
2 Mahonri Schwalger
3 Census Johnston
4 Leo Lafaiali'I
5 Kane Thompson
6 Semo Sititi
7 Justin Purdie
8 Alfie Vaeluaga

16 Silao Vaisola Sefo*
17 Naama Leleimalefaga
18 Joe Tekori*
19 Ulia Ulia
20 Steve So'oialo*
21 David Lemi*
22 Lolo Lui*

USA 21
Tries: Ngwenya, Stanfill
Con: Hercus
Pens: Hercus (3)

15 Chris Wyles
14 Takudzwa Ngwenya
13 Philip Eloff
12 Vahafolau Esikia
11 Salesi Sika
10 Mike Hercus
9 Chad Erskine
1 Mike MacDonald
2 Owen Lentz
3 Chris Osentowski
4 Alec Parker
5 Hayden Mexted
6 Louis Stanfill
7 Todd Clever
8 Fifita Mounga

16 Blake Burdette*
17 Matekitonga Moeakiola*
18 Henry Bloomfield
19 Mark Aylor*
20 Mike Petri
21 Valenese Malifa
22 Albert Tuipulotu*

Referee Wayne Barnes

28/9/2007 Parc des Princes, Paris

England 36
Tries: Sackey (2), Tait, Farrell
Cons: Wilkinson (2)
Pens: Wilkinson (2)
Drops: Wilkinson (2)

15 Josh Lewsey
14 Paul Sackey
13 Mathew Tait
12 Olly Barkley
11 Mark Cueto
10 Jonny Wilkinson
9 Andy Gomarsall
1 Andrew Sheridan
2 George Chuter
3 Matt Stevens
4 Steve Borthwick
5 Ben Kay
6 Martin Corry
7 Lewis Moody
8 Nick Easter

16 Lee Mears*
17 Phil Vickery*
18 Lawrence Dallaglio*
19 Joe Worsley
20 Peter Richards*
21 Andy Farrell*
22 Dan Hipkiss*

Tonga 20
Tries: Hufanga, T Pole
Cons: Hola (2)
Pens: Hola (2)

15 Vungakoto Lilo
14 Tevita Tu'ifua
13 Sukanaivalu Hufanga
12 Epeli Taione
11 Joseph Vaka
10 Pierre Hola
9 Sione Tu'ipulotu
1 Soane Tonga'uiha
2 Aleki Lutui
3 Kisi Pulu
4 Viliami Vaki
5 Lisiate Fa'aoso
6 Hale T Pole
7 Nili Latu
8 Finau Maka

16 Ephraim Taukafa*
17 Taufa'ao Filise*
18 Maama Molitika*
19 Inoke Afeaki*
20 Paino Hehea*
21 Hudson Tonga'uiha*
22 Aisea Havili*

Referee Alain Rolland

30/9/2007 Montpellier

South Africa 64
Tries: Burger, Steyn, Habana (2), van der Linde, du Preez, Fourie (2), Smith
Cons: Montgomery (6), James (2)
Pen: Montgomery

15 Percy Montgomery
14 Akona Ndungane
13 Jaque Fourie
12 Francois Steyn
11 Bryan Habana
10 Butch James
9 Fourie du Preez
1 Os du Randt
2 John Smit
3 BJ Botha
4 Albert van den Berg
5 Victor Matfield
6 Wickus van Heerden
7 Juan Smith
8 Schalk Burger

16 Bismarck du Plessis*
17 CJ van der Linde*
18 Bakkies Botha*
19 Bobby Skinstad*
20 Ruan Pienaar*
21 Andre Pretorius*
22 JP Pietersen*

USA 15
Tries: Ngwenya, Wyles
Con: Hercus
Pen: Hercus

15 Chris Wyles
14 Takudzwa Ngwenya
13 Philip Eloff
12 Vahafolau Esikia
11 Salesi Sika
10 Mike Hercus
9 Chad Erskine
1 Mike MacDonald
2 Owen Lentz
3 Chris Osentowski
4 Alec Parker
5 Mike Mangan
6 Louis Stanfill
7 Todd Clever
8 Dan Payne

16 Blake Burdette*
17 Matekitonga Moeakiola*
18 Mark Aylor*
19 Henry Bloomfield*
20 Mike Petri*
21 Valenese Malifa*
22 Thretton Palamo*

Referee Tony Spreadbury

* = used as replacement

FINAL POOL TABLE

	P	W	D	L	F	A	BP	PTS
South Africa	4	4	0	0	189	47	3	19
England	4	3	0	1	108	88	2	14
Tonga	4	2	0	2	89	96	1	9
Samoa	4	1	0	3	69	143	1	5
USA	4	0	0	4	61	142	1	1

8/9/2007 — Lyons

Australia 91
Tries: Sharpe, Elsom (3), Ashley-Cooper, Latham (2), Barnes (2), Mitchell (2), Smith, Freier
Cons: Giteau (3), Mortlock (7)
Pens: Mortlock (2)

Japan 3
Pen: Ono

	Australia		Japan
15	Chris Latham	15	Tatsuya Kusumi
14	Adam Ashley-Cooper	14	Tomoki Kitagawa
13	Stirling Mortlock	13	Koji Taira
12	Matt Giteau	12	Nataniela Oto
11	Lote Tuqiri	11	Hirotoki Onozawa
10	Stephen Larkham	10	Kosei Ono
9	George Gregan	9	Yuki Yatomi
1	Matt Dunning	1	Masahito Yamamoto
2	Stephen Moore	2	Taku Inokuchi
3	Alan Baxter	3	Ryo Yamamura
4	Nathan Sharpe	4	Takanori Kumagae
5	Daniel Vickerman	5	Luatangi Samurai Vatuvei
6	Rocky Elsom	6	Yasunori Watanabe
7	George Smith	7	Takamichi Sasaki
8	Wycliff Palu	8	Hajime Kiso
16	Adam Freier*	16	Yuji Matsubara
17	Guy Shepherdson*	17	Tomokazu Soma
18	Hugh McMeniman*	18	Hitoshi Ono
19	Stephen Hoiles	19	Hare Makiri*
20	Berrick Barnes*	20	Tomoki Yoshida
21	Drew Mitchell*	21	Bryce Robins
22	Mark Gerrard*	22	Kosuke Endo

Referee Alan Lewis

9/9/2007 — Nantes

Wales 42
Tries: A Jones, Charvis, Parker, S Williams (2)
Cons: S Jones (4)
Pens: Hook (3)

Canada 17
Tries: Culpan, Cudmore, Williams
Con: Pritchard

	Wales		Canada
15	Kevin Morgan	15	Mike Pyke
14	Mark Jones	14	DTH van der Merwe
13	Tom Shanklin	13	Craig Culpan
12	Sonny Parker	12	Dave Spicer
11	Shane Williams	11	James Pritchard
10	James Hook	10	Ander Monro
9	Dwayne Peel	9	Morgan Williams
1	Gethin Jenkins	1	Rod Snow
2	Matthew Rees	2	Pat Riordan
3	Adam Jones	3	Jon Thiel
4	Ian Gough	4	Luke Tait
5	Alun-Wyn Jones	5	Mike James
6	Jonathan Thomas	6	Jamie Cudmore
7	Martyn Williams	7	Dave Biddle
8	Alix Popham	8	Sean-Michael Stephen
16	Thomas Rhys Thomas*	16	Aaron Carpenter*
17	Duncan Jones*	17	Dan Pletch*
18	Michael Owen*	18	Mike Pletch*
19	Colin Charvis*	19	Mike Burak*
20	Michael Phillips*	20	Colin Yukes
21	Stephen Jones*	21	Ed Fairhurst*
22	Gareth Thomas*	22	Ryan Smith*

Referee Alain Rolland

12/9/2007 — Toulouse

Japan 31
Tries: Thompson (2), Nishiura
Cons: Onishi (2)
Pens: Onishi (4)

Fiji 35
Tries: Qera (2), Rabeni, Leawere
Cons: Little (3)
Pens: Little (3)

	Japan		Fiji
15	Go Aruga	15	Kameli Ratuvou
14	Christian Loamanu	14	Vilimoni Delasau
13	Yuta Imamura	13	Seru Rabeni
12	Shotaro Onishi	12	Seremaia Bai
11	Kosuke Endo	11	Isoa Neivua
10	Bryce Robins	10	Nicky Little
9	Tomoki Yoshida	9	Mosese Rauluni
1	Tatsukichi Nishiura	1	Graham Dewes
2	Yuji Matsubara	2	Sunia Koto
3	Tomokazu Soma	3	Henry Qiodravu
4	Hitoshi Ono	4	Kele Leawere
5	Luke Thompson	5	Wame Lewaravu
6	Hare Makiri	6	Semisi Naevo
7	Philip O'Reilly	7	Akapusi Qera
8	Takuro Miuchi	8	Sisa Koyamaibole
16	Taku Inokuchi	16	Vereniki Sauturaga
17	Ryo Yamamura*	17	Jone Railomo*
18	Takanori Kumagae	18	Netani Talei*
19	Ryota Asano	19	Aca Ratuva*
20	Yuki Yatomi*	20	Jone Daunivucu
21	Koji Taira*	21	Gabiriele Lovobalavu
22	Hirotoki Onozawa	22	Norman Ligairi

Referee Marius Jonker

15/9/2007 — Cardiff

Wales 20
Tries: J Thomas, S Williams
Cons: Hook (2)
Pens: S Jones, Hook

Australia 32
Tries: Giteau, Mortlock, Latham (2)
Cons: Mortlock (2), Giteau
Pen: Mortlock
Drop: Barnes

	Wales		Australia
15	Gareth Thomas	15	Chris Latham
14	Mark Jones	14	Drew Mitchell
13	Tom Shanklin	13	Stirling Mortlock
12	Sonny Parker	12	Matt Giteau
11	Shane Williams	11	Lote Tuqiri
10	Stephen Jones	10	Berrick Barnes
9	Dwayne Peel	9	George Gregan
1	Gethin Jenkins	1	Matt Dunning
2	Matthew Rees	2	Stephen Moore
3	Adam Jones	3	Guy Shepherdson
4	Ian Gough	4	Nathan Sharpe
5	Alun-Wyn Jones	5	Daniel Vickerman
6	Colin Charvis	6	Rocky Elsom
7	Martyn Williams	7	George Smith
8	Jonathan Thomas	8	Wycliff Palu
16	Thomas Rhys Thomas*	16	Adam Freier*
17	Duncan Jones*	17	Al Baxter*
18	Michael Owen*	18	Mark Chisholm*
19	Alix Popham*	19	Stephen Hoiles*
20	Michael Phillips*	20	Phil Waugh*
21	James Hook*	21	Scott Staniforth*
22	Kevin Morgan*	22	Julian Huxley*

Referee Steve Walsh

16/9/2007 — Cardiff

Fiji 29
Tries: Leawere, Ratuvou (2), Delasau
Cons: Little (3)
Pen: Little

Canada 16
Try: Smith
Con: Pritchard
Pens: Pritchard (3)

	Fiji		Canada
15	Kameli Ratuvou	15	Mike Pyke
14	Vilimoni Delasau	14	DTH van der Merwe
13	Seru Rabeni	13	Craig Culpan
12	Seremaia Bai	12	Dave Spicer
11	Isoa Neivua	11	James Pritchard
10	Nicky Little	10	Ryan Smith
9	Mosese Rauluni	9	Morgan Williams
1	Graham Dewes	1	Rod Snow
2	Sunia Koto	2	Pat Riordan
3	Jone Railomo	3	Jon Thiel
4	Kele Leawere	4	Mike Burak
5	Ifereimi Rawaqa	5	Mike James
6	Semisi Naevo	6	Jamie Cudmore
7	Akapusi Qera	7	Dave Biddle
8	Sisa Koyamaibole	8	Sean-Michael Stephen
16	Vereniki Sauturaga*	16	Aaron Carpenter*
17	Henry Qiodravu*	17	Dan Pletch*
18	Netani Talei*	18	Mike Pletch
19	Jone Qovu	19	Luke Tait*
20	Jone Daunivucu	20	Colin Yukes*
21	Maleli Kunavore*	21	Ed Fairhurst
22	Norman Ligairi*	22	Ander Monro*

Referee Tony Spreadbury

20/9/2007 — Cardiff

Wales 72
Tries: A Jones, Hook, R Thomas, Morgan, Phillips, S Williams (2), D James, Cooper, M Williams (2)
Cons: S Jones (3), R Thomas, Phillips, Sweeney (2)
Pen: S Jones

Japan 18
Tries: Endo, Onozawa
Con: Robins
Pens: Onishi (2)

	Wales		Japan
15	Kevin Morgan	15	Christian Loamanu
14	Dafydd James	14	Kosuke Endo
13	Jamie Robinson	13	Yuta Imamura
12	James Hook	12	Shotaro Onishi
11	Shane Williams	11	Hirotoki Onozawa
10	Stephen Jones	10	Bryce Robins
9	Michael Phillips	9	Tomoki Yoshida
1	Duncan Jones	1	Tatsukichi Nishiura
2	Thomas Rhys Thomas	2	Yuji Matsubara
3	Chris Horsman	3	Tomokazu Soma
4	Will James	4	Hitoshi Ono
5	Alun-Wyn Jones	5	Luke Thompson
6	Colin Charvis	6	Yasunori Watanabe
7	Martyn Williams	7	Hare Makiri
8	Alix Popham	8	Takuro Miuchi
16	Huw Bennett*	16	Taku Inokuchi*
17	Gethin Jenkins*	17	Ryo Yamamura*
18	Ian Evans*	18	Hajime Kiso*
19	Michael Owen*	19	Ryota Asano*
20	Gareth Cooper*	20	Chulwon Kim*
21	Ceri Sweeney*	21	Koji Taira*
22	Tom Shanklin*	22	Tatsuya Kusumi*

Referee Joël Jutge

23/9/2007 — Montpellier

Australia 55
Tries: Giteau (2), Mitchell (3), Ashley-Cooper, Hoiles
Cons: Giteau (4)
Pens: Giteau (3)
Drop: Barnes

Fiji 12
Tries: Ratuva, Neivua
Con: Bai

	Australia		Fiji
15	Chris Latham	15	Norman Ligairi
14	Drew Mitchell	14	Vilimoni Delasau
13	Adam Ashley-Cooper	13	Maleli Kunavore
12	Matt Giteau	12	Seremaia Bai
11	Lote Tuqiri	11	Isoa Neivua
10	Berrick Barnes	10	Waisea Luveniyali
9	George Gregan	9	Jone Daunivucu
1	Matt Dunning	1	Alefoso Yalayalatabua
2	Stephen Moore	2	Vereniki Sauturaga
3	Guy Shepherdson	3	Henry Qiodravu
4	Mark Chisholm	4	Isoa Domolailai
5	Daniel Vickerman	5	Ifereimi Rawaqa
6	Rocky Elsom	6	Netani Talei
7	Phil Waugh	7	Aca Ratuva
8	Wycliff Palu	8	Jone Qovu
16	Adam Freier*	16	Bill Gadolo
17	Greg Holmes*	17	Jone Railomo*
18	Hugh McMeniman*	18	Wame Lewaravu*
19	Stephen Hoiles*	19	Sisa Koyamaibole*
20	Sam Cordingley*	20	Mosese Rauluni*
21	Scott Staniforth*	21	Gabiriele Lovobalavu*
22	Julian Huxley*	22	Seru Rabeni*

Referee Nigel Owens

25/9/2007 — Bordeaux

Canada 12
Tries: Riordan, van der Merwe
Con: Pritchard

Japan 12
Tries: Endo, Taira
Con: Onishi

	Canada		Japan
15	Mike Pyke	15	Go Aruga
14	DTH van der Merwe	14	Kosuke Endo
13	Craig Culpan	13	Yuta Imamura
12	Dave Spicer	12	Shotaro Onishi
11	James Pritchard	11	Christian Loamanu
10	Ryan Smith	10	Bryce Robins
9	Morgan Williams	9	Tomoki Yoshida
1	Rod Snow	1	Tatsukichi Nishiura
2	Pat Riordan	2	Yuji Matsubara
3	Jon Thiel	3	Tomokazu Soma
4	Mike Burak	4	Hitoshi Ono
5	Mike James	5	Luke Thompson
6	Colin Yukes	6	Hare Makiri
7	Adam Kleeberger	7	Philip O'Reilly
8	Aaron Carpenter	8	Takuro Miuchi
16	Mike Pletch*	16	Taku Inokuchi
17	Dan Pletch*	17	Ryo Yamamura*
18	Scott Franklin*	18	Luatangi Samurai Vatuvei*
19	Josh Jackson*	19	Hajime Kiso*
20	Mike Webb*	20	Chulwon Kim*
21	Ed Fairhurst	21	Koji Taira*
22	Justin Mensah-Coker*	22	Hirotoki Onozawa*

Referee Jonathan Kaplan

29/9/2007 — Bordeaux

Australia 37
Tries: Baxter, Freier, Smith, Mitchell (2), Latham
Cons: Shepherd (2)
Pen: Huxley

Canada 6
Pens: Pritchard (2)

	Australia		Canada
15	Chris Latham	15	DTH van der Merwe
14	Cameron Shepherd	14	Justin Mensah-Coker
13	Lote Tuqiri	13	Mike Pyke
12	Adam Ashley-Cooper	12	Derek Daypuck
11	Drew Mitchell	11	James Pritchard
10	Julian Huxley	10	Ander Monro
9	Sam Cordingley	9	Morgan Williams
1	Greg Holmes	1	Rod Snow
2	Adam Freier	2	Pat Riordan
3	Al Baxter	3	Jon Thiel
4	Nathan Sharpe	4	Luke Tait
5	Mark Chisholm	5	Mike James
6	Hugh McMeniman	6	Colin Yukes
7	George Smith	7	Dave Biddle
8	David Lyons	8	Sean-Michael Stephen
16	Sean Hardman*	16	Aaron Carpenter*
17	Guy Shepherdson	17	Dan Pletch*
18	Rocky Elsom	18	Mike Pletch*
19	Phil Waugh*	19	Mike Burak*
20	Stephen Hoiles*	20	Mike Webb*
21	George Gregan*	21	Ed Fairhurst*
22	Matt Giteau	22	Nick Trenkel*

Referee Chris White

29/9/2007 — Nantes

Wales 34
Tries: Popham, S Williams, Thomas, Jones, M Williams
Cons: Hook, S Jones (2)
Pen: S Jones

Fiji 38
Tries: Qera, Delasau, Leawere, Dewes
Cons: Little (3)
Pens: Little (4)

	Wales		Fiji
15	Gareth Thomas	15	Kameli Ratuvou
14	Mark Jones	14	Vilimoni Delasau
13	Tom Shanklin	13	Seru Rabeni
12	James Hook	12	Seremaia Bai
11	Shane Williams	11	Isoa Neivua
10	Stephen Jones	10	Nicky Little
9	Dwayne Peel	9	Mosese Rauluni
1	Gethin Jenkins	1	Graham Dewes
2	Matthew Rees	2	Sunia Koto
3	Chris Horsman	3	Jone Railomo
4	Alun-Wyn Jones	4	Kele Leawere
5	Ian Evans	5	Ifereimi Rawaqa
6	Colin Charvis	6	Semisi Naevo
7	Martyn Williams	7	Akapusi Qera
8	Alix Popham	8	Sisa Koyamaibole
16	Thomas Rhys Thomas*	16	Vereniki Sauturaga*
17	Duncan Jones*	17	Henry Qiodravu*
18	Ian Gough*	18	Wame Lewaravu
19	Michael Owen*	19	Aca Ratuva*
20	Michael Phillips*	20	Jone Daunivucu*
21	Jamie Robinson	21	Norman Ligairi*
22	Dafydd James	22	Sireli Bobo*

Referee Stuart Dickinson

FINAL POOL TABLE

	P	W	D	L	F	A	BP	PTS
Australia	4	4	0	0	215	41	4	20
Fiji	4	3	0	1	114	136	3	15
Wales	4	2	0	2	168	105	4	12
Japan	4	0	1	3	64	210	1	3
Canada	4	0	1	3	51	120	0	2

8/9/2007 — Marseilles

New Zealand 76	Italy 14
Tries: McCaw (2), Howlett (3), Muliaina, Sivivatu (2), Jack, Collins (2) Cons: Carter (7), McAlister (2) Pen: Carter	Tries: Stanojevic, Mi Bergamasco Cons: Bortolussi, de Marigny
15 Leon MacDonald	15 David Bortolussi
14 Doug Howlett	14 Kaine Robertson
13 Mils Muliaina	13 Andrea Masi
12 Luke McAlister	12 Mirco Bergamasco
11 Sitiveni Sivivatu	11 Marko Stanojevic
10 Dan Carter	10 Roland de Marigny
9 Byron Kelleher	9 Alessandro Troncon
1 Tony Woodcock	1 Salvatore Perugini
2 Keven Mealamu	2 Fabio Ongaro
3 Carl Hayman	3 Martin Castrogiovanni
4 Chris Jack	4 Santiago Dellapè
5 Ali Williams	5 Marco Bortolami
6 Jerry Collins	6 Alessandro Zanni
7 Richie McCaw	7 Mauro Bergamasco
8 Rodney So'oialo	8 Sergio Parisse
16 Anton Oliver*	16 Carlo Festuccia*
17 Neemia Tialata*	17 Andrea Lo Cicero*
18 Chris Masoe	18 Valerio Bernabò*
19 Sione Lauaki*	19 Manoa Vosawai*
20 Brendon Leonard*	20 Paul Griffen*
21 Aaron Mauger*	21 Gonzalo Canale
22 Isaia Toeava*	22 Ezio Galon*

Referee Wayne Barnes

9/9/2007 — Saint-Etienne

Scotland 56	Portugal 10
Tries: R Lamont (2), Lawson, Dewey, Parks, Southwell, Brown, Ford Cons: Parks (5), Southwell, Paterson (2)	Try: Carvalho Con: D Pinto Pen: D Pinto
15 Rory Lamont	15 Pedro Leal
14 Sean Lamont	14 David Mateus
13 Marcus Di Rollo	13 Federico Sousa
12 Rob Dewey	12 Diogo Mateus
11 Simon Webster	11 Pedro Carvalho
10 Dan Parks	10 Duarte Cardoso Pinto
9 Mike Blair	9 José Pinto
1 Allan Jacobsen	1 Rui Cordeiro
2 Scott Lawson	2 Joaquim Ferreira
3 Euan Murray	3 Ruben Spachuck
4 Nathan Hines	4 Gonçalo Uva
5 Scott Murray	5 David Penalva
6 Jason White	6 Juan Severino Somoza
7 Allister Hogg	7 João Uva
8 Simon Taylor	8 Vasco Uva
16 Ross Ford*	16 Juan Manuel Muré*
17 Gavin Kerr*	17 João Correia*
18 Scott MacLeod*	18 Paulo Murinello*
19 Kelly Brown*	19 Diogo Coutinho*
20 Rory Lawson*	20 Luis Pissarra*
21 Chris Paterson*	21 Pedro Cabral*
22 Hugo Southwell*	22 Miguel Portela*

Referee Steve Walsh

12/9/2007 — Marseilles

Italy 24	Romania 18
Tries: Dellape, penalty try Con: Pez Pens: Bortolussi, Pez (3)	Tries: Manta, Tincu Con: Dimofte Pens: Dimofte (2)
15 David Bortolussi	15 Iulian Dumitras
14 Kaine Robertson	14 Catalin Fercu
13 Gonzalo Canale	13 Csaba Gal
12 Mirco Bergamasco	12 Romeo Gontineac
11 Andrea Masi	11 Gabriel Brezoianu
10 Ramiro Pez	10 Ionut Dimofte
9 Paul Griffen	9 Lucian Sirbu
1 Andrea Lo Cicero	1 Petrisor Toderasc
2 Carlo Festuccia	2 Marius Tincu
3 Martin Castrogiovanni	3 Bogdan Balan
4 Santiago Dellapè	4 Sorin Socol
5 Marco Bortolami	5 Cristian Petre
6 Josh Sole	6 Florin Corodeanu
7 Mauro Bergamasco	7 Alexandru Manta
8 Sergio Parisse	8 Ovidiu Tonita
16 Leonardo Ghiraldini	16 Razvan Mavrodin*
17 Matias Aguero	17 Cezar Popescu*
18 Valerio Bernabò*	18 Cosmin Ratiu*
19 Manoa Vosawai*	19 Alexandru Tudori
20 Alessandro Troncon*	20 Valentin Calafeteanu
21 Ezio Galon*	21 Ionut Tofan
22 Roland de Marigny	22 Dan Vlad

Referee Tony Spreadbury

15/9/2007 — Lyons

New Zealand 108	Portugal 13
Tries: Ellis, Hore, Mauger (2), Williams, Leonard, Hayman, Masoe, Smith (2), Toeava, Collins, Rokocoko (2), MacDonald, Evans Cons: Evans (14)	Try: Cordeiro Con: D Pinto Pen: D Pinto Drop: Malheiro
15 Mils Muliaina	15 Pedro Leal
14 Isaia Toeava	14 António Aguilar
13 Conrad Smith	13 Miguel Portela
12 Aaron Mauger	12 Diogo Mateus
11 Joe Rokocoko	11 Pedro Carvalho
10 Nick Evans	10 Gonçalo Malheiro
9 Brendon Leonard	9 Luis Pissarra
1 Neemia Tialata	1 Andre Silva
2 Andrew Hore	2 João Correia
3 Greg Somerville	3 Ruben Spachuck
4 Chris Jack	4 Marcello d'Orey
5 Ali Williams	5 Gonçalo Uva
6 Jerry Collins	6 Diogo Coutinho
7 Chris Masoe	7 Paulo Murinello
8 Sione Lauaki	8 Vasco Uva
16 Anton Oliver*	16 Rui Cordeiro*
17 Tony Woodcock*	17 Joaquim Ferreira*
18 Carl Hayman*	18 David Penalva*
19 Rodney So'oialo*	19 Tiago Girão*
20 Keven Mealamu*	20 João Uva*
21 Andrew Ellis*	21 José Pinto*
22 Leon MacDonald*	22 Duarte Cardoso Pinto*

Referee Chris White

18/9/2007 — Edinburgh

Scotland 42	Romania 0
Tries: Paterson, Hogg (3), R Lamont (2) Cons: Paterson (6)	
15 Rory Lamont	15 Iulian Dumitras
14 Sean Lamont	14 Catalin Fercu
13 Simon Webster	13 Csaba Gal
12 Rob Dewey	12 Romeo Gontineac
11 Chris Paterson	11 Gabriel Brezoianu
10 Dan Parks	10 Ionut Dimofte
9 Mike Blair	9 Lucian Sirbu
1 Gavin Kerr	1 Petrisor Toderasc
2 Ross Ford	2 Marius Tincu
3 Euan Murray	3 Bogdan Balan
4 Nathan Hines	4 Sorin Socol
5 Jim Hamilton	5 Cristian Petre
6 Jason White	6 Florin Corodeanu
7 Allister Hogg	7 Alexandru Manta
8 Simon Taylor	8 Ovidiu Tonita
16 Scott Lawson*	16 Silviu Florea*
17 Craig Smith*	17 Razvan Mavrodin*
18 Scott MacLeod*	18 Cosmin Ratiu*
19 Kelly Brown*	19 Alexandru Tudori*
20 Chris Cusiter*	20 Valentin Calafeteanu*
21 Hugo Southwell*	21 Ionut Tofan*
22 Nikki Walker*	22 Florin Vlaicu*

Referee Nigel Owens

19/9/2007 — Parc des Princes, Paris

Italy 31	Portugal 5
Tries: Masi (2), Ma Bergamasco Cons: Bortolussi (2) Pens: Bortolussi (4)	Try: Penalva
15 David Bortolussi	15 Pedro Cabral
14 Pablo Canavosio	14 David Mateus
13 Gonzalo Canale	13 Federico Sousa
12 Andrea Masi	12 Diogo Mateus
11 Matteo Pratichetti	11 António Aguilar
10 Roland de Marigny	10 Duarte Cardoso Pinto
9 Alessandro Troncon	9 José Pinto
1 Andrea Lo Cicero	1 Rui Cordeiro
2 Leonardo Ghiraldini	2 João Correia
3 Martin Castrogiovanni	3 Ruben Spachuck
4 Carlo Del Fava	4 Gonçalo Uva
5 Marco Bortolami	5 David Penalva
6 Sergio Parisse	6 Tiago Girão
7 Mauro Bergamasco	7 João Uva
8 Manoa Vosawai	8 Vasco Uva
16 Fabio Ongaro	16 Juan Manuel Muré*
17 Matias Aguero*	17 Andre Silva*
18 Salvatore Perugini*	18 Duarte Figueiredo*
19 Valerio Bernabò	19 Paulo Murinello*
20 Silvio Orlando*	20 Luis Pissarra*
21 Paul Griffen*	21 Diogo Gama*
22 Ezio Galon	22 Gonçalo Foro*

Referee Marius Jonker

23/9/2007 — Edinburgh

Scotland 0	New Zealand 40
	Tries: McCaw, Howlett (2), Kelleher, Williams, Carter Cons: Carter (2) Pens: Carter (2)
15 Hugo Southwell	15 Leon MacDonald
14 Nikki Walker	14 Doug Howlett
13 Marcus Di Rollo	13 Conrad Smith
12 Andrew Henderson	12 Luke McAlister
11 Simon Webster	11 Sitiveni Sivivatu
10 Chris Paterson	10 Dan Carter
9 Chris Cusiter	9 Byron Kelleher
1 Alasdair Dickinson	1 Tony Woodcock
2 Scott Lawson	2 Anton Oliver
3 Craig Smith	3 Carl Hayman
4 Scott MacLeod	4 Reuben Thorne
5 Scott Murray	5 Ali Williams
6 Kelly Brown	6 Chris Masoe
7 John Barclay	7 Richie McCaw
8 David Callam	8 Rodney So'oialo
16 Fergus Thomson*	16 Andrew Hore*
17 Gavin Kerr*	17 Neemia Tialata*
18 Jim Hamilton*	18 Chris Jack*
19 Allister Hogg	19 Sione Lauaki*
20 Rory Lawson*	20 Brendon Leonard*
21 Dan Parks*	21 Nick Evans*
22 Rob Dewey*	22 Isaia Toeava*

Referee Marius Jonker

25/9/2007 — Toulouse

Romania 14	Portugal 10
Tries: Tincu, Corodeanu Cons: Calafeteanu, Dumbrava	Try: Ferreira Con: D Pinto Pen: Malheiro
15 Iulian Dumitras	15 Pedro Leal
14 Catalin Nicolae	14 António Aguilar
13 Ionut Dimofte	13 Miguel Portela
12 Romeo Gontineac	12 Federico Sousa
11 Catalin Fercu	11 Pedro Carvalho
10 Dan Dumbrava	10 Duarte Cardoso Pinto
9 Valentin Calafeteanu	9 José Pinto
1 Cezar Popescu	1 Rui Cordeiro
2 Razvan Mavrodin	2 Joaquim Ferreira
3 Bogdan Balan	3 Ruben Spachuck
4 Cosmin Ratiu	4 Gonçalo Uva
5 Cristian Petre	5 David Penalva
6 Alexandru Tudori	6 Diogo Coutinho
7 Florin Corodeanu	7 João Uva
8 Ovidiu Tonita	8 Tiago Girão
16 Marius Tincu*	16 Juan Manuel Muré*
17 Paulica Ion*	17 João Correia*
18 Sorin Socol*	18 Salvador Palha*
19 Valentin Ursache*	19 Paulo Murinello*
20 Lucian Sirbu*	20 Luis Pissarra*
21 Florin Vlaicu	21 Gonçalo Malheiro*
22 Gabriel Brezoianu	22 Diogo Gama

Referee Paul Honiss

29/9/2007 — Toulouse

New Zealand 85	Romania 8
Tries: Sivivatu (2), Masoe, Rokocoko (3), Evans, Mauger, Toeava (2), Hore, Smith, Howlett Cons: McAlister (4), Evans (6)	Try: Tincu Pen: Vlaicu
15 Nick Evans	15 Iulian Dumitras
14 Joe Rokocoko	14 Stefan Ciuntu
13 Isaia Toeava	13 Csaba Gal
12 Aaron Mauger	12 Romeo Gontineac
11 Sitiveni Sivivatu	11 Gabriel Brezoianu
10 Luke McAlister	10 Ionut Dimofte
9 Andrew Ellis	9 Lucian Sirbu
1 Neemia Tialata	1 Bogdan Balan
2 Keven Mealamu	2 Marius Tincu
3 Greg Somerville	3 Silviu Florea
4 Reuben Thorne	4 Sorin Socol
5 Keith Robinson	5 Cristian Petre
6 Jerry Collins	6 Florin Corodeanu
7 Chris Masoe	7 Alexandru Manta
8 Sione Lauaki	8 Ovidiu Tonita
16 Andrew Hore*	16 Razvan Mavrodin*
17 Tony Woodcock	17 Paulica Ion*
18 Chris Jack*	18 Valentin Ursache*
19 Richie McCaw*	19 Cosmin Ratiu*
20 Brendon Leonard*	20 Valentin Calafeteanu*
21 Doug Howlett*	21 Florin Vlaicu*
22 Conrad Smith*	22 Catalin Robert Dascalu*

Referee Joël Jutge

29/9/2007 — Saint-Etienne

Scotland 18	Italy 16
Pens: Paterson (6)	Try: Troncon Con: Bortolussi Pens: Bortolussi (3)
15 Rory Lamont	15 David Bortolussi
14 Sean Lamont	14 Kaine Robertson
13 Simon Webster	13 Gonzalo Canale
12 Rob Dewey	12 Mirco Bergamasco
11 Chris Paterson	11 Andrea Masi
10 Dan Parks	10 Ramiro Pez
9 Mike Blair	9 Alessandro Troncon
1 Gavin Kerr	1 Salvatore Perugini
2 Ross Ford	2 Carlo Festuccia
3 Euan Murray	3 Martin Castrogiovanni
4 Nathan Hines	4 Santiago Dellapè
5 Jim Hamilton	5 Carlo Del Fava
6 Jason White	6 Josh Sole
7 Allister Hogg	7 Mauro Bergamasco
8 Simon Taylor	8 Sergio Parisse
16 Scott Lawson	16 Fabio Ongaro*
17 Craig Smith*	17 Andrea Lo Cicero*
18 Scott MacLeod*	18 Valerio Bernabò
19 Kelly Brown*	19 Leonardo Ghiraldini
20 Chris Cusiter*	20 Paul Griffen
21 Andrew Henderson*	21 Roland de Marigny
22 Hugo Southwell*	22 Ezio Galon

Referee Jonathan Kaplan

FINAL POOL TABLE

	P	W	D	L	F	A	BP	PTS
New Zealand	4	4	0	0	309	35	4	20
Scotland	4	3	0	1	116	66	2	14
Italy	4	2	0	2	85	117	1	9
Romania	4	1	0	3	40	161	1	5
Portugal	4	0	0	4	38	209	1	1

POOL D

7/9/2007 — Stade de France, Paris

France 12	Argentina 17
Pens: Skrela (4)	Try: Corleto Pens: F Contepomi (4)
15 Cédric Heymans	15 Ignacio Corleto
14 Aurélien Rougerie	14 Lucas Borges
13 Yannick Jauzion	13 Manuel Contepomi
12 Damien Traille	12 Felipe Contepomi
11 Christophe Dominici	11 Horacio Agulla
10 David Skrela	10 Juan Martín Hernández
9 Pierre Mignoni	9 Agustín Pichot
1 Olivier Milloud	1 Rodrigo Roncero
2 Raphaël Ibanez	2 Mario Ledesma Arocena
3 Pieter de Villiers	3 Juan Martín Scelzo
4 Fabien Pelous	4 C I Fernandez Lobbe
5 Jérôme Thion	5 Patricio Albacete
6 Serge Betsen	6 Lucas Ostiglia
7 Rémy Martin	7 J M Fernandez Lobbe
8 Imanol Harinordoquy	8 Juan Manuel Leguizamón
16 Dimitri Szarzewski*	16 Alberto Vernet Basualdo
17 Jean-Baptiste Poux	17 Santiago Gonzalez Bonorino*
18 Sébastien Chabal*	18 Rimas Álvarez Kairelis*
19 Julien Bonnaire*	19 Martín Durand*
20 Thierry Dusautoir	20 Nicolás Fernandez Miranda
21 Jean-Baptiste Elissalde*	21 Federico Todeschini
22 Frédéric Michalak*	22 Hernán Senillosa*

Referee Tony Spreadbury

9/9/2007 — Bordeaux

Ireland 32	Namibia 17
Tries: O'Driscoll, Trimble, Easterby, penalty try, Flannery Cons: O'Gara (2) Pen: O'Gara	Tries: Nieuwenhuis, van Zyl Cons: Wessels (2) Pen: Wessels
15 Girvan Dempsey	15 Tertius Losper
14 Andrew Trimble	14 Ryan Witbooi
13 Brian O'Driscoll	13 Bradley Langenhoven
12 Gordon D'Arcy	12 Piet van Zyl
11 Denis Hickie	11 Heini Bock
10 Ronan O'Gara	10 Emile Wessels
9 Peter Stringer	9 Eugene Jantjies
1 Marcus Horan	1 Kees Lensing
2 Rory Best	2 Hugo Horn
3 John Hayes	3 Jane du Toit
4 Donnacha O'Callaghan	4 Wacca Kazombiaze
5 Paul O'Connell	5 Nico Esterhuize
6 Simon Easterby	6 Jacques Nieuwenhuis
7 David Wallace	7 Heino Senekal
8 Denis Leamy	8 Jacques Burger
16 Jerry Flannery*	16 Johannes Meyer*
17 Simon Best*	17 Johnny Redelinghuys*
18 Malcolm O'Kelly	18 Michael MacKenzie*
19 Neil Best*	19 Tinus du Plessis*
20 Isaac Boss	20 Jurie van Tonder*
21 Paddy Wallace	21 Lu-Wayne Botes
22 Geordan Murphy	22 Melrick Africa

Referee Joël Jutge

11/9/2007 — Lyons

Argentina 33	Georgia 3
Tries: Borges (2), Albacete, Martin Aramburu Cons: F Contepomi, Hernández Pens: F Contepomi (3)	Pen: Kvirikashvili
15 Ignacio Corleto	15 Pavle Jimsheladze
14 Lucas Borges	14 Irakli Machkhaneli
13 Gonzalo Tiesi	13 Malkhaz Urjukashvili
12 Felipe Contepomi	12 Irakli Giorgadze
11 Federico Martín Aramburu	11 Besiki Khamashuridze
10 Juan Martín Hernández	10 Merab Kvirikashvili
9 Nicolás Fernandez Miranda	9 Irakli Abuseridze
1 Marcos Ayerza	1 David Khinchagashvili
2 Mario Ledesma Arocena	2 Akvsenti Giorgadze
3 Santiago Gonzalez Bonorino	3 David Zirakashvili
4 Rimas Álvarez Kairelis	4 Ilia Zedginidze
5 Patricio Albacete	5 Mamuka Gorgodze
6 Martín Durand	6 Giorgi Chkhaidze
7 J M Fernandez Lobbe	7 Grigol Labadze
8 Juan Manuel Leguizamón	8 Besso Udesiani
16 Alberto Vernet Basualdo*	16 Goderdzi Shvelidze*
17 Omar Hasan Jalil*	17 Avtandil Kopaliani*
18 Esteban Lozada*	18 Victor Didebulidze*
19 Martín Schusterman*	19 Zviad Maisuradze*
20 Hernán Senillosa*	20 Bidzina Samkharadze*
21 Federico Todeschini*	21 Revaz Gigauri*
22 Federico Serra Miras	22 Giorgi Shkinin*

Referee Nigel Owens

15/9/2007 — Bordeaux

Ireland 14	Georgia 10
Tries: Best, Dempsey Cons: O'Gara (2)	Try: Shkinin Con: Kvirikashvili Pen: Kvirikashvili
15 Girvan Dempsey	15 Otar Barkalaia
14 Shane Horgan	14 Giorgi Shkinin
13 Brian O'Driscoll	13 Malkhaz Urjukashvili
12 Gordon D'Arcy	12 Davit Kacharava
11 Denis Hickie	11 Giorgi Elizbarashvili
10 Ronan O'Gara	10 Merab Kvirikashvili
9 Peter Stringer	9 Bidzina Samkharadze
1 Marcus Horan	1 Mamuka Magrakvelidze
2 Rory Best	2 Goderdzi Shvelidze
3 John Hayes	3 Avtandil Kopaliani
4 Donnacha O'Callaghan	4 Ilia Zedginidze
5 Paul O'Connell	5 Mamuka Gorgodze
6 Simon Easterby	6 Ilia Maisuradze
7 David Wallace	7 Rati Urushadze
8 Denis Leamy	8 Giorgi Chkhaidze
16 Jerry Flannery*	16 Akvsenti Giorgadze*
17 Simon Best*	17 David Khinchagashvili*
18 Malcolm O'Kelly	18 Levan Datunashvili*
19 Neil Best	19 Zviad Maisuradze*
20 Isaac Boss*	20 Irakli Abuseridze*
21 Paddy Wallace	21 Irakli Machkhaneli*
22 Geordan Murphy	22 Otar Eloshvili*

Referee Wayne Barnes

16/9/2007 — Toulouse

France 87	Namibia 10
Tries: Heymans, Marty, Bonnaire, Elissalde, Nallet (2), Ibanez, Chabal (2), Dusautoir, Clerc (3) Cons: Elissalde (11)	Try: Langenhoven Con: Losper Drop: Wessels
15 Clément Poitrenaud	15 Tertius Losper
14 Vincent Clerc	14 Ryan Witbooi
13 David Marty	13 Bradley Langenhoven
12 Damien Traille	12 Piet van Zyl
11 Cédric Heymans	11 Heini Bock
10 Frédéric Michalak	10 Emile Wessels
9 Jean-Baptiste Elissalde	9 Jurie van Tonder
1 Jean-Baptiste Poux	1 Kees Lensing
2 Dimitri Szarzewski	2 Hugo Horn
3 Pieter de Villiers	3 Jane du Toit
4 Sébastien Chabal	4 Wacca Kazombiaze
5 Lionel Nallet	5 Nico Esterhuize
6 Yannick Nyanga	6 Jacques Burger
7 Thierry Dusautoir	7 Michael MacKenzie
8 Julien Bonnaire	8 Jacques Nieuwenhuis
16 Raphaël Ibanez*	16 Johannes Meyer*
17 Nicolas Mas*	17 Johnny Redelinghuys*
18 Fabien Pelous	18 Herman Lindvelt*
19 Imanol Harinordoquy*	19 Tinus du Plessis*
20 Lionel Beauxis*	20 Eugene Jantjies*
21 Yannick Jauzion*	21 Lu-Wayne Botes*
22 Aurélien Rougerie*	22 Melrick Africa*

Referee Alain Rolland

21/9/2007 — Stade de France, Paris

France 25	Ireland 3
Tries: Clerc (2) Pens: Elissalde (5)	Drop: O'Gara
15 Clément Poitrenaud	15 Girvan Dempsey
14 Vincent Clerc	14 Shane Horgan
13 David Marty	13 Brian O'Driscoll
12 Damien Traille	12 Gordon D'Arcy
11 Cédric Heymans	11 Andrew Trimble
10 Frédéric Michalak	10 Ronan O'Gara
9 Jean-Baptiste Elissalde	9 Eoin Reddan
1 Olivier Milloud	1 Marcus Horan
2 Raphaël Ibanez	2 Jerry Flannery
3 Pieter de Villiers	3 John Hayes
4 Sébastien Chabal	4 Donnacha O'Callaghan
5 Jérôme Thion	5 Paul O'Connell
6 Serge Betsen	6 Simon Easterby
7 Thierry Dusautoir	7 David Wallace
8 Julien Bonnaire	8 Denis Leamy
16 Dimitri Szarzewski*	16 Frankie Sheahan*
17 Jean-Baptiste Poux*	17 Simon Best*
18 Lionel Nallet*	18 Malcolm O'Kelly*
19 Yannick Nyanga*	19 Neil Best*
20 Lionel Beauxis*	20 Isaac Boss
21 Yannick Jauzion*	21 Paddy Wallace
22 Aurélien Rougerie	22 Gavin Duffy

Referee Chris White

22/9/2007 — Marseilles

Argentina 63	Namibia 3
Tries: Roncero, Leguizamón (2), M Contepomi, F Contepomi, Tiesi, Corleto, penalty try, Todeschini Cons: F Contepomi (4), Basualdo, Todeschini Pens: F Contepomi (2)	Pen: Schreuder
15 Ignacio Corleto	15 Heini Bock
14 Hernán Senillosa	14 Deon Mouton
13 Gonzalo Tiesi	13 Du Preez Grobler
12 Manuel Contepomi	12 Corne Powell
11 Horacio Agulla	11 Melrick Africa
10 Felipe Contepomi	10 Morne Schreuder
9 Agustín Pichot	9 Eugene Jantjies
1 Rodrigo Roncero	1 Johnny Redelinghuys
2 Alberto Vernet Basualdo	2 Johannes Meyer
3 Omar Hasan Jalil	3 Marius Visser
4 C I Fernandez Lobbe	4 Wacca Kazombiaze
5 Patricio Albacete	5 Nico Esterhuize
6 Lucas Ostiglia	6 Michael MacKenzie
7 J M Fernandez Lobbe	7 Jacques Burger
8 Juan Manuel Leguizamón	8 Tinus du Plessis
16 Mario Ledesma Arocena	16 Hugo Horn*
17 Juan Martín Scelzo*	17 Kees Lensing*
18 Rimas Álvarez Kairelis*	18 Herman Lindvelt*
19 Gonzalo Longo Elía*	19 Heino Senekal*
20 Nicolás Fernandez Miranda*	20 Jurie van Tonder*
21 Federico Todeschini*	21 Bradley Langenhoven*
22 Federico Serra Miras*	22 Piet van Zyl*

Referee Stuart Dickinson

26/9/2007 — Lens

Georgia 30	Namibia 0
Tries: Giorgadze, Machkhaneli, Kacharava Cons: Kvirikashvili (3) Pens: Kvirikashvili (3)	
15 Malkhaz Urjukashvili	15 Heini Bock
14 Irakli Machkhaneli	14 Ryan Witbooi
13 Davit Kacharava	13 Piet van Zyl
12 Irakli Giorgadze	12 Corne Powell
11 Giorgi Shkinin	11 Bradley Langenhoven
10 Merab Kvirikashvili	10 Morne Schreuder
9 Irakli Abuseridze	9 Jurie van Tonder
1 Goderdzi Shvelidze	1 Kees Lensing
2 Akvsenti Giorgadze	2 Hugo Horn
3 David Zirakashvili	3 Marius Visser
4 Levan Datunashvili	4 Wacca Kazombiaze
5 Mamuka Gorgodze	5 Heino Senekal
6 Grigol Labadze	6 Jacques Nieuwenhuis
7 Rati Urushadze	7 Jacques Burger
8 Giorgi Chkhaidze	8 Tinus du Plessis
16 David Khinchagashvili*	16 Johannes Meyer
17 Avtandil Kopaliani*	17 Johnny Redelinghuys*
18 Victor Didebulidze*	18 Jane du Toit*
19 Besso Udesiani*	19 Nico Esterhuize*
20 Bidzina Samkharadze*	20 Eugene Jantjies*
21 Revaz Gigauri*	21 Melrick Africa*
22 Besiki Khamashuridze*	22 Domingo Kamonga*

Referee Steve Walsh

30/9/2007 — Marseilles

France 64	Georgia 7
Tries: Poitrenaud, Nyanga (2), Beauxis, Dominici (2), Bruno, Nallet, Bonnaire Cons: Beauxis (5) Pens: Beauxis (3)	Try: Z Maisuradze Con: Urjukashvili
15 Clément Poitrenaud	15 Otar Barkalaia
14 Aurélien Rougerie	14 Malkhaz Urjukashvili
13 David Marty	13 Revaz Gigauri
12 Yannick Jauzion	12 Irakli Giorgadze
11 Christophe Dominici	11 Besiki Khamashuridze
10 Lionel Beauxis	10 Merab Kvirikashvili
9 Pierre Mignoni	9 Irakli Abuseridze
1 Olivier Milloud	1 Mamuka Magrakvelidze
2 Sébastien Bruno	2 Akvsenti Giorgadze
3 Jean-Baptiste Poux	3 David Zirakashvili
4 Lionel Nallet	4 Victor Didebulidze
5 Jérôme Thion	5 Zurab Mtchedlishvili
6 Serge Betsen	6 Ilia Maisuradze
7 Yannick Nyanga	7 Rati Urushadze
8 Julien Bonnaire	8 Giorgi Chkhaidze
16 Dimitri Szarzewski*	16 Goderdzi Shvelidze*
17 Nicolas Mas*	17 Avtandil Kopaliani*
18 Fabien Pelous*	18 Levan Datunashvili*
19 Rémy Martin*	19 Zviad Maisuradze*
20 Jean-Baptiste Elissalde*	20 Bidzina Samkharadze*
21 David Skrela*	21 Otar Eloshvili*
22 Vincent Clerc*	22 Giorgi Elizbarashvili*

Referee Alan Lewis

30/9/2007 — Parc des Prines, Paris

Ireland 15	Argentina 30
Tries: O'Driscoll, Murphy Con: O'Gara Pen: O'Gara	Tries: Borges, Agulla Con: F Contepomi Pens: F Contepomi (3) Drops: Hernández (3)
15 Geordan Murphy	15 Ignacio Corleto
14 Shane Horgan	14 Lucas Borges
13 Brian O'Driscoll	13 Manuel Contepomi
12 Gordon D'Arcy	12 Felipe Contepomi
11 Denis Hickie	11 Horacio Agulla
10 Ronan O'Gara	10 Juan Martín Hernández
9 Eoin Reddan	9 Agustín Pichot
1 Marcus Horan	1 Rodrigo Roncero
2 Jerry Flannery	2 Mario Ledesma Arocena
3 John Hayes	3 Juan Martín Scelzo
4 Donnacha O'Callaghan	4 C I Fernandez Lobbe
5 Paul O'Connell	5 Patricio Albacete
6 Simon Easterby	6 Lucas Ostiglia
7 David Wallace	7 J M Fernandez Lobbe
8 Denis Leamy	8 Gonzalo Longo Elía
16 Rory Best*	16 Alberto Vernet Basualdo*
17 Bryan Young	17 Omar Hasan Jalil*
18 Malcolm O'Kelly*	18 Rimas Álvarez Kairelis*
19 Neil Best*	19 Martín Durand*
20 Isaac Boss*	20 Nicolás Fernandez Miranda
21 Paddy Wallace	21 Federico Todeschini
22 Gavin Duffy*	22 Hernán Senillosa*

Referee Paul Honiss

FINAL POOL TABLE

	P	W	D	L	F	A	BP	PTS
Argentina	4	4	0	0	143	33	2	18
France	4	3	0	1	188	37	3	15
Ireland	4	2	0	2	64	82	1	9
Georgia	4	1	0	3	50	111	1	5
Namibia	4	0	0	4	30	212	0	0

Quarter-finals

6/10/2007 — Marseilles

Australia 10	England 12
Try: Tuqiri Con: Mortlock Pen: Mortlock	Pens: Wilkinson (4)
15 Chris Latham	15 Jason Robinson
14 Adam Ashley-Cooper	14 Paul Sackey
13 Stirling Mortlock	13 Mathew Tait
12 Matt Giteau	12 Mike Catt
11 Lote Tuqiri	11 Josh Lewsey
10 Berrick Barnes	10 Jonny Wilkinson
9 George Gregan	9 Andy Gomarsall
1 Matt Dunning	1 Andrew Sheridan
2 Stephen Moore	2 Mark Regan
3 Guy Shepherdson	3 Phil Vickery
4 Nathan Sharpe	4 Simon Shaw
5 Daniel Vickerman	5 Ben Kay
6 Rocky Elsom	6 Martin Corry
7 George Smith	7 Lewis Moody
8 Wycliff Palu	8 Nick Easter
16 Adam Freier*	16 George Chuter*
17 Al Baxter*	17 Matt Stevens*
18 Hugh McMeniman*	18 Lawrence Dallaglio*
19 Stephen Hoiles*	19 Joe Worsley*
20 Phil Waugh*	20 Peter Richards*
21 Julian Huxley	21 Toby Flood*
22 Drew Mitchell*	22 Dan Hipkiss

Referee Alain Rolland

6/10/2007 — Cardiff

New Zealand 18	France 20
Tries: McAlister, So'oialo Con: Carter Pens: Carter (2)	Tries: Dusautoir, Jauzion Cons: Beauxis, Elissalde Pens: Beauxis (2)
15 Leon MacDonald	15 Damien Traille
14 Joe Rokocoko	14 Vincent Clerc
13 Mils Muliaina	13 David Marty
12 Luke McAlister	12 Yannick Jauzion
11 Sitiveni Sivivatu	11 Cédric Heymans
10 Dan Carter	10 Lionel Beauxis
9 Byron Kelleher	9 Jean-Baptiste Elissalde
1 Tony Woodcock	1 Olivier Milloud
2 Anton Oliver	2 Raphaël Ibanez
3 Carl Hayman	3 Pieter de Villiers
4 Keith Robinson	4 Fabien Pelous
5 Ali Williams	5 Jérôme Thion
6 Jerry Collins	6 Serge Betsen
7 Richie McCaw	7 Thierry Dusautoir
8 Rodney So'oialo	8 Julien Bonnaire
16 Andrew Hore*	16 Dimitri Szarzewski*
17 Neemia Tialata	17 Jean-Baptiste Poux*
18 Chris Jack*	18 Sébastien Chabal*
19 Chris Masoe*	19 Imanol Harinordoquy*
20 Brendon Leonard*	20 Frédéric Michalak*
21 Nick Evans*	21 Christophe Dominici*
22 Isaia Toeava*	22 Clément Poitrenaud*

Referee Wayne Barnes

7/10/2007 — Marseilles

South Africa 37	Fiji 20
Tries: Fourie, Smit, Pietersen, Smith, James Cons: Montgomery (3) Pens: Steyn, Montgomery	Tries: Delasau, Bobo Cons: Bai (2) Pens: Bai (2)
15 Percy Montgomery	15 Norman Ligairi
14 JP Pietersen	14 Vilimoni Delasau
13 Jaque Fourie	13 Kameli Ratuvou
12 Francois Steyn	12 Seru Rabeni
11 Bryan Habana	11 Sireli Bobo
10 Butch James	10 Seremaia Bai
9 Fourie du Preez	9 Mosese Rauluni
1 Os du Randt	1 Graham Dewes
2 John Smit	2 Sunia Koto
3 Jannie du Plessis	3 Henry Qiodravu
4 Bakkies Botha	4 Kele Leawere
5 Victor Matfield	5 Ifereimi Rawaqa
6 Schalk Burger	6 Semisi Naevo
7 Juan Smith	7 Akapusi Qera
8 Danie Rossouw	8 Sisa Koyamaibole
16 Gary Botha	16 Bill Gadolo
17 Gurthro Steenkamp*	17 Jone Railomo*
18 Johannes Muller*	18 Aca Ratuva*
19 Wickus van Heerden*	19 Wame Lewaravu*
20 Ruan Pienaar	20 Jone Daunivucu
21 Andre Pretorius	21 Waisea Luveniyali
22 Wynand Olivier	22 Gabiriele Lovobalavu*

Referee Alan Lewis

7/10/2007 — Stade de France, Paris

Argentina 19	Scotland 13
Try: Longo Elia Con: F Contepomi Pens: F Contepomi (3) Drop: Hernández	Try: Cusiter Con: Paterson Pens: Parks, Paterson
15 Ignacio Corleto	15 Rory Lamont
14 Lucas Borges	14 Sean Lamont
13 Manuel Contepomi	13 Simon Webster
12 Felipe Contepomi	12 Rob Dewey
11 Horacio Agulla	11 Chris Paterson
10 Juan Martín Hernández	10 Dan Parks
9 Agustín Pichot	9 Mike Blair
1 Rodrigo Roncero	1 Gavin Kerr
2 Mario Ledesma Arocena	2 Ross Ford
3 Martín Scelzo	3 Euan Murray
4 Cl Fernandez Lobbe	4 Nathan Hines
5 Patricio Albacete	5 Jim Hamilton
6 Lucas Ostiglia	6 Jason White
7 JM Fernandez Lobbe	7 Allister Hogg
8 Gonzalo Longo Elía	8 Simon Taylor
16 Alberto Vernet Basualdo	16 Scott Lawson*
17 Omar Hasan Jalil*	17 Craig Smith*
18 Rimas Álvarez Kairelis*	18 Scott MacLeod*
19 Juan Manuel Leguizamón*	19 Kelly Brown*
20 Nicolás Fernandez Miranda	20 Chris Cusiter*
21 Federico Todeschini	21 Andrew Henderson*
22 Hernán Senillosa*	22 Hugo Southwell*

Referee Joël Jutge

Semi-finals

13/10/2007 — Stade de France, Paris

England 14	France 9
Try: Lewsey Pens: Wilkinson (2) Drop: Wilkinson	Pens: Beauxis (3)
15 Jason Robinson	15 Damien Traille
14 Paul Sackey	14 Vincent Clerc
13 Mathew Tait	13 David Marty
12 Mike Catt	12 Yannick Jauzion
11 Josh Lewsey	11 Cédric Heymans
10 Jonny Wilkinson	10 Lionel Beauxis
9 Andy Gomarsall	9 Jean-Baptiste Elissalde
1 Andrew Sheridan	1 Olivier Milloud
2 Mark Regan	2 Raphaël Ibanez
3 Phil Vickery	3 Pieter de Villiers
4 Simon Shaw	4 Fabien Pelous
5 Ben Kay	5 Jérôme Thion
6 Martin Corry	6 Serge Betsen
7 Lewis Moody	7 Thierry Dusautoir
8 Nick Easter	8 Julien Bonnaire
16 George Chuter*	16 Dimitri Szarzewski*
17 Matt Stevens*	17 Jean-Baptiste Poux*
18 Lawrence Dallaglio*	18 Sébastien Chabal*
19 Joe Worsley*	19 Imanol Harinordoquy*
20 Peter Richards*	20 Frédéric Michalak*
21 Toby Flood*	21 Christophe Dominici*
22 Dan Hipkiss*	22 Clément Poitrenaud

Referee Jonathan Kaplan

14/10/2007 — Stade de France, Paris

South Africa 37	Argentina 13
Tries: du Preez, Habana (2), Rossouw Cons: Montgomery (4) Pens: Montgomery (3)	Try: M Contepomi Con: F Contepomi Pens: F Contepomi (2)
15 Percy Montgomery	15 Ignacio Corleto
14 JP Pietersen	14 Lucas Borges
13 Jaque Fourie	13 Manuel Contepomi
12 Francois Steyn	12 Felipe Contepomi
11 Bryan Habana	11 Horacio Agulla
10 Butch James	10 Juan Martín Hernández
9 Fourie du Preez	9 Agustín Pichot
1 Os du Randt	1 Rodrigo Roncero
2 John Smit	2 Mario Ledesma Arocena
3 CJ van der Linde	3 Martín Scelzo
4 Bakkies Botha	4 Cl Fernandez Lobbe
5 Victor Matfield	5 Patricio Albacete
6 Schalk Burger	6 Lucas Ostiglia
7 Juan Smith	7 JM Fernandez Lobbe
8 Danie Rossouw	8 Gonzalo Longo Elía
16 Bismarck du Plessis*	16 Alberto Vernet Basualdo
17 Jannie du Plessis*	17 Omar Hasan Jalil*
18 Johannes Muller*	18 Rimas Álvarez Kairelis*
19 Bobby Skinstad*	19 Juan Manuel Leguizamón*
20 Ruan Pienaar*	20 Nicolás Fernandez Miranda
21 Andre Pretorius*	21 Federico Todeschini
22 Wynand Olivier*	22 Gonzalo Tiesi*

Referee Steve Walsh

3rd/4th Play-off

19/10/2007 — Parc des Princes, Paris

FRANCE	ARGENTINA
France 10 Try: Poitrenaud Con: Beauxis Pen: Elissalde	Argentina 34 Tries: F Contepomi (2), Hasan Jalil, Martin Aramburu, Corleto Cons: F Contepomi (3) Pen: F Contepomi
15 Clément Poitrenaud	15 Ignacio Corleto
14 Aurélien Rougerie	14 Federico Martín Aramburu
13 David Skrela	13 Manuel Contepomi
12 David Marty	12 Felipe Contepomi
11 Christophe Dominici	11 Horacio Agulla
10 Frédéric Michalak	10 Juan Martín Hernández
9 Jean-Baptiste Elissalde	9 Agustín Pichot
1 Jean-Baptiste Poux	1 Rodrigo Roncero
2 Raphaël Ibanez	2 Alberto Vernet Basualdo
3 Nicolas Mas	3 Omar Hasan Jalil
4 Lionel Nallet	4 Rimas Álvarez Kairelis
5 Jérôme Thion	5 Patricio Albacete
6 Yannick Nyanga	6 Martín Durand
7 Thierry Dusautoir	7 JM Fernandez Lobbe
8 Imanol Harinordoquy	8 Gonzalo Longo Elía
16 Sébastien Bruno	16 Eusebio Guiñazu
17 Pieter de Villiers	17 Marcos Ayerza
18 Sébastien Chabal	18 Esteban Lozada
19 Rémy Martin	19 Juan Manuel Leguizamón
20 Pierre Mignoni	20 Nicolás Fernandez Miranda
21 Lionel Beauxis	21 Federico Todeschini
22 Vincent Clerc	22 Hernán Senillosa

Referee Paul Honiss

RUGBY WORLD CUP 2007 – The Final

20/10/2007 — Stade de France, Paris

ENGLAND	SOUTH AFRICA
England 6 Pens: Wilkinson (2)	South Africa 15 Pens: Montgomery (4), Steyn
15 Jason Robinson	15 Percy Montgomery
14 Paul Sackey	14 JP Pietersen
13 Mathew Tait	13 Jaque Fourie
12 Mike Catt	12 Francois Steyn
11 Mark Cueto	11 Bryan Habana
10 Jonny Wilkinson	10 Butch James
9 Andy Gomarsall	9 Fourie du Preez
1 Andrew Sheridan	1 Os du Randt
2 Mark Regan	2 John Smit
3 Phil Vickery	3 CJ van der Linde
4 Simon Shaw	4 Bakkies Botha
5 Ben Kay	5 Victor Matfield
6 Martin Corry	6 Schalk Burger
7 Lewis Moody	7 Juan Smith
8 Nick Easter	8 Danie Rossouw
16 George Chuter*	16 Bismarck du Plessis*
17 Matt Stevens*	17 Jannie du Plessis
18 Lawrence Dallaglio*	18 Johannes Muller
19 Joe Worsley*	19 Wickus van Heerden*
20 Peter Richards*	20 Ruan Pienaar
21 Toby Flood*	21 Andre Pretorius
22 Dan Hipkiss*	22 Wynand Olivier

Referee Alain Rolland

* = used as replacement

RUGBY
2007